# Luke

SHARON H. RINGE

D0836016

Westminster John Knox Press
LOUISVILLE
LONDON · LEIDEN

*Book design by  Publishers' WorkGroup*
*Cover design by Drew Stevens*

*First edition*

Published by Westminster John Knox Press
Louisville, Kentucky

This book is printed on acid-free paper that meets the American National Standards
Institute Z39.48 standard. ∞

PRINTED IN THE UNITED STATES OF AMERICA

01 02 03 04 — 10 9 8 7 6 5 4 3 2

**Library of Congress Cataloging-in-Publication Data**
Ringe, Sharon H.
    Luke / Sharon Ringe.—1st ed.
        p.      cm. — (Westminster Bible companion)
    Includes bibliographical references (p.    ).
    ISBN 0-664-25259-1 (alk. paper)
    1. bible. N.T. Luke—Commentaries.    I. Title.    II. Series.
BS2595.3.R55    1995
226.4'-07—dc20                                                    95-23068

# Contents

Luke

# Westminster Bible Companion

*Series Editors*

Patrick D. Miller
David L. Bartlett

# Contents

# Series Foreword

This series of study guides to the Bible is offered to the church and more specifically to the laity. In daily devotions, in church school classes, and in listening to the preached word, individual Christians turn to the Bible for a sustaining word, a challenging word, and a sense of direction. The word that scripture brings may be highly personal as one deals with the demands and surprises, the joys and sorrows, of daily life. It also may have broader dimensions as people wrestle with moral and theological issues that involve us all. In every congregation and denomination, controversies arise that send ministry and laity alike back to the Word of God to find direction for dealing with difficult matters that confront us.

A significant number of lay women and men in the church also find themselves called to the service of teaching. Most of the time they will be teaching the Bible. In many churches, the primary sustained attention to the Bible and the discovery of its riches for our lives have come from the ongoing teaching of the Bible by persons who have not engaged in formal theological education. They have been willing, and often eager, to study the Bible in order to help others drink from its living water.

This volume is part of a series of books, the Westminster Bible Companion, intended to help the laity of the church read the Bible more clearly and intelligently. Whether such reading is for personal direction or for the teaching of others, the reader cannot avoid the difficulties of trying to understand these words from long ago. The scriptures are clear and clearly available to everyone as they call us to faith in the God who is revealed in Jesus Christ and as they offer to every human being the word of salvation. No companion volumes are necessary in order to hear such words truly. Yet every reader of scripture who pauses to ponder and think further about any text has questions that are not immediately answerable simply by reading the text of scripture. Such questions may be about historical and geographical details or about words that are obscure or so loaded with meaning that one cannot tell at a glance what is at stake. They may be about the fundamental meaning of a passage or about what connection a particular text might have to our contemporary world. Or a teacher preparing for a church school class may simply want to know: What should I say about this biblical passage when I have to teach it next Sunday? It is our hope that these volumes, written by teachers and pastors with long experience studying and teaching the Bible in the church, will help members of the church who want and need to study the Bible with their questions.

The New Revised Standard Version of the Bible is the basis for the interpretive comments that each author provides. The NRSV text is presented at the beginning of the discussion so that the reader may have at hand in a single volume both the scripture passage and the exposition of its meaning. In some instances, where inclusion of the entire passage is not necessary for understanding either the text or the interpreter's discussion, the presentation of the NRSV text may be abbreviated. Usually, the whole of the biblical text is given.

We hope this series will serve the community of faith, opening the Word of God to all the people, so that they may be sustained and guided by it.

# Introduction

## Luke in Our Context:
## Clues for Reading

### FAMILIAR STORIES AND AN
### UNKNOWN STORY

The Gospel of Luke contains some of the best-known and best-loved stories of Jesus. From the announcements of the coming births of Jesus and John the Baptist, through the visit of Mary and Elizabeth, to the account of Jesus' birth and the shepherds' visit, Luke sets the stage for Christmas hope and celebration (Luke 1 and 2). It is Luke who begins the account of Jesus' public ministry with the story of his inaugural sermon in the synagogue at Nazareth (4:16–30). Luke also is the source of such familiar stories as those about Mary and Martha (10:38–42) and Zacchaeus (19:1–10), and of such well-loved parables as the "good" Samaritan (10:29–37); the lost and found sheep, coin, and "prodigal" son (15:1–32); the rich man and Lazarus (16:19–31); and the widow and the judge (18:1–8). Finally, it is Luke who concludes his Gospel with the story of the trip to Emmaus, where Jesus was "made known to them in the breaking of the bread" (24:13–35), and with an account of Jesus' ascension (24:50–53).

In addition to the power of these stories themselves in the memory bank of Christian people, Luke's Gospel has been important in the worship of the church and in the personal devotional life of Christian people. The Emmaus story, like the account of Jesus' last meal with the disciples, has shaped the communion or eucharistic liturgy. The hymns that punctuate the first two chapters of the Gospel have been set to music many times, and they find their way into both worship and the general culture as the "Benedictus" (1:68–79), the "Nunc Dimittis" (2:29–32), and of course, the "Magnificat" (1:47–55). Luke's Gospel, more than any other, portrays Jesus at prayer at crucial junctures in his life and thus has served as a model for Christian piety. The Gospel and the sequel by the same author (the book of Acts) both carry the hallmark of the Holy Spirit as the foundation of Jesus' own life and ministry and as the energizing power of the church convened in his name.

Luke has also provided a number of teachings about the Christian life that have challenged and empowered people in the church. An example of the challenge of this Gospel can be found in Luke's reflection on Christian life as part of a long, ongoing history. Most, if not all, of the earliest Christians understood Jesus' resurrection as simply the "first fruits" of the general resurrection that would mark the end of history and the triumph of divine judgment. They saw themselves as living in a brief interval before the risen Christ would return to participate in God's final judgment of the people. The focus of their attention was on being prepared for that judgment, not on the meaning of the Christian life as an ethical calling.

Luke's second volume, the book of Acts, provides one example of how seriously Luke took the church's responsibility as an institution in ongoing human history. Acts tells about the early years of the church as a time when God continued the work brought to a climax in Jesus Christ. The powerful preaching, deeds, and faithful witness even to death of such leaders as Stephen, Peter, and Paul, had as a consequence the spread of the gospel throughout the then-known world, and followers of Jesus could be charged with "turning the world upside down" (Acts 17:6).

The same concern for the ongoing life of the church has led Luke to emphasize the "daily-ness" of both our responsibility and God's presence and care in the Christian life of discipleship. "Taking up the cross" initially referred to the action of someone condemned to crucifixion by Rome for some capital crime (usually treason). The condemned person had to carry the horizontal bar of the cross to the place of execution, or if previous torture had left the condemned person too weak to carry it, another was pressed into service (23:26). Luke, however, says a disciple must take up the cross "daily" (9:23; see also 14:27–32). Clearly, this did not mean that one should face execution each day, nor did it simply urge the Christian to have patience with life's burdens. Instead, for Luke it demanded of each disciple a lifestyle of faithfulness to the gospel that would in fact be "indictable" if one were charged with being a Christian.

Similarly, God's presence was promised to be an abiding presence. Nowhere can this be seen more clearly in Luke than in the petition for bread in the Lord's prayer (11:3). Unlike the more familiar version in Matthew, "Give us this day our daily bread" (Matt. 6:11), Luke's version reads literally "Be giving us (repeatedly or continually) *each* day our daily bread." Just as discipleship is a long-term commitment for which one ought to reckon the cost from the outset (14:28–32), so also God's nurture and sustenance can be counted on to suffice.

Luke's Gospel has also sounded a liberating voice for many groups of people who have been excluded from the benefits of the dominant cultures of their days. In Luke's own context, he championed ethnic inclusiveness in the church by his affirmation of the inclusion of both Jews and Gentiles in the church and in the salvation that God intended for "all flesh" (3:6). That affirmation has allowed racial and ethnic minority groups in all ages to find in Luke support for their claims for justice and a source of strength in the face of unyielding systems of apartheid and segregation.

Luke also speaks often about the poor, and they are mentioned at key points when the agenda of his Gospel is being defined (4:18; 6:20; 7:22; 14:13, 21; 18:22; 19:8; 21:2–3). He also recognizes "giving alms" or taking care of the poor as a crucial dimension of one's Christian responsibility (11:41; 12:33; and 19:1–10). Luke's Gospel thus provides an important foundation for the church as it struggles with the dimensions of its mission that address economic justice (see below "The Gospel and 'the Poor'").

Similarly, Luke's Gospel contains more stories than the other Gospels about women who play significant roles among Jesus' followers. The prominence of Mary and Elizabeth in the first two chapters, the story of Mary and Martha (10:38–42), and the parables of the leaven (13:21) and the lost coin (15:8–10) have all figured prominently in women's affirmation of their importance in the life of the church alongside men (see below "Women in the Gospel of Luke"). Clearly, Luke understood that women were included among that larger group of "disciples" gathered around Jesus (8:1–3), who are the principal bearers of his message, as distinct from such "officials" of the church as "the twelve" or "the apostles" (9:1, 10, 12–16).

Despite these themes in Luke's Gospel that have empowered, encouraged, and challenged its readers, other themes have had a more hurtful effect. For example, the teaching prohibiting remarriage after divorce that Luke attributes to Jesus (16:18) has been lifted out of its context, and it has been used to condemn many people to the alternative of staying in loveless or even abusive marriages, spending the rest of their lives alone, or shouldering a tremendous burden of guilt and shame for defying scripture to marry again.

Similarly, Luke's witness concerning such justice issues of the gospel as

the role of women and advocacy for the poor also is read by many as ambiguous. They consider his advocacy for inclusion, participation, or compassion to be expressed within the framework of oppressive social structures and systems that remain unchallenged (see below "The Dominance
of a Worldview").

In short, many people "know"—and either celebrate or condemn—
Luke's Gospel through such themes and individual stories, reflecting the
usual ways scripture is incorporated into worship and Bible study. We
read "lections," or brief passages assigned or chosen as the basis for sermons, or we skip through the book to examine its perspective on a theme
or a question of interest to us. It is unlikely, however, that many people
will have had an opportunity to reflect on these themes and stories as part
of the larger whole of Luke's Gospel or as factors in the theological reflection of Luke's community. Thus for many people Luke's Gospel as a
whole is unknown territory.

## THE ROLE OF LUKE'S CONTEXT

Becoming attuned to Luke's Gospel as a whole is a task that encompasses
several dimensions. First, just as we modern readers come to our faith—
and to the reading of a Gospel—rooted in our own life's circumstances
(both individual and social), so also did Luke and his original readers. It is
thus important to become familiar with Luke's context—the social, economic, political, cultural, and historical circumstances and the wider
Christian movement in which Luke and his church participated. The
pressures and possibilities of that context have contributed a great deal toward shaping the way Luke has portrayed Jesus. To put the matter another
way, if the account of the life, death, and resurrection of Jesus was to be
able to proclaim good news to Luke's audience, he had to make clear how
the story of Jesus addressed the particular relationships, experiences, concerns, pains, fears, and joys that the people to whom he wrote were expe-
riencing.

Today preachers and theologians accomplish that interpretative task by
the way they reflect on the various biblical accounts in essays and sermons.
Instead of *reflecting on* the Gospel as a book that exists in final written form
as we do today, Luke lived in a time when interpretation could take place
in how he *retold* the story itself. All of the Gospels were written several
decades after Jesus' life, drawing on memories and traditions about Jesus
that had passed through generations of retelling and shaping. The Gospel

writers were principally preachers of the good news of Jesus Christ, and not biographers interested in factual accuracy. Thus, for them the concern to tell the "truth" about Jesus, in the sense of reporting information about Jesus, was secondary. Their primary concern was for the "truth" of the proclamation of God's presence with and in Jesus, and of the consequences of that truth for the life of the Christian community to which the particular Gospel was addressed.

As the story of Jesus was retold by each Gospel writer, the particular stories that each included, how each writer emphasized or minimized details within the stories, and how each combined individual stories and teachings into larger narrative blocks allowed the writer to develop the theological concerns most central to the writer's community or to his own theological agenda.

At the same time, the work of each Gospel writer allowed the stories of Jesus to move from the circumstances of rural Palestine in the early years of the first century to the various urban contexts in the century's closing decades. Another meaning of "context" thus comes into play, in the sense of the several life settings in which the various stories and teachings that make up the Gospel, as well as its final form, have found a home. In that sense, each Gospel is like a set of transparencies on which can be found the traces of the various communities that wrestled with the underlying traditions about Jesus and adapted them to their own pastoral circumstances. Thus, in order to grasp the breadth and depth of meaning conveyed in any of the Gospels, a careful reader needs to distinguish between elements of the Gospel writer's circumstances and assumptions about life, those that characterized the original stories of Jesus, and those of the various Christian communities that told the stories in the intervening years. The point of such investigation is not to scrape away the various interpretative lines and shadings in order to recover some allegedly pure form of the story of Jesus, but rather to appreciate the human experiences, needs, and strengths that are chronicled in the church's own record of its wrestling to affirm the gospel of Jesus Christ as the story of its faith and salvation.

Far from being simply the province of scholars interested in obscure information, questions about the various social, historical, and cultural contexts that have shaped the Gospel are fundamental to our efforts as Christians to grasp the good news that the Gospels convey. Luke, like all of the Gospels, is a story told from faith to faith. Getting to know our ancestors from whom the stories have come, and to appreciate how faith and life intersected in their experience, is essential if we are to join them in the long line of communities born out of and shaped by the story of Jesus' life, ministry, death, and resurrection.

## THE GOSPEL AS A LITERARY AND
## THEOLOGICAL WHOLE

Each of the Gospels has woven the various individual stories and teachings into a single story of Jesus, and not simply presented a collection of isolated traditions and reminiscences. That fact introduces another dimension of the word "context" as it relates to reading the Gospels in general and Luke in particular. If one were to sit down and read the Gospel of Luke from beginning to end, as one might read a novel or short story, it would show itself to be a remarkably coherent whole. Words and themes recur through the narrative like threads in a tapestry that surface, then disappear, and then emerge again to create the pattern of the whole. Similarly, in the Gospels the various individual stories coalesce into a coherent picture or design representing the author's view of what it means to confess Jesus as "Messiah" or "Christ" and "Lord." The stories and teachings that are woven together give shape to Jesus' ministry and to the content of "the good news of the kingdom of God" which is Jesus' agenda (4:43).

Thus it becomes important to consider the literary "context" of various passages in the Gospel—how the part functions in the larger whole. For example, one might ask how Luke uses a particular story to further the larger narrative he is presenting. How do stories that precede or follow shade the meaning of a particular passage? How does the narrative setting Luke has provided—geographical location, characters, circumstances—shape the meaning of a parable or other teaching?

## THE AUTHORITY OF THE GOSPEL

Luke's literary artistry is an important facet of the authority that readers grant to his Gospel. Fundamental to the authority of this or any biblical book is the church's affirmation that it is part of "Scripture"—that is, part of what is called "the Word of God." In parts of the church where such designations are understood to mean that God is the source of the very words of the text transmitted through the human authors, obviously the message conveyed by the book as a whole, or even the tiniest of its parts, is of paramount importance.

Such understandings of biblical authority, however, are part of the belief structure of parts of the church, and they do not appear to have been
shared by Luke himself. Luke appears to be unaware that he is writing
"scripture" himself, in the sense of some eternally and divinely sanctioned
document. Rather, he writes his Gospel for a very specific and limited audience and purpose (1:1–4).

Furthermore, Luke does not treat the Bible of his church (a Greek
translation of the Hebrew Bible, or what the later Christian church has
called the "Old Testament") as a collection of divine utterances that can
"prove" something about Jesus. Instead, he cites and alludes to those traditions in order to set his account of God's presence in and work through
Jesus in the context of the ongoing narrative of God's redemptive will for
God's people and God's relationship with them.

Luke's sense of an ongoing history of God's involvement in a saga of
divine love and human rebellion is played out in the care with which he
sets the story of Jesus in the context of the faith of Israel and the concrete
life circumstances of his own people. That sense is confirmed in the fact
that for Luke even the entire Gospel is only a part of the whole story to
which he wants his audience to pay attention, as his reflections on the early
years of the church in the book of Acts bear witness. Whether or not Luke
is factually accurate in his representation of that story is beside the point.
Rather, his artistically powerful and theologically persuasive narrative
compels our attention to the deeper truth he conveys.

Two consequences of the power of Luke's artistry need to be mentioned and reflected on before we turn to a study of the Gospel itself.

## THE GOSPEL-IN-THE-WORLD

The first consequence Luke's two-volume work has bequeathed to the
Christian church is a sense of itself as participating in a social world shaped
by many factors of the secular society—its politics, economics, culture,
and social institutions. Luke has not written literature for a "sect" or separated group hovering on the sidelines of history, preoccupied with other-
worldly concerns or a narrowly defined religious sphere of life. Instead,
the story of Jesus itself is set both explicitly and implicitly in a historical
context that establishes both limits and possibilities for what happens and
how events are understood. The religion, or, more properly, the "discipleship" to which the Gospel calls those who hear or read it engages people in specific activities and encounters with the institutions, customs, and

relationships of their own (and our own) contexts. For Luke, Jesus the Christ is indeed fully human as well as fully transparent to God's presence and will, and the gospel Jesus brought points to God's sovereignty over every aspect of human life.

## THE DOMINANCE OF A WORLDVIEW

The second consequence of Luke's artistry in telling his story is that readers are drawn into the particular view of human life and of the world that Luke himself assumes. Stories build on assumed social institutions (slavery, the practice of absentee ownership of rural lands, women's roles, and family or household structures, for example) and ways of symbolizing divine presence (for instance, able-bodiedness as a sign of God's reign). Evidence from other sources (including one's own life experience) that Luke's worldview is partial and—like every view of the world—biased has to hold its own against a tightly constructed narrative world where all the pieces fit. Speaking a counter-voice to Luke is no easy task!

An example may illustrate the problem. In my seminary class, the students and I were discussing the parable of the "prodigal" son (15:11–32). We discussed the fact that, despite the traditional title of the parable, the loving father who goes out to greet *both* of his sons is clearly the central figure of the parable. We noted also that the whole parable operates in a man's world. Despite the family and household context, there is no mention of a mother or any sisters, for the world of inheritance laws and journeys to a far country—at least in Luke's day—belongs to men. As the discussion neared its conclusion a woman spoke up: "What about the servants?" she asked. Then she elaborated, "My mother has been a domestic worker all her life, and every time the people for whom she works throw a party, she comes home exhausted. In this parable, the servants merely provide information to the elder son; then they are sent to cook the food for the family's party: Business as usual! If this is a story about God's grace and the generosity of God's reign, where is the party for the servants?" The class—myself included—sat in silence. Most of us had not even noticed the servants, who functioned for Luke and for us as merely part of the stage setting for the "real" story. Even others in the class whose family members have worked as servants, or whose ancestors were slaves, had dismissed the servants as not really important to the story. Luke's artistry, supported by common wisdom about what and who is important, created a "world" of the parable, which itself embodied injustice and discrimination that negated the very story the parable claimed to tell. Until the woman's question forced the recognition that we were accepting a world in the parable that otherwise we would disavow, we had not even noticed that we were being taken in.

## THEOLOGICAL CONCERNS FOR THE CONTEMPORARY CHURCH

Although Luke's central concern is to present a portrait of Jesus as the Christ and bearer of God's reign, he carries out that project indirectly. Instead of focusing on Jesus himself—the titles ascribed to him, or the "metaphysics" that explains his connection to God, for example—Luke allows Jesus to be known through a variety of pastoral or ethical encounters. Luke's Gospel invites his hearers or readers to meet Jesus in arenas of human concern, pain, joy, and hope. Two such arenas that are of particular importance in the life and theology of the church near the end of the twentieth century illustrate both the strength and the problem of the persuasiveness of Luke's Gospel. Those two arenas are (1) the concern celebrated in liberation theologies of God's "option for 'the poor'," and (2) the question of gender.

### The Gospel and "the Poor"

Luke is welcomed by many theologians of liberation as the Gospel that paints most vividly the implications of the message and ministry of Jesus for the marginalized people of society. Luke's first beatitude pronounces a blessing on the "poor," without Matthew's apparent spiritualizing of that category (6:20). Luke also contains a number of stories that contrast people who are rich and powerful with others who are poor or otherwise outside the mainstream of society's benefits—those who are maimed, lame, blind, deaf, or ill (see Luke 14 and the many stories of Jesus' healing ministry). Wealth that is simply amassed as a hedge against the future or a source of security is condemned (6:24–26; 12:13–21; 16:1–13, 19–31). "Alms-giving" as the redistribution of wealth and not a charitable dole is presented as an important expression of one's discipleship or following of Jesus.

Clearly, on such matters the Gospel of Luke appears to have been written from the "underside" of the dominant society of Luke's day. Similarly, it is to persons on the margins of the dominant society of our own day that this Gospel speaks most comfortingly and persuasively. It presents a vision of God's sovereign will for humankind that involves what the Gospel of John calls "abundant" life for all people. There is no condemnation of a comfortable life as evil in itself, any more than there is romanticism or idealization of poverty. For Luke the problem lies in imbalance—when some have nothing, while others have more than enough. The strength of the themes of wealth, poverty, and possessions in Luke is striking, because it is not what one would expect, given the time and place where Luke wrote. His Gospel clearly comes from a time in the church's life when it was moving from the status of a reform movement on the margins of the small Roman colony of Palestine, to that of an institution taking its place alongside others in the Roman Empire. Not yet an institution *of* power as it would become several centuries later under Constantine, the church was already an institution that *related to* power and that was looking toward its own long-term needs.

Despite the weight of such a historical moment pulling in the direction of political accommodation and economic conservatism, Luke sustains the vision of a divine project designed according to other norms. When Luke is read in light of its context, it is clear that the Gospel calls into question social relationships built on inherited structures that delineate insiders and outsiders, and that depend on patterns of dominance and dependency. Shame as a device of social control and status determination is negated in favor of the celebration of the initiative of people on the margins to take their place as "subjects"—self-determining actors—of their own lives and histories. The Gospel of Luke thus stands—if we are honest—as an offense to our own self-interest as beneficiaries of a system of honor and shame, and of relationships of "patronage," that rewards people who are wealthy, powerful, or able-bodied, and that penalizes those who are not. Through this Gospel, the good news of God's reign confronts us from outside the norms of business as usual and requires our response.

## Women in the Gospel of Luke

On the other hand, when we examine the Gospel of Luke asking about its treatment of questions of gender, the verdict is different. For a long time Luke has had the reputation of being a "friend" to women—even an early Christian "feminist"—because of the larger number of stories featuring women in this Gospel than in any of the others (see, for example, chaps. 1 and 2; 7:36–50; 8:1–3; 10:38–42; 13:10–17; 15:8–10; 18:1–8; 23:27–31, 49, 55–56). Since so many of these examples are found only in

Luke, some scholars have even suggested that Luke drew on a source of traditions about Jesus that came from a community led by women, or that his own community was led by women, or even that the author we call "Luke" was really a woman whose identity was disguised by the later church.

Closer study, however, leads to another conclusion. Although there are indeed many stories that feature women, women actually appear in very traditional roles. Typically, they serve at table, keep house, suffer from illnesses and are healed by Jesus, and bear children. Even Mary, Jesus' mother, fades into the background once she has given birth to Jesus. Her response to God's call is never celebrated as her own "discipleship," and Luke leaves unanswered the question of whether she is part of the new "family" constituted by his followers (8:19–21).

The famous argument between Mary and Martha (10:38–42) is similarly ambiguous in its portrayal of women. On one hand, the story counters stereotypical pictures of women as valued only in domestic roles like preparing meals for guests. Mary is praised for choosing to listen to Jesus instead of joining her sister's hostessing frenzy. On the other hand, however, women's traditional work is put down as of lesser value, and the woman who is clearly running her own household with all the energy she can muster is held up to ridicule. Luke shows Jesus praising the woman who sits like a mouse in the corner quietly listening to him. Unlike events where male followers learn from Jesus in order to preach the gospel and to carry out their own ministries, Mary's education is not said to equip her for leadership in the community. She simply listens, and nothing more.

Two women are portrayed as taking initiatives to meet their needs and, in one case, to obtain healing from Jesus. One of the women—the tenacious widow—remains only a figure in a parable (18:1–8), and the other—after her proclamation transforms a "crowd" into a "people"—simply disappears from the Gospel account (8:43–48). Thus, while it is true that women's stories are more plentiful in Luke than in other Gospels, women are often present as themes in or passive recipients of Jesus' teaching, and as objects of healing. They are voiceless learners, remaining in the background in supporting roles. They serve on the margins, embodying what is identified as the lifestyle of discipleship (9:46–48; 22:24–27), but at the same time, they are given no leadership or responsibility in the community that formed around Jesus.

In the end, then, Luke's Gospel seems to legitimize male dominance rather than standing as a manifesto for women's affirmation and leadership. Some feminist interpreters have even suggested that Luke and Acts might have been intended—at least in part—as handbooks for good Christian women who are to be quiet, grateful, prayerful, and supportive of their male leaders. The picture is a sad one for many women who feel we have lost a potential ally in Luke and his Gospel.

But for Luke the point of the Gospel emerges only gradually, and at the end it is the women who model the key to the gospel's power. At the empty tomb the women "remembered" Jesus' words (24:8), and that memory is the key that turns mourning into Easter joy. These quiet, background people— the women who have been with Jesus from the beginning—have not been passive objects, as at first might seem to be the case. Instead, they have been active witnesses who in the moment of crisis are prepared to testify on behalf of the crucified and now risen Jesus. In a dynamic that characterizes Luke's Gospel from the very beginning (see Luke 1 and 2), categories of strong and weak, rich and poor, insider and outsider, subject and object are overturned in the logic of the reign of God—God's sovereign will for the world and for the redemption of humankind. The women carry the story on.

## Luke in Its Context: Questions of "Introduction"

### FINDING THE QUESTIONS

How should one begin the study of a Gospel? At first the answer seems obvious: The Gospels are about Jesus, so one should begin with Jesus. To say that, though, catches us in a circular argument, for all we know about Jesus is what is contained in the Gospels. We have four Gospels in the Bible (and a number of others that are "apocryphal"—early Christian writings not included in the Bible), and they differ in the stories they tell about Jesus and even in the claims they make about him. Sometimes they differ in the details of particular stories, and at other times they differ in the order in which the stories are told or even in which ones are included.

The differences among the Gospels are troubling if we assume that they are intended to be biographies providing accurate information about what Jesus said or did. In that case, we find ourselves caught up in ques- tions of what is factually "true," and the discrepancies pose problems of determining which version is correct. We then must deal with the dilemma of "mistakes" or "errors" in what the church has called the "Word of God."

The situation is quite different when we recognize that the Gospels are preaching, rather than reporting, about Jesus. The word "Gospel" itself means "good news." The noun is not found in the Greek of Luke's Gospel. Instead, Luke uses a verb—a single word—that means "to-preach-the-good-news" or "to-preach-the-gospel." Preaching always involves the intersection of content and audience. The question governing the Gospel writers' work appears to have been, How can I make clear the meaning of Jesus as good news for my particular community?

That question requires that each Gospel writer have a specific community in mind, and that the writer know that community well. What events and relationships are shaping the community? From what chronic or acute pain are its members suffering? What are the principal qualities of its cultural, economic, political, and social identity? Of what are people afraid? What causes of joy, comfort, beauty, and peace do people celebrate?

Today when we think of a preacher addressing the needs of a particular community, we think of someone working to understand how a text that we have in fixed form, as part of a collection of "books" that are bound in the single book we call the Bible, relates to the life of the contemporary community. The "text" and the resulting sermon are clearly distinguished. When one proclaims the good news of Jesus as the Christ, one preaches "from" or "about" a particular story about or teaching of Jesus.

For the Gospel writers, on the other hand, the traditions about Jesus still circulated in collections of stories of his life and teachings associated with him that were not yet seen as "fixed." Instead, they could be adapted, reorganized, and commented upon within the text itself, in order to make the author's point about Jesus as good news. Material coming from a variety of places of origin in the life of the earlier Christian communities could be woven together in a narrative that retold the gospel (in the sense in which Mark uses that noun, to name the story of Jesus' ministry). The "truth" of such a story lies not in the factual accuracy of the information it presents about Jesus but in its power to comfort, inspire, and transform the lives of its hearers. It is the truth of art, literature, or music, not the truth we hope to find in news reports.

Given the importance of the community to which a Gospel was directed, and of the author's relationship to that community, we might do well to begin our study of Luke's Gospel by inquiring into the identity of this person we call "Luke" and the community to which he wrote. That too is easier said than done.

"Introductions" to biblical books—discussions of who wrote the book,

using what sources, when, where, to whom, and why—often cause readers' eyes to glaze over from boredom and total frustration. The number
of times words like "perhaps," "possibly," "likely," and "unknown" dot the
text of the most responsible of those discussions convinces readers that a
fabric of such a sheer and even flimsy weave cannot bear any weight of interpretation. The details are elusive, and it is often hard to see what difference a few years in the date of composition, or in the precise identification of the city where Luke lived, could possibly make.

On the other hand, our curiosity still makes us pull and twist the threads
of the introductory fabric, and legitimately so. These biblical books that
have become so central to our faith and our lives evoke questions. What
can we know about the author of a particular book? For whom was it written, and why? What was the daily life of those people like? Was it anything like our own? What made their lives pleasant, exciting, or full of
hope? What pains, fears, or anxieties haunted them? How were joys confirmed and hurts comforted by their faith? Who are these ancestors in the
faith with whom our own lives become entangled through the Bible we
share?

The task of reconstructing the everyday life of the communities to
which the Gospels were written is difficult, for we have to accomplish that
task from clues within the Gospels themselves. Those communities and
their concerns are addressed indirectly, through the way the story of
Jesus is told. Some of the "background data" we pick up from the story
reflects Jesus' own context in rural Palestine in the first third of the first
century. At other points we find remnants of the life of the earlier communities (living between the time of Jesus and when a particular Gospel
was written) that told the stories or remembered the teachings. The context and concerns of the Gospel writer must be read largely between the
lines and through the particular points that author emphasizes.

In the case of the Gospel of Luke, the author has provided additional
clues about himself, about the purpose and audience for which the book
was written, and about the sort of work it is intended to be. The first of
those clues is in the fact that this same author has given us a second volume in addition to the Gospel that bears his name, the book of Acts. Luke
himself tells us that Acts is a sequel to the "first book" written to
"Theophilus" (Acts 1:1; see the discussion of Theophilus below).

The kinship of these two books is masked by their placement in the
Bible. Those who gathered the books we know as the "New Testament"
into their present order apparently decided to begin with Gospels, or stories of Jesus' life. The first three—Matthew, Mark, and Luke—are very

similar, and so it is not surprising that they were kept together. The fourth book is also clearly a Gospel, but very different from the first three. It was thus tucked in at the end of the collection of Gospels. As understandable as this rationale is, it resulted in the Gospel of John "interrupting" Luke's narrative.

The fact that Luke's narrative continues into the history of the church provides a clue about Luke's historical context. It situates him, not as a contemporary of the events of Jesus' life, but as someone for whom the story of the early church—at least through the careers of Peter and Paul—is part of the history of God's saving presence in and through Jesus the Christ.

## LUKE'S PREFACE
## Luke 1:1–4

The second set of clues that the writer we call "Luke" has given us about himself and his context can be found in the brief preface with which the Gospel begins (1:1–4):

> 1:1 **Since many have undertaken to set down an orderly account of the events that have been fulfilled among us,** 2 **just as they were handed on to us by those who from the beginning were eyewitnesses and servants of the word,** 3 **I too decided, after investigating everything carefully from the very first, to write an orderly account for you, most excellent Theophilus,** 4 **so that you may know the truth concerning the things about which you have been instructed.**

As modern readers of various types of nonfiction, we are used to authors' prefaces, in which they explain why their project is significant, how it differs from other similar works, and to which predecessors and colleagues they are particularly indebted. We often skip over such paragraphs as merely tips of the hat to scholarly courtesy and integrity at best, or self-commendation at worst. In the case of the preface to Luke's Gospel, though, we would do well to pay close attention to his preface, for it gives us several important hints for understanding what follows.

Luke is the only Gospel writer who begins with such a preface. In contrast, Matthew begins with a genealogy (similar to the genealogies found in the Hebrew Bible and in Luke 3:23–38), Mark jumps right into the middle of the story of John the Baptist's preparation for Jesus' ministry, and John begins with a hymn. Clearly, Luke is not simply following a recipe for starting a Gospel. But Luke's use of a preface appears to be deliberate, for he begins his second volume, the book of Acts, in a similar way (Acts 1:1–5). What do the content and very existence of this preface add to our knowledge of the author?

We have to go outside of the Bible to find other authors who begin their works as Luke does. In fact, it was common for writers of historical and scientific works at the time when this Gospel was written to use such statements of purpose and method. Even the grammar, vocabulary, and style of these opening verses of Luke resemble their secular parallels (for example, the beginning of Josephus's *Against Apion*), and they differ from Luke's style in the rest of the Gospel and Acts. The fact that Luke follows this rhetorical practice of beginning his work with a preface places him in the company of formal scholars and academicians of his day. This formal scholarly precision suggests that it is important to the writer that this Gospel be seen as credible by such an audience. The content of the preface, however, makes it clear that Luke does not intend the Gospel to be seen as an academic exercise.

## WRITTEN FROM FAITH TO FAITH

The author is writing as an insider—one of those among whom the events to be described have been "fulfilled." In other words, the author is a Christian, and not someone who has researched the events as a disinterested scholar. However, the author is not one of Jesus' own disciples—an eyewitness to the events being described. Instead, the preface acknowledges that there are already other "orderly accounts" of these events (what we would call "Gospels"), and other materials as well (1:1–2). When Luke refers to his use of those sources, he uses formal language for the passing on of tradition within the Christian community ("handed on"; see also 1 Cor. 11:23 and 15:3). Luke clearly sees himself as one link in a chain of people who reflect on and interpret the events that form the foundational story of the Christian faith.

## THE QUESTION OF SOURCES

Luke does not provide us with a bibliography of sources used, and it is difficult to know what exactly should be included on that list. To a large extent, one's response to that question depends on how one understands the process by which the first three Gospels came to be written in their present form, with both their strong similarity (even to the point of identical wording in some sections) and their equally striking differences. For a long time Matthew was accepted by the church and by scholars alike as the earliest Gospel. Because of the high degree of agreement among Matthew, Mark, and Luke (so high, in fact, that they are called the "Synoptic" Gospels, because they can be "viewed together"), the consensus was that Mark and Luke in some way drew on Matthew, adapting that original Gospel for their own communities' needs.

Some scholars still view Matthew as the oldest Gospel and the basis for Mark and Luke, but by far the largest number of scholars now view Mark as the earliest Gospel. The evidence they cite is Mark's use of a number of Aramaic terms, the lack of a clear reference to the destruction of Jerusalem that took place in 70 C.E. ("Common Era"—formerly designated "A.D.") as having already taken place, and the generally rough and unpolished language that is "improved" when the same stories are told in Matthew or Luke.

Besides the basic story found in Mark, the large amount of additional material found in both Matthew and Mark (often with largely identical wording, but in different places in the overall narrative) suggests that they shared another source in common. For many years that source was assumed to be a written document, and it was referred to as "Q," from the German word *Quelle* or "source." No such document has ever been found (though the apocryphal Gospel of Thomas is the sort of collection of teachings and very little narrative material that "Q"—if it existed—appears to have been). In the absence of evidence of such a document, many of us prefer to refer simply to the source shared by Matthew and Luke, leaving open the question of whether it was a written document or an oral collection consisting mostly of parables and other teachings of Jesus.

In addition to the basic structure of Mark's narrative and this additional common material, Matthew and Luke each contain some teachings and stories about Jesus that are unique to that Gospel. This material probably includes stories about and teachings of Jesus that had circulated in the author's community (but apparently not in those of the other Gospel writers) as well as the author's own comments and editorial work.

Although all the Gospel writers—and, by his own admission, Luke in particular—clearly drew on sources of information about Jesus to compose their Gospels, none of them should be seen as a biographer bent on factual accuracy. Neither should any of them be seen as wooden compilers stringing together material they received simply for the sake of preserving it. Instead, it is important to respect the Gospel writers as the preachers, theologians, and artists they in fact were, as each crafted a beautiful and powerful narrative portrait of Jesus of Nazareth.

## THE DATE OF THE GOSPEL

Luke's use of sources helps us get an idea of when that Gospel was written. The Gospel of Mark was probably written around 65–70 C.E. Mark 13 suggests that the Jewish-Roman War was close at hand, if not already in process. Furthermore, it is unlikely that other Gospels would have been written much before that date. The expectation that the risen Christ would soon return in triumph meant that in the early decades of the church's life people in general were not making long-range plans. During the first few decades after Jesus' death, the memories of eyewitnesses and their immediate apprentices would have been seen as adequate to preserve Jesus' teachings and the stories about him as guidance for the life and faith of the community.

The Gospel of Luke, then, would have come even later than these early accounts. The Gospel also indicates the author's familiarity with the events of the Jewish-Roman War (66–70 C.E.) and with the trauma of the loss of Jerusalem and the Temple (see for example 19:41–44; 21:20–24). An additional clue to when the author wrote can be found in the book of Acts. Paul's missionary activity is a major focus of that narrative, but the reports of his travels are hard to coordinate with the references to his travels in Paul's own letters. In addition, the report contained in Acts 15 of Paul's important meeting with the Christian leaders in Jerusalem differs markedly from Paul's own version of that event in Galatians 2. Furthermore, summaries of Paul's theology according to Acts do not correspond to what is found in his letters. Those discrepancies suggest that Luke worked before collections of Paul's letters were widely circulated through the church—in other words, before about 90 C.E. Luke, then, appears to have written both the Gospel and Acts sometime between 80 and 90 C.E.

## WHO IS "LUKE"?

The discrepancies between Acts and Paul's letters cause us also to look at the name we give to our author. The name "Luke" has been associated with the third of the four biblical Gospels at least since late in the second century. Drawing on Col. 4:14, Philem. 24, and 2 Tim. 4:11, Irenaeus, Bishop of Lyons (c. 185 C.E.), identified the author of this Gospel and the book of Acts with Luke, the physician and companion of Paul—a tradition in which Irenaeus was later joined by such other early theologians as Tertullian, Origen, and Clement of Alexandria. That same tradition led to the name being used to identify the Gospel in the headings supplied in the biblical manuscripts.

As widespread as its acceptance was in the early church, that identification of the author does not hold up under careful study. The conclusion that the author was a companion of Paul is based on the travel diaries in Acts that are written in the first person plural (Acts 16:10–17; 20:5–21:18; 27:1–28:16). Those diaries that place the author on the journey with Paul might well be a source on which the author of Acts drew (just as he drew on others' writings to compose his Gospel), rather than his own reminiscences. The discrepancies noted above between Acts and Paul's letters support the judgment that the two were not co-workers. It should be noted, however, that some scholars explain these discrepancies by suggesting that Paul and Luke only collaborated for a short time, and thus Luke did not know Paul's theology very well.

Corroborating evidence of medical terms and insights that would fit the profession of physician also does not hold up. Instead, Luke's careful use of language, his sometimes elegant style, his familiarity with both the content and style of the Greek translation of the Hebrew Bible known as the Septuagint (commonly designated by the Roman numeral LXX, following the tradition that seventy scholars arrived independently and spontaneously at that same translation), his use of formal rhetorical devices, and his general historical bent in consulting and adapting various sources, mark him as a well-educated person. That education would have provided him with a foundation in the natural sciences as well as history, literature, and rhetoric, and evidence of such a foundation is all that Luke's writings reveal.

Thus, we must finally conclude that the author of both the third Gospel and the book of Acts—like the authors of the other Gospels—is anonymous. Even though we cannot know exactly who the author was, for convenience's sake I will continue to use the traditional name to refer to him. After all, we have to call him something. I will also use masculine pronouns to refer to the author, but not simply because they are appropriate for the name "Luke." I am convinced that the author was writing from a man's perspective. He seems to take men's reality and men's leadership in the community around Jesus for granted. Conversely, though Luke often refers to women, they are always shown in subordinate or traditional roles. He appears to be offering guidelines for women's appropriate behavior in the context of the late-first-century church, which was modeled on a benevolently administered but hierarchical household (see, for example, Eph. 5:21–6:9 for a more prescriptive statement of such a model; see also the discussion of issues of gender in Luke in the first part of this introduction).

## WHO IS "THEOPHILUS"?

In addition to providing clues to his own background, Luke's preface also shows that he has a very specific audience in mind, whom he holds in great respect ("most excellent Theophilus"). Unfortunately, we do not know who Theophilus was. Theophilus (which means something like "friend of God" or "one who loves God") might be the name of a specific person Luke wants to instruct (or perhaps convince) about the "truth" of the gospel. On the other hand, the name may be a general reference to members of Luke's community, many of whom may have been Gentile "God-fearers" attracted to the theology and moral principles of Judaism, but not full converts to Judaism. That segment of the population was a rich source of members for Christian communities in many cities of the Roman Empire (such as Antioch in Syria, Rome itself, or a city in southern Greece, all of which are suggested as possible locations of Luke's community). In fact, Luke himself may have come from its ranks.

Several details in the Gospel fit such a Gentile community on the edge of Judaism. For example, Luke traces Jesus' genealogy not only through various key figures of Israel's history, but back to Adam, the ancestor of all the peoples of the world (3:23–38). Furthermore, the few portions of Mark's Gospel that Luke does not incorporate into his Gospel (for example, Mark 7:1–23) include some that are specifically concerned with questions of Jewish law or "Torah" that go beyond basic food laws and laws about sabbath keeping that Gentile God-fearers would be expected to observe. In a similar vein, the book of Acts discusses the mission to the Gentiles without much attention to the issue of circumcision that was so crucial to Paul's mission and to his interaction with other Jewish Christians. Alongside this lack of attention to matters of concern principally within the Jewish community, the author is careful to set the Gospel in the context of secular history (2:1–3 and 3:1–2), "for this was not done in a corner" (Acts 26:26). Finally, the question of the relationship between Jews and Gentiles occupies a great deal of attention in Luke. Running through the Gospel is Luke's emphasis on God as an actor on the stage of world history, carrying out a plan of salvation that encompasses Israel and the nations alike.

## LUKE'S "ORDERLY ACCOUNT"

Luke's preface also provides clues about the sort of work Luke is creating. He acknowledges his indebtedness to others who have offered their versions of "the events that have been fulfilled among us" (1:1), but he is not merely a passive recipient of these traditions. His concern for "truth" does not entail meticulous repetition of words or data found in those sources. Instead, Luke has felt free to carry out his own investigation and present his own "orderly account" of the events in order to help Theophilus know "the truth" about things he has already learned.

Luke's claim to have presented "an orderly account" and "the truth" leads us to ask what sort of order, and what kind of truth. Luke gives clues rather than clear answers. For instance, the Greek word translated "account" does not mean a list of data (such as the financial records or "accounts" of a business), but a narrative—a continuous story. To call that narrative "orderly" need not mean that Luke has investigated the facts and now (in contrast to more careless predecessors) presents them in the accurate chronological sequence in which they occurred. Instead, it can refer to the presentation of a coherent narrative in a literary sense. In other words, the transitions between sections or scenes are smooth, and the plot development is coherent. An "orderly account" can also mean simply an account appropriate to the development of the author's agenda and purpose for writing, whatever that might have been.

This last type of "order" seems to be the one probably meant here, and that order is related to the author's concern to convey "truth." The "truth" relates to what Theophilus has been "instructed," which is a technical term for the "catechism" by which Christians received the essential elements of their religion. In other words, Luke's purpose is theological—to help Theophilus better understand the gospel as the account of how God's intent has been "fulfilled" in their midst. To be more specific, Luke is a preacher and a theologian at the same time, for he engages in his reflection and interpretation in the very process of proclaiming the gospel.

Luke's own emphasis on the narrative or "orderly account" directs our attention as readers beyond the individual teachings and stories that make up the narrative. As important as each of these is, the way they are arranged and how they function as parts of a larger whole are essential factors in setting forth the truth Luke is trying to communicate. Thus, while using this study, for example, the reader should refer frequently to the outline of the structure of the Gospel that serves as the table of contents, in order to keep in mind just where a particular passage fits into Luke's vision of the whole.

Luke's preface thus sets limits on what we can expect from the narrative that follows, and at the same time emphasizes the importance of the story he has set out to tell. We should not look to the Gospel as a deposit of historical facts to be carefully mined from the ore of church tradition. By the same token, Luke's Gospel should not be seen as the definitive biography of Jesus, every detail of which is presented in the precisely accurate chronological order that Luke's research uncovered. This Gospel is, however, a carefully crafted presentation and interpretation that both stretches and redefines what we have already learned about Jesus—the life-sustaining truth that the gospel proclaims.

# 1. Origins and Definitions

*Luke 1:5–4:13*

# 1. Births and Beginnings
## Luke 1:5–2:52

Three distinct styles of writing mark segments of Luke's Gospel. After the formal scholarly preface, Luke's tone shifts dramatically. In place of academic jargon (a first-century equivalent of such notes as "Submitted in partial fulfillment of the requirements of the degree of Doctor of Philosophy"), Luke's language becomes "biblical," reflecting the forms and cadences of the Septuagint. Just as suddenly, with the beginning of the account of Jesus' public ministry in Luke 3, Luke's language changes again, this time to a more everyday usage. From that point on, he writes carefully and correctly, but with neither the formality of the preface nor the deliberately religious tone of the first two chapters. The contrast is like what happens in a worship service where all the prayers are in Elizabethan English ("thou dost," "thy name") and the sermon in modern speech.

It would be interesting to know why Luke decided to make those dramatic shifts in language, but unfortunately he did not tell us. The best we can do is to be aware of the *effect* of those shifts—what happens to us when we encounter them—and then to see if possible motives suggest themselves. The modern parallel might be helpful. Some people, to be sure, are offended by the use of archaic language in prayer, seeing it as artificial or pretentious. Others, however, feel that it expresses greater respect, whether because of its heightened formality or because it seems to convey a deeper intimacy. In any event, it is not the language we use for everyday communication, but rather, it is reserved for speaking to God.

In addition, for many people who were brought up on earlier English translations of the Bible such as the King James Version, the rhythms of Elizabethan English connect them to the entire biblical story. The language itself is strengthening and reassuring because of the memories and associations it invokes, and in that way it makes real again the presence, power, and love of God. It does not require a great deal of imagination to see the peculiarly biblical-sounding Greek of the beginning of Luke's narrative having a similar effect on his hearers. Whatever twists and turns Luke's story may eventually take, it is from the outset recognizable as an account that connects the hearers to the God they have already come to know, to count on, and to trust.

On Christmas Eve, surrounded by candlelight, those of us for whom Christmas memories of our childhood and youth are happy ones (though, sadly, for far too many people that is not the case) find ourselves transported into those warm and happy memories as soon as we hear the first words of Luke 2. Christmas Present is enveloped in all the Christmases Past, and we draw strength not only for all the Christmases Yet-To-Come, but also for the seasons in between. Even those for whom memories of Christmas recall times of pain or sadness often find in the rhythms of these songs and stories a glimpse of God's persistent longing for humankind and determination to be the God of "good news" or "gospel" in the midst of pain.

When we are caught up in the power of such awareness, questions that might normally concern us—What exactly might the shepherds have heard? or How was the child Jesus really conceived?—are held in suspension for a time, as the images sing their carols, dazzle us with their splendor, and cradle us in their warmth. Information and factual accuracy take second place to the effect the narrative and the hymns have on us.

Similarly for Luke's audience, the fact that he really does not quote particular passages of the Septuagint would have been overshadowed by the effect evoked by the whole picture he presents. The story of Hannah (1 Samuel 1 and 2), her song as well as those of Miriam (Exodus 15) and Deborah (Judges 5), and the prophecies of Isaiah, for example, flow together into a pattern of divine presence and promise given new substance in the account that Luke is undertaking.

## PARALLEL BEGINNINGS

Luke's Gospel narrative begins with parallel accounts of the annunciations and births of John the Baptist and Jesus. The design is what many call "step-parallelism," since every affirmation made concerning John is heightened in the parallel passage about Jesus: John is born to an elderly woman who has previously been childless, whereas Jesus is born to a "virgin"; John "will be great in the sight of the Lord" (1:15), but Jesus "will be called Son of God" (1:35); and so on. The two narratives are braided together, with first one and then the other coming into focus, blending into a single account only to relate the visit of Mary to Elizabeth (1:39–56). The two chapters can be divided as follows (asterisks indicate hymns or canticles in the narrative):

The variation in length of the various sections makes Luke's points of emphasis clear, both within and between the two narrative strands. For example, in the story of John, Luke focuses on the annunciation of his coming birth and on the giving of his name. His actual birth and the summary of his childhood merit barely a mention. In the story of Jesus, on the other hand, the time surrounding the birth and presentation in the temple receives the greatest attention, with the annunciation told in just over half as many verses as either of these episodes or as the annunciation of John. Incorporated into the narratives at key points are hymns or canticles. These songs of praise and thanksgiving (attributed to Mary, Zechariah, and Simeon) invite us to linger a while and let the wonder of it all sink into our hearts.

## JOHN'S BIRTH FORETOLD
## Luke 1:5–25

1:5 **In the days of King Herod of Judea, there was a priest named Zechariah, who belonged to the priestly order of Abijah. His wife was a descendant of Aaron, and her name was Elizabeth. 6 Both of them were righteous before God, living blamelessly according to all the commandments and regulations of the Lord. 7 But they had no children, because Elizabeth was barren, and both were getting on in years.**

8 Once when he was serving as priest before God and his section was on duty, 9 he was chosen by lot, according to the custom of the priesthood, to enter the sanctuary of the Lord and offer incense. 10 Now at the time of the incense offering, the whole assembly of the people was praying outside. 11 Then there appeared to him an angel of the Lord, standing at the right side of the altar of incense. 12 When Zechariah saw him, he was terrified; and fear overwhelmed him. 13 But the angel said to him, "Do not be afraid, Zechariah, for your prayer has been heard. Your wife Elizabeth will bear you a son, and you will name him John. 14 You will have joy and gladness, and many will rejoice at his birth, 15 for he will be great in the sight of the Lord. He must never drink wine or strong drink; even before his birth he will be filled with the Holy Spirit. 16 He will turn many of the people of Israel to the Lord their God. 17 With the spirit and power of Elijah he will go before him, to turn the hearts of parents to their children, and the disobedient to the wisdom of the righteous, to make ready a people prepared for the Lord." 18 Zechariah said to the angel, "How will I know that this is so? For I am an old man, and my wife is getting on in years." 19 The angel replied, "I am Gabriel. I stand in the presence of God, and I have been sent to speak to you and to bring you this good news. 20 But now, because you did not believe my words, which will be fulfilled in their time, you will become mute, unable to speak, until the day these things occur."

21 Meanwhile the people were waiting for Zechariah, and wondered at his delay in the sanctuary. 22 When he did come out, he could not speak to them, and they realized that he had seen a vision in the sanctuary. He kept motioning to them and remained unable to speak. 23 When his time of service was ended, he went to his home.

24 After those days his wife Elizabeth conceived, and for five months she remained in seclusion. She said, 25 "This is what the Lord has done for me when he looked favorably on me and took away the disgrace I have endured among my people."

The story begins simply. It is set during Herod's reign over Judea, but the theme is a common one in the Bible. A husband and wife, Zechariah and Elizabeth, have reached old age without having children. Abram and Sarai shared this fate (Genesis 16—21), as did Hannah and Elkanah (1 Samuel 1). For all these couples, any emotional pain from longing for but being unable to conceive children would have been compounded by the social stigma. Women of the more privileged classes (which these women clearly were) would have been seen to have fulfilled their purpose in life only by bearing sons. In the absence of knowledge about the biological process of conception and the reasons for infertility, ancient cultures usually held the women responsible for a couple's inability to conceive children. Her "failure" was often interpreted as God's judgment against her, by which she brought suffering and shame on her husband.

Luke quickly silences any such malicious suggestions in this case by emphasizing the exemplary character of both husband and wife (1:6–7). In human terms their childlessness is simply the sad truth. For Luke, it becomes an occasion for God to act. Luke sets the stage with care and precision. At the climax of a typical liturgy while Zechariah is on duty in the temple (1:8–10), he is addressed by a messenger from God. The Greek word translated as "angel" means "messenger." It can refer to either a human messenger, as it does in 7:24 and 9:52, or a divine messenger, as it does in the first two chapters of the Gospel and in 22:43.

This messenger, who later identifies himself as the angel Gabriel, seems to specialize in birth announcements in this narrative, for he gets to deliver the news of her pregnancy to Mary as well (1:26). In both cases he is said to begin with the reassurance, "Do not be afraid." Since that refrain also greets the shepherds at the time of Jesus' birth (2:10), Gabriel should probably be understood as the spokesperson for the heavenly chorus as well. In any event, the presence and role of angels is taken for granted. Their role in Luke, as in the earliest parts of the Hebrew Bible, is a simple one: They are interpreters of God's plan and comforters of human fears. They are recognized as personifications of God's blessing and help to God's people and as bearers of God's grace. And they will be heeded.

Zechariah appears to have forgotten that last point about angels, for Gabriel's words evoke a skeptical question (1:18). From a human point of view, who could blame Zechariah for having his doubts? But as a priest he should have been attuned to the angel's real message. The promised baby was not to be merely God's gracious blessing upon the parents—something for which the Bible offers several precedents. This time the focus was to be on the life and calling of the child, who was "to make ready a people prepared for the Lord" (1:17). "With the spirit and power of Elijah," the child was to shift the focus of attention to God's future as the locus of God's presence—not to turn the children back to the ways of their parents, but "to turn the hearts of parents to their children." The child was to call the holy people into the future God was planning for them, just as tradition held that the prophet Elijah would do when he returned just before God's final triumphant act of judgment and redemption at the end of time.

The consequence of Zechariah's unbelief is that this priestly spokesperson charged to address God on behalf of the people and the people on behalf of God is rendered silent, unable even to explain to the people what has happened. The messenger's news remains a secret. It would be a mistake to read this account as meaning that a person's inability to speak is a punishment from God. Luke is not writing a manual for the ethical interpretation of human illness: "Symptom x results from misbehavior y." Instead, Luke is unfolding a specific narrative in which the contradiction represented by a skeptical response to God's messenger—whom Zechariah of all people should have recognized as the bearer of truth—is mirrored in other reversals. Zechariah, who is used to speaking, is silenced, while Elizabeth, whose body itself communicates what Zechariah cannot, articulates God's favor (1:24–25). We who know the message of the angel to Zechariah recognize that Elizabeth's interpretation is not adequate, for it is limited to the way God has healed the suffering of the past. But, for the moment, it will suffice.

## JESUS' BIRTH FORETOLD
## Luke 1:26–38

> 1:26 **In the sixth month the angel Gabriel was sent by God to a town in Galilee called Nazareth, [27] to a virgin engaged to a man whose name was Joseph, of the house of David. The virgin's name was Mary. [28] And he came to her and said, "Greetings, favored one! The Lord is with you." [29] But she was much perplexed by his words and pondered what sort of greeting this might be. [30] The angel said to her, "Do not be afraid, Mary, for you have found favor with God. [31] And now, you will conceive in your womb and bear a son, and you will name him Jesus. [32] He will be great, and will be called the Son of the Most High, and the Lord God will give to him the throne of his ancestor David. [33] He will reign over the house of Jacob forever, and of his kingdom there will be no end." [34] Mary said to the angel, "How can this be, since I am a virgin?" [35] The angel said to her, "The Holy Spirit will come upon you, and the power of the Most High will overshadow you; therefore the child to be born will be holy; he will be called Son of God. [36] And now, your relative Elizabeth in her old age has also conceived a son; and this is the sixth month for her who was said to be barren. [37] For nothing will be impossible with God." [38] Then Mary said, "Here am I, the servant of the Lord; let it be with me according to your word." Then the angel departed from her.**

Both relative time ("in the sixth month") and the same messenger connect the two annunciations. Otherwise the details are contrasting. Instead of in the temple in Jerusalem, this annunciation takes place in the remote village of Nazareth in Galilee. The recipient of the news is not an elderly priest during his official service in the temple, but a young, unmarried woman engaged to a certain Joseph, identified only as a descendant of David. The credibility gap relative to Gabriel's message is not that an elderly and (to this point) childless woman will finally conceive a son, but rather that the

promised birth will come to a woman living still in the time between betrothal and "home-taking," when the marriage would become official.
While the first promised child is to be the preparer of the way, the second
is to be the one awaited (1:32–33). While Zechariah's question to the angel's message leads to his becoming speechless, Mary's is greeted by renewed assurance about the identity of the child, who "will be called Son of
God" (1:35b), and about God's power to effect such a promise (1:36–37).
Zechariah is left unable even to convey the angel's message to the crowd
or to Elizabeth, but Mary has another chance to accept the word (1:38).

The angel's message that Jesus is to be called Son of God introduces a
motif that will reappear like a brightly colored thread woven through
Luke's account, which comes to prominence to highlight crucial points in
the narrative. Twice—at the baptism (3:22) and the transfiguration
(9:35)—a divine voice calls Jesus God's chosen or beloved Son. In the
story of Jesus' testing in the wilderness, the phrase "if you are the Son of
God" is used twice by the devil as the hook on which to try to catch Jesus
(4:3, 9). Demons (or the people possessed by them) recognize Jesus' identity when ordinary mortals are still unable to do so (for example, 4:41;
8:28). Finally, the charge that Jesus is blaspheming by claiming to be Son
of God is brought against Jesus in his hearing before the Sanhedrin that
eventually leads to his crucifixion (22:70).

The scene between Mary and the messenger Gabriel is dotted with
question marks concerning what exactly is being claimed about the coming
birth. The matter is complicated by the similarities and differences between
Luke's version of Jesus' origins and that presented in Matthew 1—2.
In order to understand what Luke is affirming, it will be important to explore both the divergences and the points of connection between the two
accounts.

In both Gospels, Mary is called a "virgin." The Greek word, which can
be used of men or of women, identifies someone who has not had sexual
intercourse. Before we jump immediately to the conclusion that Luke has
in mind the virginal conception of Jesus, however, other details of the narratives need to be explored. For instance, in Matthew, where the announcement of Jesus' approaching birth is made to Joseph, the birth is
identified as the fulfillment of Isaiah 7:14 (Matt. 1:23). The Hebrew text
of that verse refers only to a "young woman." In the LXX, however, the
Greek word for "virgin" is used. In its current setting in Matthew, the
Greek meaning is clearly intended, but in Luke the situation is not as clear.

In the first place, while the annunciation in Matthew refers to a pregnancy already under way, in Luke the verbs are in the future tense: She

will conceive. Nothing is to prevent the interpretation that the pregnancy will occur in due order, after the home-taking, with Joseph as the promised child's father. Such a reading is supported by the promise that the child will be given "the throne of his ancestor David" (1:32), to which lineage Joseph is the crucial link (1:27). Mary's question "How can this be?" (1:34) is then a simple human quest for reassurance that all will happen in due time and in due order, in keeping with the commitments made in her betrothal.

The messenger's reply to Mary's question provides precisely such assurance, and it need not be read as referring to anything but a conception involving human parents. The explanation is that the Holy Spirit will "come upon" and "overshadow" Mary. The way the underlying Greek words are used elsewhere in the New Testament is significant. In the accounts of the transfiguration of Jesus in all three of the Synoptic Gospels, a cloud is said to "overshadow" Jesus, Moses, Elijah, and the three disciples (Matt. 17:5; Mark 9:7; Luke 9:34), and in Acts 5:15, Peter's shadow falling on or overshadowing people is said to convey healing. In these places the verb clearly refers not to impregnation, but to divine presence and power. The word translated as "come upon" sometimes carries a neutral meaning of "occur" or "happen", or even simply "come" or "arrive" (for example, Acts 1:8; 14:19), but it often conveys a threatening sense of overpowering by a stronger adversary (Luke 11:22), threatening circumstances (Acts 8:24; James 5:1), or even the woes of the end-time (Luke 21:26; Eph. 2:7). In short, nothing in the language of the passage itself requires the interpretation of a "virginal conception" or a birth any more "miraculous" than every occasion of new life.

What Luke does proclaim by this annunciation is that the child whose birth is foretold is to play a unique role in the fulfillment of God's purposes and in mediating God's presence in the world. For Luke to affirm that the child "will be called Son of God" refers not to biological paternity, but to the acclamation of God's self-evident, indelible commitment and engagement in this human life from before its beginning.

Mary's assent to this project (1:38) is the step Zechariah could not take. The pattern of reversal of status and privilege that will become the hallmark of the good news Jesus brings is already set in the annunciation stories. Zechariah becomes powerless to continue his formal liturgical duties, while Mary becomes the first to participate knowingly and willingly in God's future that has been announced to her. The messenger is free to leave now that there are human characters who can carry the message forward—Mary having heard the promise itself, and Elizabeth following the wisdom of her own body.

## MARY'S VISIT TO ELIZABETH
## Luke 1:39–56

1:39 In those days Mary set out and went with haste to a Judean town in the hill country, 40 where she entered the house of Zechariah and greeted Elizabeth. 41 When Elizabeth heard Mary's greeting, the child leaped in her womb. And Elizabeth was filled with the Holy Spirit 42 and exclaimed with a loud cry, "Blessed are you among women, and blessed is the fruit of your womb. 43 And why has this happened to me, that the mother of my Lord comes to me? 44 For as soon as I heard the sound of your greeting, the child in my womb leaped for joy. 45 And blessed is she who believed that there would be a fulfillment of what was spoken to her by the Lord."

46 And Mary said,
"My soul magnifies the Lord,
47   and my spirit rejoices in God my Savior,
48 for he has looked with favor
    on the lowliness of his servant.
    Surely, from now on all generations will call me blessed;
49 for the Mighty One has done great things for me,
    and holy is his name.
50 His mercy is for those who fear him
    from generation to generation.
51 He has shown strength with his arm;
    he has scattered the proud in the thoughts of their hearts.
52 He has brought down the powerful from their thrones,
    and lifted up the lowly;
53 he has filled the hungry with good things,
    and sent the rich away empty.
54 He has helped his servant Israel,
    in remembrance of his mercy,
55 according to the promise he made to our ancestors,
    to Abraham and to his descendants forever."

56 And Mary remained with her about three months and then returned to her home.

In this scene the two narrative strands of Luke 1—2—stories about John and about Jesus—come together. The scene is a touching one. The young girl Mary—apparently now pregnant—hurries to the home of her older female relative, who is herself in the middle of a joy-filled, wondrous, and somewhat perplexing pregnancy. We are given no reason for the trip. Was it joyful exuberance? Or the need to think through her situation with someone older and presumably wiser? On the level of human feelings, we can imagine both. But Luke is not interested in answering such human questions, any more than he is concerned to tell us where the silent

Zechariah is during the visit. Luke's focus has already shifted from the mothers (and fathers) to the awaited babies, and especially to Mary's child.

According to Luke, Elizabeth's body teaches her theological truths. At Mary's greeting, Elizabeth feels a stirring in her womb that evokes her recognition of who it is to whom Mary will give birth (1:43). By calling the coming baby "my Lord," Elizabeth gives voice to the first confession of faith in Jesus that is recorded in Luke's Gospel. Blessings pour from Elizabeth's mouth, blessing the child who is to come (1:42) and blessing Mary, not for bearing the child, but for her faith: "And blessed is she who believed that there would be a fulfillment of what was spoken to her by the Lord" (1:45).

Mary's response is to sing the song known as the "Magnificat," which is the first word of its Latin translation. The best manuscripts attribute the song to Mary, as has the tradition of the church. Some manuscripts, though, attribute the song to Elizabeth, and that possibility must at least be considered. In the first place, the form and content of the song resemble very closely Hannah's song recorded in 1 Samuel 2:1–10. It is Elizabeth's story that clearly echoes Hannah's: Both are older women, wives of priests, childless until a pregnancy late in life that is interpreted as a special blessing by God, and that is to result in a child dedicated in a special way to divine service. Elizabeth's "disgrace" (1:25) makes her at least as fitting a candidate for the self-description of lowly "servant" (1:48) as Mary would be. That is especially true, since the word translated "lowliness" does not mean "humility" or "meekness" as we would understand those words, but rather carries a social connotation. One was "lowly" in the sense of "humiliated" or "marginalized" because of one's failure to live up to the demands of honor and respectability that characterize a society such as that into which Jesus and John were born. The word could be used, for example, of a woman like Elizabeth who was unable to conceive a child, or it could be used of a woman who had been raped. By having Mary apply such a word to herself, Luke may be communicating information about her actual situation as a victim of rape, or at least about her solidarity with such despised women.

The power of the song itself and its prominence in the liturgy and tradition of the church might well explain why a song once connected to Elizabeth found a new voice in the one whom the church too called "blessed," both for her own faith and faithfulness, and as the mother of Jesus the Christ. That she should sing this song that links God's blessing of her in her "lowliness" to God's promises for the whole people makes Mary into the lead singer in a chorus of all those whose dreams and yearnings are given voice in its words.

The song itself would never be confused with a calming lullaby being rehearsed by two pregnant women. The first part of the song (1:46–49) comes closest to fitting the immediate circumstances, as the singer praises God for looking on her "with favor," in spite of or perhaps even because of her "lowliness" and humiliation. Even future generations will recognize that she has been blessed by God's mighty deeds on her behalf.

In the second half of the song (1:50–55), the focus shifts to a more general celebration of God's deeds and ways. That portion of the hymn is in three parts. The first (1:50) and last (1:54–55) celebrate God's mercy. That mercy is accorded to those who "fear" or are in awe of God, and it comes to bear specifically on Israel, in keeping with God's promises that began with God's covenant with Abraham (Gen. 17:7; 18:18; 22:17). The question of how God's covenants with Israel are expressed in the context of God's new act in Jesus Christ is an issue of great concern to Luke, and one that recurs throughout the Gospel and Acts. As the concluding affirmation of this hymn already makes clear, God's faithfulness to God's promises, and to those people or peoples with whom God is joined in covenant, is at the heart of Luke's theology.

The center of the song elaborates on what happens when God's strength is displayed (1:51–53). The theme is developed in two sets of contrasting parallels or reversals. In the first (1:51b–52), the "proud" and "powerful" are scattered and brought down, respectively, and the "lowly" are lifted up. The second set (1:53) begins with the hungry being filled and ends with the rich being sent away empty. The human categories represent economic and political opposites, and as a result of God's action, they are said to move toward a common middle ground.

It is important to recognize how the framing celebration of God's mercy and the center describing a reversal of fortunes interpret each other. Within the frame of God's mercy, the center loses any tone of vengeance or triumphalism. Instead, an economy marked by scarcity and competition is replaced by an economy of generosity in which all have enough: Those who are hungry get to enjoy good things, and those who are rich do not get to add to their riches. The powerful no longer get to exercise power over others, but nothing is said about the "lowly" now getting to do what has been done to them. Conversely, the social transformation portrayed in the central verses prevents our sentimentalizing the affirmation of God's mercy. For Luke, God's mercy is never divorced from God's justice, nor can that mercy be understood except in the context of God's faithfulness to God's own commitments and covenants.

The themes and style of the hymn would have sounded vaguely familiar to Luke's audience. The cadence of the poetry and the images of God's

mercy and power recall Hannah's song in particular, but if we check the
text of that song, we find that it is not quoted. Perhaps a psalm, then?
There are echoes of several psalms in the biblical book of Psalms, as well
as in Jewish literature not found in the Bible (such as the hymn scroll that
is part of the library found at Qumran by the Dead Sea), but again none
seems to have been quoted directly. In these very "biblical"-sounding first
two chapters of Luke, it is the songs or canticles that are most "biblical"
of all. But they seem to have come fresh to the Christian tradition, either
in the various sources on which Luke drew, or as Luke's own poetic celebration of the gospel he has undertaken to proclaim. By their very form,
they affirm God's commitment to continue the mercy and strength that
have grounded Israel's life and confidence from the beginning. The story
may already have taken some unusual twists and turns, and certainly more
lie ahead, but the hymns assure us that we can trust it.

Following Mary's hymn, Luke tells us only that the two women stayed
together for the remaining months of Elizabeth's pregnancy. Did Mary
see the baby John before she returned home? That is another one of those
human questions to which Luke does not bother to respond, as the curtain closes on this scene and the times of birth are at hand.

## THE BIRTH, NAMING, AND
## CHILDHOOD OF JOHN
### Luke 1:57–80

1:57 **Now the time came for Elizabeth to give birth, and she bore a son.**
58 **Her neighbors and relatives heard that the Lord had shown his great
mercy to her, and they rejoiced with her.**
59 **On the eighth day they came to circumcise the child, and they were
going to name him Zechariah after his father.** 60 **But his mother said, "No;
he is to be called John."** 61 **They said to her, "None of your relatives has this
name."** 62 **Then they began motioning to his father to find out what name he
wanted to give him.** 63 **He asked for a writing tablet and wrote, "His name
is John." And all of them were amazed.** 64 **Immediately his mouth was
opened and his tongue freed, and he began to speak, praising God.** 65 **Fear
came over all their neighbors, and all these things were talked about
throughout the entire hill country of Judea.** 66 **All who heard them pondered
them and said, "What then will this child become?" For, indeed, the hand
of the Lord was with him.**
67 **Then his father Zechariah was filled with the Holy Spirit and spoke this
prophecy:**

⁶⁸ "Blessed be the Lord God of Israel,
     for he has looked favorably on his people and redeemed them.
⁶⁹ He has raised up a mighty savior for us
     in the house of his servant David,
⁷⁰ as he spoke through the mouth of his holy prophets from of old,
⁷¹    that we would be saved from our enemies and from the hand of
         all who hate us.
⁷² Thus he has shown the mercy promised to our ancestors,
     and has remembered his holy covenant,
⁷³ the oath that he swore to our ancestor Abraham,
     to grant us  ⁷⁴ that we, being rescued from the hands of our enemies,
     might serve him without fear,  ⁷⁵ in holiness and righteousness
         before him all our days.
⁷⁶ And you, child, will be called the prophet of the Most High;
     for you will go before the Lord to prepare his ways,
⁷⁷ to give knowledge of salvation to his people
     by the forgiveness of their sins.
⁷⁸ By the tender mercy of our God,
     the dawn from on high will break upon us,
⁷⁹ to give light to those who sit in darkness and in the shadow of
         death,
     to guide our feet into the way of peace."
⁸⁰ The child grew and became strong in spirit, and he was in the wilderness until the day he appeared publicly to Israel.

John's birth is simply reported, with appropriate recognition by neighbors
and family as yet another sign of God's mercy (1:57–58). Luke's attention
is focused on events surrounding the circumcision of the child (1:59–79),
in particular the selection of his name. The usual practice in Palestine
early in the first century appears to have been to name a child at birth.
Other than in this account, several centuries elapse before there is another
record among Palestinian Jews of naming being linked to circumcision.
Selection of the name was the responsibility of the parents (not of the
neighbors, as this narrative suggests). Though there is evidence from the
time of Jesus of Jewish babies being named after their fathers (as indeed
was commonly the case among Gentiles), the usual practice would have
been to name a boy after his grandfather. Luke's narrative at this point
may reflect the practice of Jews living in his own community outside of
Palestine—a practice that he assumed would have been followed in the
time and place of which he was writing. In any event, the public setting of
the naming of the child allows Luke to focus the event on the child's importance for the larger narrative he is developing.

According to Luke's story, the neighbors assume that the baby will be named for his father, but instead, the still-speechless Zechariah writes what Gabriel had told him at the annunciation, "His name is John" (1:63). Just as Mary's acceptance of Gabriel's word to her (1:38) set the stage for her visit to Elizabeth, for Elizabeth's own praises, and for Mary's song, so now Zechariah's acceptance of the angel's word finds his speech restored. The neighborhood buzzes with speculation about the future of the child (1:65–66), and Zechariah speaks a "prophecy" (1:67) in the form of another hymn (1:68–79).

This hymn too leaves us wondering if some psalm or prophetic oracle is being quoted, but whereas individual images can be found that have precedents in the Hebrew Bible, the hymn as a whole is new. Several motifs echo Mary's song: God's "mercy," God's looking "favorably," and the promises to Abraham, for example. But the focus here is different. It is as if Luke has picked up the closing affirmation of Mary's song—God's mercy and covenant faithfulness to Israel—and, with the voice of this priest of Israel, embroidered those themes into a rich tapestry of Israel's longing, hope, and confidence.

This hymn can also be divided into two parts. The first (1:68–75) is a hymn of praise to God who "has looked favorably" on the people and "redeemed them." The verb tenses are puzzling in a song of Zechariah, for they point to what God has already done, yet the reference to the "mighty savior" (or more literally, "horn of salvation") raised up in the house of David seems to look forward to Mary's child yet to be born. In a hymn of the Christian community, of course, the verb tenses are appropriate, and they serve as a reminder that we need to recognize Luke's narrative as Christian literature and theology, and not a transcript of historical events.

Furthermore, such poetic telescoping of chronological time reminds us of the theological point (which also would not have been alien to Luke) that in the certainty of God's faithfulness, what is promised is as good as done. On that score, Luke appears to have taken a most daring step: Twice in the hymn he refers to the people being saved from their enemies (1:71, 74). In the first instance, it is implied as the work of the "mighty savior," just as God promised through the prophets. In the second, it is part of the "mercy" promised in the covenant with Abraham, and the basis for the people's being able to serve God without fear. But for Luke's community the Roman-Jewish war (66–70 C.E.) was recent history. Far from being saved from their enemies, the people were badly beaten, the temple destroyed, and the city of Jerusalem sacked! And still Zechariah's song is sung, reminding the people of the reliability of God's promises and calling them, in turn, to serve God "without fear, in holiness and righteousness" (1:75).

The second part of the song (1:76–79) focuses on John's task of preparing the people to receive the one who is to come. He is to educate them concerning this salvation that expresses God's "tender mercy." Salvation is described in images that echo oracles attributed to the exilic or post-exilic contributor to the book of Isaiah (Isa. 58:8; 60:1–2): "The dawn from on high will break upon us, to give light to those who sit in darkness and in the shadow of death, to guide our feet into the way of peace" (Luke 1:78b–79). Salvation is also linked to "forgiveness" or release of sins (1:77), a term that for Luke recalls the imagery of the Year of Jubilee, central to Jesus' proclamation of God's reign (see comment on 4:18).

Luke concludes the account of John's beginnings with a summary statement (1:80). Again, curiosity leads us to wonder what John was doing in the wilderness during the years prior to his public appearance in Luke 3. Some interpreters have concluded from his subsequent role in the Gospel that he must have been living as a hermit in the desert in order to prepare for his eventual mission. Others have suggested that his emphasis on a coming time of judgment, when lines between evil and good, acceptable and unacceptable, will be clear and without compromise, resembles what is found in some of the scrolls written by the community at Qumran by the Dead Sea. These echoes suggest that John may have spent time in that community, and then left to pursue his different calling. Still other interpreters suggest that he may have spent some of the intervening years with terrorist bands fighting Roman occupation and the oppressive economic system it imposed, only to have despaired, finally, of that solution and turned to the proclamation of repentance. In the end, we do not know because Luke abandons John's story to pick up again the narrative about Jesus.

## JESUS' BIRTH
## Luke 2:1–20

2:1 **In those days a decree went out from Emperor Augustus that all the world should be registered.** 2 **This was the first registration and was taken while Quirinius was governor of Syria.** 3 **All went to their own towns to be registered.** 4 **Joseph also went from the town of Nazareth in Galilee to Judea, to the city of David called Bethlehem, because he was descended from the house and family of David.** 5 **He went to be registered with Mary, to whom he was engaged and who was expecting a child.** 6 **While they were there,** the time came for her to deliver her child. [7] And she gave birth to her first-born son and wrapped him in bands of cloth, and laid him in a manger, because there was no place for them in the inn.

[8] In that region there were shepherds living in the fields, keeping watch over their flock by night. [9] Then an angel of the Lord stood before them, and the glory of the Lord shone around them, and they were terrified. [10] But the angel said to them, "Do not be afraid; for see—I am bringing you good news of great joy for all the people: [11] to you is born this day in the city of David a Savior, who is the Messiah, the Lord. [12] This will be a sign for you: you will find a child wrapped in bands of cloth and lying in a manger." [13] And suddenly there was with the angel a multitude of the heavenly host, praising God and saying,

[14] "Glory to God in the highest heaven,
    and on earth peace among those whom he favors!"

[15] When the angels had left them and gone into heaven, the shepherds said to one another, "Let us go now to Bethlehem and see this thing that has taken place, which the Lord has made known to us." [16] So they went with haste and found Mary and Joseph, and the child lying in the manger. [17] When they saw this, they made known what had been told them about this child; [18] and all who heard it were amazed at what the shepherds told them. [19] But Mary treasured all these words and pondered them in her heart. [20] The shepherds returned, glorifying and praising God for all they had heard and seen, as it had been told them.

No summary statements suffice to cover the events of Jesus' birth, circumcision, and presentation at the temple, or the years of Jesus' childhood. In each case, the event or time period is highlighted by narrative detail, and either by hymns (of human characters or of angels) or by a saying of the boy Jesus himself. The rich details—as if a zoom-lens has suddenly been slid forward for a close focus—compel the reader to move more slowly and to become caught up in the imagery, the interplay of characters, and the thickly textured narrative settings.

The story of Jesus' birth begins with a complex historical rationale to explain why Mary and Joseph ended up in a suburb of Jerusalem instead of at home in Nazareth when the baby was born (2:1–5). The reasoning seems good—that a Davidite would need to go to his ancestral city in order to be counted on the appropriate lists in a census. A problem occurs, however, when we examine secular records from the period to learn more about the census, for there is no report of such a census in Palestine in the years surrounding Jesus' birth. Matthew also records the tradition that Jesus was born in Bethlehem (though without attempting to explain why, Matt. 2:1), and there is no reason to argue against it. But the confusion about the census, coupled with the richly detailed and symbol-laden descriptions of various moments in the narrative should lead us to suspect that something other than historical reporting is on Luke's agenda.

The connection of Jesus' birth to a census offers a good place to begin exploring what that agenda might be. A census seems harmless enough: What could be more straightforward and unbiased—even harmless—than a simple counting of inhabitants? Yet census-takers usually report hesitancy and even fear from residents of poor communities or communities whose residents are not part of the dominant racial, ethnic, or political group. Finding oneself on government lists can have consequences: military conscription, investigation by social services or immigration officials, or taxation.

In occupied Palestine the census would have served especially to expand the tax system, particularly for the residents of outlying areas such as Galilee. Peasants and artisans (like the carpenter Joseph) would have found probably more than half of their income consumed by the various levels of Roman taxes, with the yearly tax due to the temple adding to the burden.

Luke's community also would have understood the link between census-taking and taxation, for the urban populations of the Empire were also counted periodically in order to keep the tax rolls current. Never mind that this particular census is hard to identify; there were plenty of others that made the setting clear. According to Luke's narrative, the promised child—the one about whom so many splendid things had been sung only moments before—was born in the shadow of the Roman eagle and in a context where the "institutional violence" of the Roman tax structure was about to be escalated yet again.

Following the long introduction dealing with the census, the actual birth is reported in terse language: The time came and she gave birth, and then she carefully wrapped the child (2:6–7b). But suddenly the fuzzy, warm, generic birth scene comes into specific focus (2:7c–d). This baby is laid in an animal's feeding trough, "because there was no place for them in the inn." The word "inn" is not a good translation of the underlying Greek word, which does not refer to a place of public accommodation such as one might find along the highway. The word is not the same one found in 10:34, for example, referring to the place to which the wounded man was brought by the compassionate traveler. Rather, it is the same word used to refer to the guest room or "upper room" in a private home in Jerusalem, where Jesus and the disciples would celebrate the Passover meal (22:11–12).

Homes in small towns like Bethlehem, as well as in the city proper, would have consisted of one room to accommodate the family who lived there. Separating the living quarters from any animals' stalls would have been a manger area, where food and farm implements were stored, and where births often took place a bit apart from the ongoing life of the family. Over the manger area would have been the "upper room," where visiting relatives or acquaintances, or persons linked to the family by political or economic ties, could be given hospitality. Joseph, having returned with his pregnant wife to his ancestral village, would have anticipated such accommodation. The fact that none was available meant that others from a higher rung on the social ladder and in the hierarchy of obligations and honor that characterized Palestinian society had already claimed the space. Not even Mary's obvious need could dislodge such a firmly implanted order of rights and privileges. Instead of having a guest room, then, Mary, Joseph, and the baby are left to spend their nights in Bethlehem in the manger area where the birth has taken place.

The specific family into which Jesus is born is thus identified as not a family of great prestige or privilege, even if they were not necessarily among the destitute poor. They are thus vulnerable, especially when they have to leave the security of their own village and move into more public arenas of reckoning of honor and prestige. In that context, to use a modern idiom, they become street people, forced to grab shelter where they can, even while they are caught up in the machinery of a political and economic system that is interested in counting them only for its advantage.

No scholars or court officials visit the baby in Luke's version of the story. Instead of the magi bearing lavish gifts that Matthew describes (Matt. 2:1–11), in Luke only some shepherds come (2:8–20). Shepherds too were among the poor, and by the standards of the most religiously meticulous people, they were outcasts. They lived a hard life out in the fields, far removed from the comforts and leisure that would allow them to follow the rules for food preparation, purification, and other aspects of religious practice. They lived a life wrapped in danger as they tried to protect their animals from both human marauders and various wild beasts (see John 10:1–18 for a sketch of the shepherd's life).

The pattern of reversal of circumstances between rich and poor, powerful and powerless, that was expressed in Mary's song and illustrated in the contrast between the splendid future forecast for the child and the humble and even marginal circumstances of his birth, is repeated in the fact that it is shepherds who are said to be the recipients of a divine visitation. The time is the night watch, the bleakest and most dangerous time on the hillsides. Luke grants no space for imaginary night noises or the hallucinations of tired sentries. He does not take refuge in general references to a sense of God's presence or even of divine "overshadowing." As was the case with Gabriel's earlier visits to Zechariah and Mary, Luke does not debate the existence or physical composition of angels, or the grammar of angelic speech. Instead, he describes in simple, direct language the most amazing scene: "Then an angel of the Lord stood before them, and the glory of the Lord shone around them, and they were terrified" (2:9).

Their terror at the sight is addressed by the angel's speech (2:10–12). The speech moves from assurance, to proclamation, to a sign by which they can verify the event. The proclamation is all too common, yet completely unprecedented. It is common in that it takes the form of a royal birth announcement. Each time a Caesar was born, or even one of the lesser royal figures, the birth was "proclaimed-as-good-news" (a single word in Greek). All the people were compelled to celebrate the event, even though for most of them it would only mean a new lease on life for an oppressive system, whose splendor and pretense the poor were forced to finance by the products of their fields and workshops. The angel's proclamation is unprecedented in that it heralds an event that does bring joy to *all* the people. The birth is not of another king who will keep the system going; instead, it is the birth of "a Savior, who is the Messiah, the Lord" (2:11).

The news of the recent birth is so wonderful that its consequences are broadcast by a heavenly chorus: Glory in the highest heavens and peace on earth (2:14). The actual meaning of the second line of the angels' refrain is not clear, as the note to the NRSV and the variations among other translations illustrate. Some of the occasions where similar expressions occur in Greek clearly refer to "good will" as an attitude of human beings, whereas others use the same expression to mean that divine favor rests on the person in question. The point is that this is not a celebration of the Pax Romana—the "pacification" of the peoples of the eastern Mediterranean under the armies and imperial bureaucracy of the Roman Empire. It actually is the opposite, a peace that is an occasion of God's blessing and of rejoicing throughout the creation.

The qualities celebrated by the heavenly chorus clarify the earlier proclamation of the birth of "a Savior, who is the Messiah, the Lord." For Luke's community as well as for our own, these titles would have been equated with Jesus, and would have been understood to mean everything he means as Savior, Lord, and Christ. In the present literary context, however, Luke has introduced those titles before telling any of the story of

Jesus. They are thus part of the context for hearing the story Luke will go on to tell. While the first-century Jewish longing for a Messiah in the tradition of the Davidic kings, who would be a political liberator from Roman domination, is part of the background Luke appears to assume, that is not the whole story. Instead, Luke has identified the "anointed one" (that is what the words "Messiah" and "Christ" mean) by the consequences of his coming: "Joy" for the whole people, and "peace." In that sense, the emerging character of this one who was awaited and now has arrived continues the patterns of reversal of circumstances and overturning of business-as-usual found in the canticles of Mary and Zechariah and in the details Luke has emphasized in the setting of the birth itself.

The shepherds' story concludes with the report that they found everything in Bethlehem to be just as the angels said (2:15–16). With that reassurance, they tell others what they have learned about the child. In effect, they take up the heavenly messengers' words, both of interpretation (2:17) and of praise (2:20). The pattern of reversal thus continues, as the economically poor and religiously marginalized shepherds, and not persons of power or exceptional piety, become the first human "evangelists" or proclaimers of the good news.

The story ends on a note of quiet anticipation, as the shepherds return to their flocks and Mary ponders what she has heard.

## JESUS' CIRCUMCISION AND PRESENTATION IN THE TEMPLE
### Luke 2:21–39

2:21 **After eight days had passed, it was time to circumcise the child; and he was called Jesus, the name given by the angel before he was conceived in the womb.**

[22] **When the time came for their purification according to the law of Moses, they brought him up to Jerusalem to present him to the Lord** [23] **(as it is written in the law of the Lord, "Every firstborn male shall be designated as holy to the Lord"),** [24] **and they offered a sacrifice according to what is stated in the law of the Lord, "a pair of turtledoves or two young pigeons."**

[25] **Now there was a man in Jerusalem whose name was Simeon; this man was righteous and devout, looking forward to the consolation of Israel, and the Holy Spirit rested on him.** [26] **It had been revealed to him by the Holy Spirit that he would not see death before he had seen the Lord's Messiah.** [27] **Guided by the Spirit, Simeon came into the temple; and when the parents brought in the child Jesus, to do for him what was customary under the law,** [28] **Simeon took him in his arms and praised God, saying,**

<sup>29</sup> "Master, now you are dismissing your servant in peace,
   according to your word;
<sup>30</sup> for my eyes have seen your salvation,
<sup>31</sup>  which you have prepared in the presence of all peoples,
<sup>32</sup>  a light for revelation to the Gentiles
   and for glory to your people Israel."

<sup>33</sup> And the child's father and mother were amazed at what was being said about him. <sup>34</sup> Then Simeon blessed them and said to his mother Mary, "This child is destined for the falling and the rising of many in Israel, and to be a sign that will be opposed <sup>35</sup> so that the inner thoughts of many will be revealed—and a sword will pierce your own soul too."

<sup>36</sup> There was also a prophet, Anna the daughter of Phanuel, of the tribe of Asher. She was of a great age, having lived with her husband seven years after her marriage, <sup>37</sup> then as a widow to the age of eighty-four. She never left the temple but worshiped there with fasting and prayer night and day. <sup>38</sup> At that moment she came, and began to praise God and to speak about the child to all who were looking for the redemption of Jerusalem.

<sup>39</sup> When they had finished everything required by the law of the Lord, they returned to Galilee, to their own town of Nazareth.

The story of Jesus' circumcision is told in a single verse (2:21). The ritual itself and the naming (following Gabriel's instructions, 1:31) proceed without incident. The drama that accompanied the naming ritual of John is reserved for the next episode in Jesus' story, the ritual of Mary's purification and the presentation of Jesus in the temple.

The account of the purification of Mary and presentation of Jesus in the temple is framed by references to the law of Moses (2:22–24, 27, 39). According to Leviticus 12:2–8, forty days following the birth of a male child (or eighty days following the birth of a female child) the mother had to present an offering in the temple, so that the priest on duty could make atonement on her behalf and she could be clean. The usual offering was a lamb, but if the woman could not afford the lamb she could substitute two pigeons or two turtledoves. According to Luke, Mary makes the less costly offering (2:24), which confirms Luke's earlier picture of the family's humble circumstances. The only puzzling point in Luke's version of the purification is the initial reference to "their" purification, since only the mother required such a ritual. There really is no way to get around the awkwardness of that pronoun, other than to recognize it in the context of Luke's description of the pilgrimage as involving the whole family. One might even see the plural pronoun as affirming that upon the completion of this obligation, the whole family would be ready to resume its life after the dramatic intervention of the birth of the baby.

The second part of the ritual at the temple centers on the baby Jesus him-self. Jesus is presented to God, much as Samuel was presented by his mother Hannah (1 Sam. 1:22–24). The rationale cited, however, is not that narra-tive parallel (which the reader would simply need to recognize). Instead, Luke refers to the law concerning the firstborn animal or human, which was to be consecrated to God and then "redeemed" by the payment of money to one of the priests (Exod. 13:1–2, 11–16; 22:29b–30; Num. 3:13, 47–48; 18:15–16). However, nothing in Luke's story suggests that money was paid to redeem the child Jesus, and the result is that this becomes a unique rit-ual of "presentation," not simply one of the rituals prescribed by law or de-scribed as a custom either in the Bible or in rabbinic writings that can be traced. Jesus' dedication to the Lord remains in effect, and it is a fact of Jesus' life that Luke assumes as the Gospel narrative unfolds.

In any event, Luke's principal point in describing Jesus' presentation seems to have been to get the family to the temple as the setting for the scene with Simeon and Anna (2:25–38). Both Simeon and Anna are mod-els of faithfulness and piety (2:25, 36–37). Simeon's exemplary life is re-warded by the assurance of the Holy Spirit that his longing for the con-solation of Israel would be satisfied by his seeing the Messiah before he died (2:26). His recognition of the baby Jesus as the promised one evokes yet another song of acclamation (2:27–32). This song echoes the earlier themes of peace and salvation, then adds a new dimension to the divine purpose—one that is said to amaze even the parents, despite all they have heard (2:33). The earlier songs and the angel's proclamation focused on God's covenant promises to Israel now coming to fruition, despite the suf-ferings the people were enduring. The songs and the narratives pointed to a particular meaning of the birth as good news in the specific histori-cal, social, and economic reality of the poor. In Simeon's song the good news is explicitly extended to "all peoples," Gentiles as well as Israel (2:31–32).

Simeon's closing words (2:34–35) cast the shadow of the cross over this joyful celebration. The child will be a catalyst provoking opposition and revealing the truths of human hearts, and the result will bring his mother pain. He will bring about a time of sorting and division in Israel, and some will "fall" because of him (as Luke, of course, has already witnessed). Luke leaves Simeon's words in all their stark truth without comment.

Anna is identified as a prophet who lived a life of prayer and fasting dur-ing her long widowhood. The temple is her home in every sense of that word. Her pious discipline, like Simeon's focused longing for Israel's con-solation, have prepared her also to recognize the child, and she praises

God and interprets Jesus' importance "to all who were looking for the redemption of Jerusalem" (2:36–38). That concluding phrase would have touched the longing of Luke's audience as well, in the specific context of the city's recent destruction: The good news that expresses the ancient longing continues to comfort and to satisfy.

## JESUS' CHILDHOOD
## Luke 2:40–52

2:40 **The child grew and became strong, filled with wisdom; and the favor of God was upon him.** [41] **Now every year his parents went to Jerusalem for the festival of the Passover.** [42] **And when he was twelve years old, they went up as usual for the festival.** [43] **When the festival was ended and they started to return, the boy Jesus stayed behind in Jerusalem, but his parents did not know it.** [44] **Assuming that he was in the group of travelers, they went a day's journey. Then they started to look for him among their relatives and friends.** [45] **When they did not find him, they returned to Jerusalem to search for him.** [46] **After three days they found him in the temple, sitting among the teachers, listening to them and asking them questions.** [47] **And all who heard him were amazed at his understanding and his answers.** [48] **When his parents saw him they were astonished; and his mother said to him, "Child, why have you treated us like this? Look, your father and I have been searching for you in great anxiety."** [49] **He said to them, "Why were you searching for me? Did you not know that I must be in my Father's house?"** [50] **But they did not understand what he said to them.** [51] **Then he went down with them and came to Nazareth, and was obedient to them. His mother treasured all these things in her heart.** [52] **And Jesus increased in wisdom and in years, and in divine and human favor.**

The one glimpse Luke gives into Jesus' childhood is framed by parallel summary statements about his growth in wisdom, strength, and favor (2:40, 52). Between the two summaries is the story of a precocious but apparently inconsiderate child who, in pursuit of his vocation, manages to worry and annoy his parents. Luke's narrative gives divine justification to the beginning independence of a teenager, and Jesus looks like something less than the son one dreams of.

Luke is the only canonical Gospel to say anything about Jesus' life between infancy and adulthood, though several of the Gospels that were not included in the Bible include fantastic stories of the child Jesus' magic tricks and unusual wisdom. This story is really quite restrained by comparison. It portrays Jesus as having been brought up within the customs and traditions of Judaism (2:41–42), and thus as accepting for himself the implications of his dedication to God as an infant (much like the confirmation of young adults in the church today) and of the unusual vocation attributed to him earlier by others: "Did you not know that I must be in my Father's house?" (2:49).

Except for the statement about his subsequent obedience to his parents (2:51), the other details of the story are very realistic. In a caravan of friends and relatives traveling back to Galilee, a young boy could easily not be missed until the end of the day's journey. The parents' frenzied search and Mary's rebuke of the child seem completely appropriate.

But Luke leaves us with several jarring details. The narrator calls Mary and Joseph Jesus' "parents," and Mary's rebuke refers to "your father and I." If we are intended to understand Jesus' birth as "miraculous" in a biological sense, we can only conclude that the editor was careless or else was taking liberties in order to set up a pun in the reference to "my Father's house." If, however, Luke intended us to understand Jesus as "Son of God" (1:35) more in terms of presence and vocation than biological relationship, the picture of the young man's acceptance of prior commitments made on his behalf is completely appropriate. In that case, the parents' failure to understand (2:50), despite having heard the promises and predictions about their child, is jarring. We are left with Mary "treasuring" all these things (2:51), but somehow also unsettled about what will take place before the angels can sing again.

# 2. A Time of Preparation
## Luke 3:1–4:13

Luke has already established the fact that the lives and vocations of Jesus and John are intertwined. He has left us waiting for news of how the fantastic forecasts and promises made about them at birth (and, in Jesus' case, confirmed by his own words as a young adult) will come to fruition. And he has assured us by the style as well as the content of the opening stories that the account he is presenting furthers the biblical witness to God's will and ways.

When Luke's story resumes, the mood changes. Instead of a smooth transition into accounts of the next phases of Jesus' life, he reintroduces his story by an intricate process of dating the incidents he is about to report (3:1–2a). At first, we might think Luke has satisfied some of our modern curiosity for historical facts about Jesus. Our optimism is short-lived, however, when we realize that his references to the terms of the various government officials give us at best a range of years (25–30 C.E.), which only some scholars dare to date more precisely, perhaps to 28–29 C.E. Furthermore, his mention of the high priesthood of Annas and Caiaphas introduces additional ambiguity, since there was only one high priest at any given time. (He may reflect a practice similar to that in the United States of referring to Presidents, members of Congress, and other public officials by their titles even after their term of office ends. Unfortunately, there is no clear evidence that such a practice prevailed in the ancient world.)

What, then, would Luke have accomplished by this elaborate description of when the ensuing events took place? By situating them against the background of other public events, he establishes his own account also as being one of public, historical significance. He affirms that he is recounting events of real human time, not some placeless or timeless mythic tales without real contexts. And he establishes the relevant context of his account as the double system of authority—Empire and temple—that prevailed in Palestine. Whichever of those systems was most important in lending shape and meaning to the lives of his audience or their ancestors, Luke alerted his readers to pay attention to how his story came to bear on historical circumstances in Jesus' day, and, by extension, in their own specific context as well.

Luke's second formal introduction, parallel in style to the earlier one in 1:1–4, is also important because it introduces what for Luke is the heart of the story of Jesus. If you read Luke's Gospel and the book of Acts as a continuous narrative, you will see that the stories he has related in the first two chapters about the unusual circumstances surrounding the births of Jesus and John are not referred to again. Some of the motifs of the canticles and of the statements about Jesus' and John's vocations will be taken up and developed more fully, but not the narratives themselves. When Luke summarizes the story of Jesus in Peter's sermon in Acts 10:37–43, he begins, not with Jesus' birth, but with his baptism. While the first two chapters are important in setting the stage and preparing the readers or hearers of Luke's Gospel for what is to come, the focus of the Gospel is on the account of Jesus' public ministry and its consequences. All four Gospels, however, begin the story of Jesus' ministry by looking at John the Baptist.

## THE MINISTRY OF JOHN THE BAPTIST
## Luke 3:1–20

3:1 **In the fifteenth year of the reign of Emperor Tiberius, when Pontius Pilate was governor of Judea, and Herod was ruler of Galilee, and his brother Philip ruler of the region of Ituraea and Trachonitis, and Lysanias ruler of Abilene,** 2 **during the high priesthood of Annas and Caiaphas, the word of God came to John son of Zechariah in the wilderness.** 3 **He went into all the region around the Jordan, proclaiming a baptism of repentance for the forgiveness of sins,** 4 **as it is written in the book of the words of the prophet Isaiah,**
> **"The voice of one crying out in the wilderness:**
> **'Prepare the way of the Lord,**
> **make his paths straight.**
> 5 **Every valley shall be filled,**
> **and every mountain and hill shall be made low,**
> **and the crooked shall be made straight,**
> **and the rough ways made smooth;**
> 6 **and all flesh shall see the salvation of God.'"**

7 John said to the crowds that came out to be baptized by him, "You brood of vipers! Who warned you to flee from the wrath to come? 8 Bear fruits worthy of repentance. Do not begin to say to yourselves, 'We have Abraham as our ancestor'; for I tell you, God is able from these stones to raise up children to Abraham. 9 Even now the ax is lying at the root of the trees; every tree therefore that does not bear good fruit is cut down and thrown into the fire."

10 And the crowds asked him, "What then should we do?" 11 In reply he said to them, "Whoever has two coats must share with anyone who has none; and whoever has food must do likewise." 12 Even tax collectors came to be baptized, and they asked him, "Teacher, what should we do?" 13 He said to them, "Collect no more than the amount prescribed for you." 14 Soldiers also asked him, "And we, what should we do?" He said to them, "Do not extort money from anyone by threats or false accusation, and be satisfied with your wages."

15 As the people were filled with expectation, and all were questioning in their hearts concerning John, whether he might be the Messiah, 16 John answered all of them by saying, "I baptize you with water; but one who is more powerful than I is coming; I am not worthy to untie the thong of his sandals. He will baptize you with the Holy Spirit and fire. 17 His winnowing fork is in his hand, to clear his threshing floor and to gather the wheat into his granary; but the chaff he will burn with unquenchable fire."

18 So, with many other exhortations, he proclaimed the good news to the people. 19 But Herod the ruler, who had been rebuked by him because of Herodias, his brother's wife, and because of all the evil things that Herod had done, 20 added to them all by shutting up John in prison.

All three Synoptic Gospels locate John's ministry in the "wilderness." The reference is to the stark and not very hospitable desert region along the Jordan River, but if we read this account with sensitivity to Israel's story, the "wilderness" evokes many connections. It is the territory through which the Israelites wandered on their journey from Egypt to the promised land. It is full of dangers from hostile peoples, wild beasts, and the constant scarcity of food and water. It is a place of testing, where the people are challenged to rely on God for sustenance, and the place from which the wanderers are born as a new people, chosen and precious to God.

Luke alone of all the Synoptic writers identifies John as the son of Zechariah. Elizabeth disappears from the story once she has fulfilled her traditional role of childbearing, whereas Zechariah's public role as priest makes him relevant for locating their son on the social landscape of his day. Despite John's priestly origins, Luke portrays him as a prophet, but without using that specific label. The introductory dating, for example, mirrors the beginnings of such prophetic books as Jeremiah and Ezekiel, and (more briefly) Isaiah and Hosea. Similarly, Luke alone claims that "the word of God came to John," using a phrase that is a standard way of introducing authoritative pronouncements of the great prophets whose messages are included in the Bible.

John's role as preparer of the way was already identified in the stories of his conception and naming (1:17, 76–77), but Luke follows Mark in declaring it again in the account of John's public ministry, using the words of Isaiah 40:3–5. (Like Matthew, Luke omits Malachi 3:1, which Mark has blended with that text). Luke alone continues the quote from Isaiah, including lines that mirror themes of leveling and reversal found in the "Magnificat" and other parts of the first two chapters of the Gospel, and concluding with the affirmation that "all flesh" will see salvation, as Simeon's song earlier celebrated. In the context of Luke's community, that meant in particular that Jews and Gentiles alike were to be recipients of God's promised salvation.

Matthew, Mark, and Luke agree in summarizing John's message as a call to repentance, and Luke follows Mark in giving the purpose of repentance as to lead to "the forgiveness of sins," a message that will be attributed to Jesus (5:17–32) and the church (24:47) as well. (Matthew omits the reference to forgiveness of sins as part of John's message, reserving that for Jesus and the church.) Matthew, Mark, and Luke all agree also in associating John so closely with "baptism" that it became part of the way he was identified, namely as John "the Baptist" (or, in Mark 1:4, "the baptizer"). The word is from a verb meaning "to dip," suggesting that John's rite did involve immersion in the water. It has echoes of purification rituals common to other Jewish groups too, but unlike those rituals that had to be repeated, John's appears to have been a one-time event, and it was linked to repentance rather than to cleansing. Unlike the "proselyte baptism" that came later to be performed on converts to Judaism, John's "dipping" was not an entrance ritual into a new religion (although baptism took on that role in the church), but a mark of repentance or "turning"— a reorientation of one's life on a new course.

Both Matthew and Mark include a description of John's clothing and diet that links him closely to the prophet Elijah, but Luke omits that detail. The annunciation to Zechariah already associated John with Elijah (1:17), and his role as forerunner and preparer of the way of the coming one also links him to the expectation of Elijah as the prophet of God's end-time, so Luke is clearly not afraid to suggest that connection. Perhaps he has concluded that the description will not be recognized by his community, or that they might draw wrong conclusions from it about the credibility of John's message. Later on (Luke 4 and 7) Luke connects Jesus' ministry to those of Elijah and Elisha, so perhaps he does not want to put too much emphasis on the association of John with Elijah. In any event, for Luke, John's importance seems to lie in the content of his message, and not in his physical appearance.

The first segment of John's preaching, which contains vivid imagery of judgment (3:7–9), is from the source shared by Luke and Matthew. In Matthew, the warnings are directed to religious leaders in particular, but Luke directs them to all who have gathered. According to Luke, it is not only the pious who call in vain on Abraham to help them avoid the judgment lodged against them (16:24–25). The warning not to presume on one's religious heritage is also a reminder of God's grace. "God is able from these stones to raise up children to Abraham" (3:8) recalls the story told in Joshua 4, where stones were piled at the place where the people had crossed the Jordan as a reminder of God's granting safe passage to the people and the ark of the covenant when they entered the promised land. The implication is that just as God created a people once before by God's gracious act, God could do so again.

In Luke 3:10–14, a passage found only in Luke, John's preaching is taken beyond mere warning of impending judgment to provide some guidelines for living in the meantime. Though the crowds in general are said to pose the question, the response is directed specifically to those wealthy enough to have extra food or clothing, to tax collectors, and to soldiers. In each case, they are instructed not to use their position of relative power to take advantage of others (a principle central to the story of Zacchaeus as well, 19:1–10).

The similarity between John's message and Jesus' led to some confusion and competition among their respective followers concerning whether John or Jesus was the "coming one" toward whom their longing and expectation were directed. Luke already had begun to address that problem in the clear delineation of their roles in the first two chapters, but here again the issue arises. In addition to the confusion because of the similarity of their messages, there is the rather uncomfortable point that Jesus was baptized by John (and not the other way around), suggesting, at least in that event, that John is the figure of greater authority.

Each of the Gospel writers finds particular ways to address the problem. In Luke there are at least three details in the way the story is told that make the case for the "Christian" version of the debate, which grants Jesus priority over John. First, the concluding segment of John's message (3:16–18), which Luke shares with Matthew and in part with Mark, is presented as John's own response to such speculation (3:15). Second, prior to Jesus' arrival on the scene, Luke reports John's imprisonment by Herod (3:19–20), which Mark and Matthew describe in greater detail later in their narratives (Matt. 14:3–12; Mark 6:17–29). Later in Luke's account (7:18–23), Jesus again interacts with John through the intermediaries of John's disciples, so it would be wrong to see the two as being confined by Luke to separate narrative (or theological) periods. But this shift of sequence assures that Jesus and John never share the narrative spotlight. Third, Luke minimizes the place of the actual baptism and emphasizes the consequences of Jesus' prayer in the events that follow (3:21).

## THE BAPTISM OF JESUS
Luke 3:21–22

3:21 **Now when all the people were baptized, and when Jesus also had been baptized and was praying, the heaven was opened,** 22 **and the Holy Spirit descended upon him in bodily form like a dove. And a voice came from heaven, "You are my Son, the Beloved; with you I am well pleased."**

Jesus' baptism is merely reported as part of a general baptism. Just as Zechariah and Anna were said to be at prayer at the moment when they received a revelation (1:10; 2:37), so here Jesus also is praying. In fact, it is already clear that, in Luke's Gospel, prayer signals an important event about to take place, and the reader would do well to pay special attention. In this case, prayer becomes a window to the divine presence.

That encounter with God is communicated by three images. The first is the opening of the heavens. Mark writes of this as something perceived by Jesus alone (Mark 1:10), but Luke portrays it as an objective event presumably observed by anyone who was present (Luke 3:21). The ancient understanding of the heavens was that they were like an inverted stack of bowls of graduated sizes, with the smaller ones nested inside the larger ones. These bowls would protect the earth from the waters above the heavens (Gen. 1:6–7). In light of that understanding, this story suggests that people looked up and saw a crack in the nearest bowl. It is a scary picture, for it portrays the people as vulnerable to the chaos of the heavenly waters flooding the earth. They would also be vulnerable to the even scarier prospect of an encounter with God.

The second image is the descent of the Holy Spirit "in bodily form like a dove." The Holy Spirit has already emerged as an important element in Luke's Gospel (1:15, 35, 41, 67; 2:25–27; 3:16), and it will continue to express divine presence and power at key points throughout the Gospel and Acts. Wind and fire are also common symbols of the Spirit's presence (3:16; Acts 2:2–4), but the dove too appears in Christian literature and art from the very earliest period as a way to signify the Spirit. While Matthew and Mark compare the Spirit's manner of alighting on Jesus to the way a dove might alight, Luke depicts the physical symbol of the bird. Studies of the way symbols function in religious experience show that the longer and more frequently they are used, the more concrete and specific they tend to become. By the time Luke's Gospel was written, it would appear that the dove as a symbol of the presence of the Holy Spirit had already become common in the language of the church.

The third image is the heavenly voice. According to the oldest manuscripts (and thus the ones least likely to have been influenced by the wording of the other Gospels), the words spoken by the voice, "You are my Son, the Beloved; with you I am well pleased," blend Isaiah 42:1, which describes the servant of God, with Psalm 2:7, a psalm sung at the coronation of Israel's kings as "sons of God." It would be fruitless to debate whether the royal imagery or the servant imagery is the principal one intended, for the two are combined. The are joined both in the tradition (the king was to be God's servant as well as God's son) and in Luke's affirmation of the leveling process that is part of God's new agenda (1:46–55). That agenda will be played out most specifically in the life of the new community that will gather around Jesus (22:24–27). The voice does what Gabriel foretold to Mary (1:35), namely call Jesus "Son of God."

The role of this story in Luke's Gospel is difficult to grasp. In Mark it is clearly the occasion when Jesus' vocation and unique relationship to God are communicated. Luke follows Mark's account of the heavens opening, the Spirit descending, and the voice speaking, with variations only in details. Yet he has already proclaimed in carefully crafted narratives who Jesus is and how he is related to God. This account of the beginning and authorization of Jesus' ministry clearly was central to the church's tradition by the time of Luke's writing, and apparently it had to be included as the first scene of that ministry. Furthermore, it functions, along with the genealogy that follows, to set up the subsequent testing of Jesus in 4:1–13, in which two of the devil's three challenges begin, "If you are the Son of God . . . ," and the third plays on the image of the reigning servant.

# THE GENEALOGY OF THE "SON OF GOD"
## Luke 3:23–38

> 3:23 **Jesus was about thirty years old when he began his work. He was the son (as was thought) of Joseph son of Heli,** [24] **son of Matthat, son of Levi, son of Melchi, son of Jannai, son of Joseph,** [25] **son of Mattathias, son of Amos, son of Nahum, son of Esli, son of Naggai,** [26] **son of Maath, son of Mattathias, son of Semein, son of Josech, son of Joda,** [27] **son of Joanan, son of Rhesa, son of Zerubbabel, son of Shealtiel, son of Neri,** [28] **son of Melchi, son of Addi, son of Cosam, son of Elmadam, son of Er,** [29] **son of Joshua, son of Eliezer, son of Jorim, son of Matthat, son of Levi,** [30] **son of Simeon, son of Judah, son of Joseph, son of Jonam, son of Eliakim,** [31] **son of Melea, son of Menna, son of Mattatha, son of Nathan, son of David,** [32] **son of Jesse, son of Obed, son of Boaz, son of Sala, son of Nahshon,** [33] **son of Amminadab, son of Admin, son of Arni, son of Hezron, son of Perez, son of Judah,** [34] **son of Jacob, son of Isaac, son of Abraham, son of Terah, son of Nahor,** [35] **son of Serug, son of Reu, son of Peleg, son of Eber, son of Shelah,** [36] **son of Cainan, son of Arphaxad, son of Shem, son of Noah, son of Lamech,** [37] **son of Methuselah, son of Enoch, son of Jared, son of Mahalaleel, son of Cainan,** [38] **son of Enos, son of Seth, son of Adam, son of God.**

It seems as though Luke realizes that his audience needs a breathing space after the drama of the previous scene. What better way to provide a rest than with a roll call of Jesus' ancestors? Beyond that helpful pause, there may be other functions that the genealogy has for Luke, and specifically at this place in his narrative. For example, since we were told Jesus' age when we last heard about him (twelve years old), we now find out how much time has passed. Jesus is a thirty-year-old man, more or less at midlife, given the life expectancy of that place and time.

To take another approach to interpreting the genealogy, much critical ink has been used in discussing patterns in the list, and in comparing it to the genealogy of Jesus provided in Matthew's Gospel. Suffice it to say that there is no convincing design or numerical pattern of the generations, and that there are some points in common but even more differences between the two genealogies. For example, both Matthew and Luke include Abraham and David among Jesus' ancestors. His connection to these two key ancestors is an important way of establishing Jesus' role as savior for all of Israel. Both genealogies also trace Jesus' ancestry through Joseph, despite the fact that in both Gospels the birth narratives have served as the basis for the church's tradition of Jesus' birth to Mary through the action of the Holy Spirit.

On the latter point, Luke acknowledges that Joseph's paternity is not to be assumed, calling Jesus "the son (as was thought) of Joseph" (3:23). Although the parenthetical comment seems to support the traditional understanding of Jesus' "miraculous" conception without a human father, the meaning is not clear. This is the only place outside of the first two chapters that Luke seems to question Joseph's relationship to Jesus. Some interpreters suggest that the genealogy might represent a tradition about Jesus that is older than the stories of his birth. Following that explanation, then, Luke would have added the parenthetical comment to adapt the genealogy to the birth narrative. Other interpreters suggest that the parenthetical comment was not added by Luke at all, but by an early reader who found the combination of the birth narrative and the genealogy puzzling. (Note, though, that there is little manuscript support for viewing the comment as added later.) Despite the comment, however, Luke proceeds with the list of Joseph's ancestors as something relevant to his story of Jesus.

As far as their differences are concerned, in addition to including a number of different names, the two genealogies are listed in opposite orders. Luke begins with Joseph and works backward, while Matthew begins with Abraham and works down to Jesus. Perhaps the most important difference between the two is that Matthew traces Jesus from Abraham, but Luke continues to name the ancestors to the very beginning: ". . . son of Enos, son of Seth, son of Adam, son of God" (3:38). In Luke, Jesus' ancestry establishes him not only as the savior of all of Israel, but as one whose kinfolk include all the nations and families of the earth. The theme of inclusiveness found in the song of Simeon (2:30–32) and in the prophecy of Isaiah cited in Luke 3:6 is thus confirmed in the genealogy. And as Gabriel promised to Mary (1:35) and the voice from heaven confirmed (3:22), Jesus once again is called the "son (of the son of the son, through seventy-seven generations) of God."

The genealogy in that way rounds out the introductory material of the first three chapters. Jesus' identity has been established and his vocation determined by angelic announcement, prophetic precedent, human sensitivity, a heavenly voice, and a catalog of ancestors. A number of themes have been introduced that will be developed and elaborated as the narrative unfolds. What Luke still has to tell us is what Jesus does with these beginnings, how all of the claims and commissions work themselves out in the very specific historical context whose lack of hospitality toward such a project has already been reflected in the circumstances of Jesus' birth (2:1–7).

## A TIME OF TESTING
## Luke 4:1–13

4:1 Jesus, full of the Holy Spirit, returned from the Jordan and was led by the Spirit in the wilderness, 2 where for forty days he was tempted by the devil. He ate nothing at all during those days, and when they were over, he was famished. 3 The devil said to him, "If you are the Son of God, command this stone to become a loaf of bread." 4 Jesus answered him, 'It is written, 'One does not live by bread alone.'"

5 Then the devil led him up and showed him in an instant all the kingdoms of the world. 6 And the devil said to him, "To you I will give their glory and all this authority; for it has been given over to me, and I give it to anyone I please. 7 If you, then, will worship me, it will all be yours." 8 Jesus answered him, "It is written,

'Worship the Lord your God,
    and serve only him.'"

9 Then the devil took him to Jerusalem, and placed him on the pinnacle of the temple, saying to him, "If you are the Son of God, throw yourself down from here, 10 for it is written,

'He will command his angels concerning you,
    to protect you,'

11 and

'On their hands they will bear you up,
    so that you will not dash your foot against a stone.'"

12 Jesus answered him, "It is said, 'Do not put the Lord your God to the test.'" 13 When the devil had finished every test, he departed from him until an opportune time.

Before the account of Jesus' public ministry can begin, though, Luke has one more story to tell. It will make clear the specific space within the panorama of divine vocation, human longing, and socio-political reality that Jesus' ministry will occupy. Framed by assurances that the presence and power of the Holy Spirit still surround Jesus and, indeed, direct his path (4:1, 14), the story relates Jesus' own time in the wilderness—an experience like that of John, of the prophets of old, and of Israel itself on its God-directed journey.

Forty days is a symbolic number for a long period of time rather than a specific calendar measurement—a period of time recalling, among other things, Moses' time of fasting (Exod. 34:28; Deut. 9:9) and Elijah's time of seclusion (1 Kings 19:4–8). It is a long time to be isolated and to go without food. Such disciplines frequently accompany rites of passage in various world religions, where fasting and isolation often function as the first stage of a ritual that is supposed to reveal the identity and vocation of the person engaging on it. In this case, though, the wilderness period is not part of a "vision quest," for the revelation is said already to have happened. Jesus' experience is described instead as a time of "testing" by the devil, apparently with the collusion of the Holy Spirit.

The devil functions in each of the three tests as a sort of prosecuting attorney, not as an independent evil power with whom Jesus must do battle. Not only is the Holy Spirit said to have led Jesus to the encounter, but the devil's tests, like Jesus' replies, are all drawn from biblical models and promises. For two of the three tests, the "hook" used by the devil to evoke Jesus' response recalls the heavenly voice Jesus has just heard: "If you are the Son of God, . . ." The challenge might be considered in various ways: "If you believe what you say you heard, you can do this, so why don't you prove you're telling the truth?" "If you are the son of God, let *God* prove it!" "If you wonder if you imagined the whole thing, why don't you test it?"

The three tests, taken individually and together, are highly symbolic. The tests described in Luke are the same as those found in Matthew (Matt. 4:1–11), but with the second and third reversed. Both begin with the challenge that Jesus turn a stone (or stones) into bread. In the context of Jesus' own hunger, making bread could hardly be seen as evil. In the context of a people for whom famine was a frequent experience, and whose poor members experienced scarcity even in years of good harvests, the ability to make bread from the abundant stones scattered on the west bank of the Jordan could be a lifesaver. Also, Moses is said to have been the catalyst for a similar provision of bread for Israel on their wilderness journey. What could be wrong with turning stones into bread? Nothing really is wrong with it. Jesus rejects the challenge not because it is wrong, but because it is inadequate: "One does not live by bread alone" (Deut. 8:3b). Even the fundamental human longing for bread is not sufficient to define Jesus' calling.

The second test (according to Luke) is that the devil shows Jesus all the kingdoms of the world in a split-second vision (in Matthew the view is said to have been provided from a mythically high mountain), and Jesus is offered "their glory and all this authority" simply for agreeing to worship the devil. At first thought there is no contest about this question, but it too is really ambiguous. Consider Jesus' context. The heavy foot of Rome is on the people's neck, and that alien occupation is itself a denial of God's sovereignty and an obstacle to the coming of God's promised reign of justice and peace (see the promises scattered through Isaiah 40—66, for example). If Jesus' vocation is to participate in that divine reign, surely the means are secondary to the end, and the theological details can be ironed out later. But Jesus' response is the first commandment: "Worship the Lord your God, and serve only [God]" (Luke 4:8; Deut. 6:13). As tempting as such political rationales might be to an occupied and suffering people, the tradition is harsh in its linking political compromise with betrayal of the most basic commandment to worship only God.

For Matthew, Jesus' quoting of the first commandment concludes the account, but Luke offers another ending. The third test in Luke is that Jesus should jump from the pinnacle of the temple in Jerusalem, trusting the angels to protect him. The devil offers a biblical precedent for such an act (Ps. 91:11–12): The truly righteous are promised God's special protection. To do something like that in the heart of Jerusalem would certainly solve any problem of public credibility of Jesus and his program. But Jesus again responds from Deuteronomy: "Do not put the Lord your God to the test" (Deut. 6:16). Public relations stunts also contradict the gospel, and indeed, the heart of Jerusalem will prove to have another welcome for Jesus because of the nature of the gospel he brings.

On one level, Jesus' being tested by the devil is yet another chapter in the story of the Son of God. Adam, the first son of God, failed his test by the devil (Gen. 3:1–19), and thereby set all humankind at odds with God's purposes. This Son of God, however, by passing the devil's tests, sets in motion a whole new era in God's relationship with all of humankind.

None of the tests proposed by the devil in Luke 4:1–13 would have had Jesus do anything inherently harmful or evil, and in each case good could result from what the devil proposed. In fact, later in the Gospel, Jesus is described, not as turning stones into bread, but as feeding a huge multitude when it appears that there is no food (9:12–17). He is said to possess a "kingdom," and to be able to confer it on others (22:29). And by going to the cross, Jesus trusts not in his own power to save himself (23:35, 37, 39), but in the salvation that comes from God alone (24:5–7, 46). Jesus' responses to the devil's tests, however, all drawn from the account in Deuteronomy of Israel's various tests in the wilderness, remind us that Luke and the earlier tradition on which he was drawing saw those tests as relating not just to the activity of a leader but also to the whole people's relationship with God.

The three specific tests described in 4:1–13 also involve something else—something that would have been clear to Jesus' contemporaries, as well as to his followers who told and retold this story. In each of the tests, the devil proposes to Jesus that he take on one of the forms expected for God's coming Anointed One. Perhaps the awaited one would be anointed as a prophet like Moses, who could lead the people in their wilderness—

feeding them, caring for them, and preparing them to enter God's promised dwelling place. Perhaps the coming one would be a political leader, a royal messiah, who could bring the people to freedom from the rule of their enemies and then establish a reign of justice, peace, and plenty. Or the one in whom hope was lodged might come as a righteous, pure, and worthy priest, who would "live in the shelter of the Most High" and "abide in the shadow of the Almighty" in such a way that he and the whole people with him would see God's salvation (Ps. 91:1, 16).

Given the responses attributed to Jesus, each of these possibilities is portrayed as being like the Israelites' misunderstanding of God's purposes and their failure to trust God during the period in the wilderness. Jesus' responses deny each possibility presented, but he provides no positive statement or summary of his purpose, his identity, or his vocation. To find out what shape that will take, we have to read the rest of the account.

For this reason it is important that in Luke's version the tests move from hunger in the wilderness, through the question of sovereignty over all the earth, to the temple in Jerusalem. Luke's Gospel will take us on a parallel journey from this beginning, through Jesus' ministry and teaching, to Jerusalem, where Jesus will be crucified and where the resurrected Jesus will appear, and from where the testimony to Jesus will go out "to the ends of the earth" (Acts 1:8).

The rest of the story is forecast also in the ominous note sounded by the devil's departure "until an opportune time" (4:13). Although this program of tests has been completed, and Jesus apparently has won the day, the devil will be back (22:3). Luke apparently has no illusions that the satanic sabbatical extends into the time of the church. Instead, the story that is about to begin gives us a glimpse into a brief and unique time in the complex relationship between God and humankind.

By assuring us that the same Spirit that filled Jesus and led him into the wilderness (4:1) filled him also at the end of the time in the wilderness, Luke is not only closing the parentheses around this episode. He is also assuring us that Jesus is equipped for the more subtle challenges and more difficult days ahead. Unlike Mark and Matthew, who affirm that angels "waited on" or served Jesus in the wilderness (Matt. 4:11; Mark 1:13), Luke leaves Jesus in the care of the Holy Spirit alone, both there and in his whole ministry. In Luke, the angel's care for Jesus comes only on the Mount of Olives (22:43), when a time of renewed and even harsher human testing is about to begin. It is clear from the stories in the first two chapters of Luke's Gospel that he is no stranger to angels, and that he has no qualms about granting them key roles in conveying information, understanding, or comfort. However, other than in that one episode early in the passion narrative, angels play no further active roles in Luke's Gospel. Instead, they are mentioned only in connection with the heavenly final judgment (9:26; 12:8–9; 15:10; 16:22) and with the women's experience at the empty tomb on Easter morning (24:23). In between, Luke's account will tell a very human story, with only the abiding power and presence of the Holy Spirit to assure its outcome.

# 2. Jesus' Ministry in and around Galilee

*Luke 4:14–9:50*

# 3. Preaching, Power, and Controversy: To Proclaim the Good News
## Luke 4:14–44

## JESUS IN NAZARETH: THE JUBILEE AGENDA
## Luke 4:14–30

4:14 Then Jesus, filled with the power of the Spirit, returned to Galilee, and a report about him spread through all the surrounding country. [15] He began to teach in their synagogues and was praised by everyone.

[16] When he came to Nazareth, where he had been brought up, he went to the synagogue on the sabbath day, as was his custom. He stood up to read, [17] and the scroll of the prophet Isaiah was given to him. He unrolled the scroll and found the place where it was written:

[18] "The Spirit of the Lord is upon me,
   because he has anointed me
       to bring good news to the poor.
He has sent me to proclaim release to the captives
   and recovery of sight to the blind,
       to let the oppressed go free,
[19] to proclaim the year of the Lord's favor."

[20] And he rolled up the scroll, gave it back to the attendant, and sat down. The eyes of all in the synagogue were fixed on him. [21] Then he began to say to them, "Today this scripture has been fulfilled in your hearing." [22] All spoke well of him and were amazed at the gracious words that came from his mouth. They said, "Is not this Joseph's son?" [23] He said to them, "Doubtless you will quote to me this proverb, 'Doctor, cure yourself!' And you will say, 'Do here also in your hometown the things that we have heard you did at Capernaum.'" [24] And he said, "Truly I tell you, no prophet is accepted in the prophet's hometown. [25] But the truth is, there were many widows in Israel in the time of Elijah, when the heaven was shut up three years and six months, and there was a severe famine over all the land; [26] yet Elijah was sent to none of them except to a widow at Zarephath in Sidon. [27] There were also many lepers in Israel in the time of the prophet Elisha, and none of them

**was cleansed except Naaman the Syrian."** [28] **When they heard this, all in the synagogue were filled with rage.** [29] **They got up, drove him out of the town, and led him to the brow of the hill on which their town was built, so that they might hurl him off the cliff.** [30] **But he passed through the midst of them and went on his way.**

The account of Jesus' ministry begins in earnest, immediately following the story of his time in the wilderness. In fact, Luke 4:14 serves a double purpose. It closes the parentheses around the previous story by the reference to Jesus being "filled with the power of the Spirit," just as earlier he was said to be "full of the Holy Spirit" and "led by the Spirit" into the wilderness. At the same time, 4:14–15 introduces the following section. The action is set in Galilee, and the specific incidents are narrated against the background of Jesus' growing fame and his practice of beginning his teaching in the Galilean synagogues.

In the narratives about Jesus' birth and childhood, and in the narratives that introduce his ministry, Luke provides clear indicators of his agenda. Messages from heaven—through angels or through direct speech—declare God's purposes and interpret the meaning of events. Hymns, reminiscent of biblical psalms and the poetry of prophets, provide key images and a framework for theological interpretation. Even the style and language serve to remind Luke's audience that the events carried in the narrative should be recognized as furthering the commitment of God that "all flesh shall see the salvation of God" (3:6).

With the beginning of Jesus' ministry in Galilee, he is left on his own, without angels or heavenly voices to comment on the action (until the Transfiguration in 9:28–36). Jesus himself is now Luke's principal interpretive lens. We learn to trust other characters when they exhibit an understanding of Jesus' vocation that he accepts, or when they are described as doing what he has instructed. Instead of the devil taking the stage to offer the "wrong" answers and to misread the Bible, Jesus' neighbors, his followers, and various others of his contemporaries provide the negative backdrops and the false readings against which the good news Jesus brings can be understood.

The incident set in the synagogue at Nazareth establishes the agenda of Jesus' ministry in two ways. First, it provides the occasion for Luke to have Jesus give a biblical warrant for his own work (4:18–19). Second, the reactions of the congregation provide a way to introduce what Luke considers to be the basis for inappropriate responses to Jesus and his message.

Although Matthew, Mark, and Luke all tell of an episode when Jesus and his message were rejected by his neighbors in Nazareth, Luke is the only one of the three to present an extended account of what happened. In both Matthew (13:54–58) and Mark (6:1–6a) the incident at Nazareth is set later in Jesus' ministry. In their versions of the story, the townspeople express amazement that the Jesus whose origins and upbringing they knew could exhibit such wisdom and power. The offense they take at him is interpreted by the proverb about prophets' lack of honor in their own homes (a variation on the modern proverb, "Familiarity breeds contempt"). The people's lack of faith is said to account for Jesus' unwillingness (Matthew) or inability (Mark) to do "deeds of power"—healings or exorcisms—there.

Luke's version of the story is set against the background of only the brief summary statement about the favorable response to his teaching. "Deeds of power" do not yet enter the discussion, and despite the mention of deeds done in Capernaum (4:23), no account of Jesus' ministry there is given until after he has left Nazareth (4:31). The people's amazement instead is focused on what Jesus says in this account itself (4:22a). The many details in the narrative and its importance as an inaugural episode of Jesus' ministry in Luke's Gospel tempt us to treat this account as the reminiscence of a particular historical episode in Jesus' life, but those same factors remind us instead to focus on how the story functions for Luke, and to recognize that he is probably the one who gave it its present shape. After all, no one would have been following Jesus around like a modern press corps on the trail of a political candidate, taking notes on his speeches and on the crowd's response.

The account begins with Jesus reading from the prophet Isaiah. Luke says nothing about how or why the specific verses would have been chosen on that day, and what we know about worship in the synagogues of Jesus' day or Luke's day does little to clarify the situation. Some scholars have suggested that Luke presented Jesus as following a "lectionary" or set of readings prescribed for the various sabbaths and other festivals of the year (or perhaps over a cycle of several years, like the three-year lectionary now used in many Christian churches). We cannot be sure, however, that such an accepted pattern of readings was followed in the early or middle years of the first century, since all of the evidence cited to support the suggestion comes from a later period. Again, the text itself does not make it clear whether we should understand Jesus as looking for a passage that had been assigned to him to read, or if we should understand this as something that he selected himself. Since the point of the story is not to present a report of a specific event but to move us along through a crucial interval of Luke's "account," such questions are really not crucial.

The passage from Isaiah is drawn mostly from the Septuagint of Isaiah 61:1–2a, with the addition of a phrase that seems to be from Isaiah 58:6. Luke may have been using a version of Isaiah that already combined those verses (since there were a number of variations in the texts of biblical manuscripts, especially during the centuries before the advent of modern printing techniques), or he may have been quoting from memory and been guided by the common content to include "to let the oppressed go free" with the other lines from Isaiah 61:1–2. What is clear is that the quotation of those verses stops before the reference to God's "day of vengeance." It is impossible to know whether Luke stopped there in order to avoid those words or if he wanted to emphasize "the year of the Lord's favor" as the final words cited.

Following the reading, Jesus is said to sit down, and both Luke's readers and a Galilean synagogue congregation would have seen that as the signal for the beginning of an interpretation of the text just read. No such "sermon" or explanation of the passage appears, however, but only the declaration, "Today this scripture has been fulfilled in your hearing" (4:21). That declaration is enough to evoke the amazement of the congregation. Why? How would this passage from Isaiah have been understood in Jesus' day or in Luke's?

Isaiah 61 builds on the imagery of the Jubilee year mandated in Leviticus 25. According to the laws effecting the Jubilee year, every fifty years Israel was to declare a "year of liberty" marked by four types of "release" or "rest." Like the earlier laws concerning the sabbath year to be observed every seven years (Exod. 21:2–6; 23:10–11; Deut. 15:1–18), the Jubilee laws required that the land be granted a year of rest (a "fallow" year, when no crops would be sown); debts were to be canceled; and any Israelite who had become an indentured servant would be set free. According to both the sabbath year and the Jubilee year laws, the reason for such requirements on the part of the people was God's prior action in freeing them from slavery and hard labor in Egypt. The Jubilee year laws included an additional provision, that any of the ancestral lands that had been sold out of financial necessity (the only conceivable reason why one would part with the land on which one's long-term livelihood depended) would be returned to those to whom God had originally allocated them when the Israelites entered the land. The reason for that last provision had to do with Israel's recognition of God's sovereignty. Like the kings of medieval Europe, the sovereign God was understood to own the land, which human beings could merely cultivate and enjoy at the "king's" discretion, in exchange for their unquestioning allegiance. The earth always belongs to

God, and thus we have no right to dispose of it in perpetuity, but only to trade the produce of the land (Lev. 25:23).

It is clear that the implementation of such laws would result in periodic economic upheavals throughout the land. That was the point. The laws would have prevented the accumulation of wealth—particularly capital, in the form of land—in anyone's hands. Rather, once in a lifetime the entire economy would be given a fresh start. Similar laws (even formulated in the same language) were decreed by the rulers of some of Israel's Canaanite neighbors when those rulers ascended their thrones. Rather than periodic economic restructurings, such as the laws in Leviticus prescribed, these other royal decrees had the effect of clearing out traces of the previous regime so the new sovereign would have free space in which to work out the programs of the new administration.

Although there are records stating that these other royal decrees were enacted in lands surrounding Israel, history gives us no evidence that a Jubilee year ever was celebrated. To conclude from that silence that no such year was celebrated seems warranted, for it would seem likely that so thoroughgoing an economic and social restructuring would have been noted somewhere. If it had been observed, such a year would surely have been a cause for celebration among the poor and for consternation among those whose investments were threatened.

Instead, the imagery of the Jubilee—of a royal decree of amnesty, of rest, and of liberty—is found in Isaiah 61 linked not to recurring human political and economic activity, but to the inaugural celebration of God's reign. The imagery came to represent the utter change of allegiance required from loyalties to the systems and structures of the present order, to a new participation in God's reign of justice and peace. The prophet becomes a herald leading the inaugural parade of that reign, trumpeting God's Jubilee or "liberty," which is what the underlying Hebrew word meant.

The words were a message of tremendous comfort and promise, both in the time of the Exile (or shortly after), when the passage from Isaiah was written, and in occupied Palestine of the first century, when the presence of Rome weighed heavily on the people. In Jesus' day, that weight was borne especially by the poor of the land, such as many of the townspeople of Nazareth. Isaiah 61:1–2 figured prominently among biblical passages cited by Jesus' contemporaries to recall to the people the promised future God had in store for them, in spite of their present reality of oppressive colonization. A study of the Gospels of Matthew and Mark, as well as Luke, reveals that the themes of this passage—good news to the poor, healing, release (or, as the Greek word is often translated, "forgiveness") from various kinds of captivity—figure prominently in the accounts of Jesus' ministry and teaching. Thus it is certainly not impossible that Jesus drew on this text himself, and that the passage itself, as well as its principal themes, was part of the memory bank and interpretive categories available to the early church in its proclamation of and about Jesus.

In any event, this passage, with its introductory affirmation of the empowering role of the Holy Spirit in "anointing" (the verb related to the titles of "Messiah" and "Christ"), served Luke well as a programmatic or inaugural text for Jesus' ministry. The affirmation that in Jesus that text has taken on flesh and been "fulfilled" is certainly something Luke could have proclaimed about Jesus to introduce his account of Jesus' ministry. And the amazement of the townspeople at such a declaration has a ring of truth, especially when they saw Jesus as simply "Joseph's son"—an identification that Luke's readers know is at best only partly true.

Subsequent verses make clear, though, that the problem goes deeper than the people's failure to understand that not only Jesus' human father Joseph was involved in Jesus' birth, or than the truism that prophets (and especially those who speak of God's "acceptable year") are themselves not "accepted" (4:29) by those who hear a word of judgment—or, at best, wishful thinking—in that message. The proverb cited in 4:23, "Doctor [or 'healer'], cure yourself!" underlines the contrast between the revolutionary changes promised in the text from Isaiah and Jesus' own situation, where the people were hemmed in by the structures and rules of the present age, especially in the form of Roman occupation. By that proverb, the people are said to ask for evidence of the fulfillment Jesus has just declared—a most understandable request.

Luke makes it clear that although the declaration that the text has been fulfilled is true, the results will not be what the people might expect. The references to the Elijah and Elisha traditions in 4:25–27 (1 Kings 17:8–9; 2 Kings 5:14) are to episodes when those prophets performed their healing or redeeming acts among Gentiles, and not for Israelites who were equally in need. If we read those stories in their entirety, it is clear that the redeeming work of Elijah and Elisha did eventually touch Israel as well, but it began outside the community. Coming on the heels of the proverb in 4:23, the recalling of this precedent in 4:25–27 portrays Jesus as telling the townspeople that their longing for evidence of the fulfillment of which he spoke might well not come to them first of all. They have no priority of place, and, as John had warned earlier (3:8), no basis on which to claim privilege in this divine project.

The ensuing wrath of the townspeople (4:28–29) is thus a fulfillment of the warning that God's faithfulness always includes God's freedom to make good on God's promises in unexpected—even unwanted—ways. In his account of the episode at Nazareth, Luke has thus provided both a guiding text for Jesus' ministry (Isa. 61:1–2) and a key to its interpretation—the prophetic affirmation of God's freedom to work in unexpected ways. For Luke's audience, the specific references to Gentiles, in contrast to the presumed inside track of Jesus' Jewish hearers, would not be lost. But Luke has carefully avoided setting up a simple reversal of roles—privileging Gentiles to the exclusion of Jews—by the references to the Elijah and Elisha stories, in which redemption does indeed come to Israel as well as to the specific Gentiles with whom the prophets' work began.

The death threat by the townspeople—intending to hurl Jesus off the cliff outside of town—is unsuccessful (4:30), but it serves as a harbinger of what is to come. The agenda provided by the Jubilee text from Isaiah read in prophetic affirmation of God's freedom to ignore human categories of privilege will set the contours of Jesus' message and ministry that will continue to evoke hostility and opposition. The forecast of Jesus' passion and death is clear. But just as Jesus here is said to pass through the very heart of the crowd and continue with his mission, so Luke will affirm that crucifixion also will fail to have the last word. From Jesus' preaching and teaching, to his ministry of healing and liberation of captives of every sort, to his death at the hands of his adversaries, to the victory of the resurrection, Luke's Gospel is sketched here in miniature, as Jesus leaves Nazareth (never to return, according to Luke's narrative) on the road that eventually will lead him to Jerusalem.

The parentheses are then closed around this episode by a summary statement emphasizing his successful teaching (4:31–32), echoing the introductory summary in 4:14–15, and moving the narrative forward to its next phase. Despite the near disaster in Nazareth, Luke affirms this aspect of Jesus' ministry—an affirmation mirrored in the response of Jesus' own hearers, who recognize that he teaches "with authority."

## A SABBATH IN CAPERNAUM

### The Good News Enacted (Luke 4:31–44)

4:31 He went down to Capernaum, a city in Galilee, and was teaching them on the sabbath. 32 They were astounded at his teaching, because he spoke with authority. 33 In the synagogue there was a man who had the spirit of an unclean demon, and he cried out with a loud voice, 34 "Let us alone! What have you to do with us, Jesus of Nazareth? Have you come to destroy us? I know who you are, the Holy One of God." 35 But Jesus rebuked him, saying, "Be silent, and come out of him!" When the demon had thrown him

down before them, he came out of him without having done him any harm.
[36] They were all amazed and kept saying to one another, "What kind of ut-
terance is this? For with authority and power he commands the unclean spirits, and out they come!" [37] And a report about him began to reach every
place in the region.

[38] After leaving the synagogue he entered Simon's house. Now Simon's
mother-in-law was suffering from a high fever, and they asked him about
her. [39] Then he stood over her and rebuked the fever, and it left her. Immediately she got up and began to serve them.

[40] As the sun was setting, all those who had any who were sick with various kinds of diseases brought them to him; and he laid his hands on each of
them and cured them. [41] Demons also came out of many, shouting, "You are
the Son of God!" But he rebuked them and would not allow them to speak,
because they knew that he was the Messiah.

[42] At daybreak he departed and went into a deserted place. And the
crowds were looking for him; and when they reached him, they wanted to
prevent him from leaving them. [43] But he said to them, "I must proclaim the
good news of the kingdom of God to the other cities also; for I was sent for
this purpose." [44] So he continued proclaiming the message in the synagogues of Judea.

The passage read from Isaiah speaks of both proclamation and action.
The actions, like the words, communicate good news, particularly in the
form of release from captivity and healing from disease. Whereas the synagogue in Nazareth provides the setting in which Luke can introduce the
proclamation and teaching about its implications, the synagogue in Capernaum becomes the place where the actions are introduced that will
complement the words. Luke follows Mark with only a few differences in
detail in his narration of this series of sabbath healings—healings, we
should note, that go unchallenged, unlike the stories of Jesus' sabbath
healings set later in his ministry.

The first of the stories (4:31–37) tells of the effectiveness of Jesus' "authority" over "demons." Gospel accounts that portray Jesus as an exorcist
are troubling to many modern readers. They invoke gruesome images of
horror movies, or of evil creatures, grotesque in appearance, lurking in the
shadows and waiting for someone to harm or to "take over" as an agent of
evil. Many of us, however, simply do not believe in demons, and we have
difficulty relating to stories that assume their reality.

Two angles of investigation might help us get inside stories such as this
one, in order better to understand how those stories function in the
Gospel narrative. The first direction we might take is to ask what condition is being attributed to demon possession, and what is said to happen

to the person in the course of the story. In this story, for example, the man is described as shouting angry and accusatory words. "What have you to do with us?" should be understood as an accusation that Jesus is a threat to what is making the person not an integrated "I," but a fragmented "we." Were we to hear someone shouting like that, we would think immediately of mental illness or a severe personality disorder: Something is making the person "not him- or herself." Our concern would be for the person to get care in the short term, and treatment over the long haul, to attempt to bring the broken parts of the personality back together into the sort of integrated whole that we recognize as healthy human life.

That is precisely what the exorcism narratives are attempting to communicate. In the language of the world from which the Gospels emerged, demons are recognized in conditions of physical or mental suffering, not where there is moral wrongdoing. In these stories, as in the world from which they came, the symptoms indicating demon possession were seen as frightening (as such symptoms are to many people today as well). The person seen as "possessed" might be avoided or ignored—not acknowledged until an outburst forces people to notice—or physically removed to the margins of society. But what is recognized to be needed is healing, or perhaps for the person to be freed from captivity or enslavement to the alien and self-alienating forces that are in control. What is not called for is judgment or punishment. Thus, in this story the "demon" is simply said to be silenced (resulting in the cessation of the principal symptom), and after provoking something like a seizure in the person, to leave the person unharmed and restored to an integrated whole.

A second way to get inside such narratives is to look at what claims the narrator makes about Jesus. In this story, it is while the person is shouting as a fragmented self that "they" are said to recognize Jesus, to realize that he represents a threat, and to identify him as "the Holy One of God" (4:34). As a power beyond the realm of everyday human interaction (the demon has been able to conquer and take over a human being), the demon can recognize that greater-than-human power in Jesus. The narrator thereby makes a claim about Jesus' own identity as involving more than simply the human authority of, for example, a great teacher. Power is at issue, and Jesus is not only recognized as moving in the realm of greater-than-human power that so often has destructive manifestations. He is also able to control even that sort of power when it functions to harm a person (4:35). Just as the people were astounded at the authority of his teaching (4:32), so now they are amazed at this other sort of authority and power that he manifests (4:36).

The story of Jesus' first successful exorcism of a demon stands in striking contrast to the preceding episode at Nazareth. In the synagogue at
Nazareth, the people misconstrue Jesus' identity, and they ridicule his authority. In contrast, the demon correctly identifies "Jesus of Nazareth" as
"the Holy One of God" and obeys his command, "Be silent, and come out
of him!" In Nazareth, the people unsuccessfully try to kill Jesus by throwing him down from a cliff, but the demon throws the man to the ground,
leaving him not only unharmed, but actually healed. Jesus demonstrates
authority over the demon, but he manages only to survive the wrath of his
neighbors. He does not heal or change the obduracy of the townspeople.
Taken together, the two episodes preview the pattern and apparent inconsistency of Jesus' ministry. His authority over demons and other powers is expressed repeatedly, but the intransigence of human hearts poses a
threat to the very death. The inconsistency is only in appearance, however, for God's own verdict of life in the drama of the resurrection (Luke
24) will finally triumph even over human hard-heartedness.

The second story in this collection deals not with the disintegrative
power of "demons," but with the physical ravages of disease—a fever
(4:38–39). The time is still the sabbath, but the setting has shifted from
the public arena of the synagogue to the privacy of Simon's house. Luke
has not yet identified Simon, though in Mark the story of Jesus' calling of
Simon, Andrew, James, and John (Mark 1:16–20) has preceded this series
of stories of healings and exorcisms (Mark 1:21–34), so Mark's readers
would know him as one of Jesus' followers. The person who is ill is identified as "Simon's mother-in-law," and we know neither her name nor that
of her daughter, Simon's wife.

The story gives none of the sort of information we would like to have,
such as the nature and cause of the fever or what medical procedures were
undertaken. Mark mentions only that Jesus took the woman's hand and
helped her up (Mark 1:31), but Luke does not mention even that touch.
Instead, just as Jesus "rebuked" the demon in the earlier narrative, he now
"rebukes" the fever, and the same authority is evidenced: she gets up and
begins to "serve them" (4:39).

The picture we have is of the woman getting up from her sickbed and
bringing them some food, and that may be the meaning intended here.
The verb "serve" does refer to serving food, and thus is connected to the
importance of meals in the life of early Christian communities. "Serve" is
also the word Jesus uses later in the Gospel to identify the appropriate activity and posture of disciples (22:26). By portraying the woman as engaging in this act of ministry as a consequence of her having been healed

by Jesus early in his ministry, Luke already hints at the continuing life of the Christian community.

It is interesting that the first person actually to carry out the duty of ministry or service is this unnamed woman. She is not the only woman in Luke's Gospel described as "serving" Jesus and those with him (Martha's work described in 10:38–42 is another well-known example). Other women will learn from Jesus (Mary in 10:38–42) and even "preach" (the woman who had been cured of hemorrhages, according to 8:47)—despite the fact that in Luke's Gospel and in Acts only men are officially commissioned to preach. By this little story, then, Luke not only amplifies the picture he is sketching of Jesus, but he also sets the stage for the continuing work of carrying forward the gospel, which comes into focus in Luke's second volume telling about the Acts of the Apostles.

The exorcism and healing stories thus continue to prepare the readers for, and to provide previews of, what Luke will narrate in the rest of the Gospel. They portray Jesus as not only proclaiming the good news, release, and liberty that is our first encounter with God's reign but also as doing deeds to make that proclamation a reality. The concluding verses of the section remind us, by means of summary statements, of the dual direction Jesus' ministry has taken—deeds of healing and exorcism that make clear Jesus' power (4:40–41), and preaching of the message, which is "the good news of the kingdom of God" (4:42–44). Jesus' earlier departure from Nazareth may have been under duress, but he goes out from Capernaum compelled only by the clarity of his vocation: "I must proclaim the good news of the kingdom of God to the other cities also; for I was sent for this purpose."

# 4. Disciples Called in Power, Chosen in Conflict
*5:1–6:19*

Something is still missing in Luke's Gospel: No disciples have been called to follow Jesus. Both Matthew and Mark mention the first disciples joining Jesus immediately after the initial report of his preaching in Galilee (Matt. 4:18–22; Mark 1:16–20). In Luke, though, we have already heard about the episode in the synagogue at Nazareth and about several healings. Luke has sketched an outline of the "good news" that is Jesus' agenda of teaching and action before anyone is invited to follow him, so that those who do become disciples should have a fairly clear idea of the design of Jesus' project.

That general evidence is supplemented by a personal demonstration of Jesus' power, before Simon, James, and John are called to follow Jesus (5:1–11). Between their call and the completion of Jesus' team of co-workers in the choosing of the twelve (6:12–16), Luke presents a series of episodes giving further evidence of Jesus' power and authority, and of the emerging opposition to him. These episodes are introduced by vague indications of changes in time or place ("once," "one day," "then"), and are not connected by any subtle narrative links or developments. Instead, they have a cumulative effect as each adds its details to the emerging picture. According to Luke, those who join Jesus in his mission should know what they are getting into. Responsibility for any subsequent confusion or second thoughts is lodged squarely at their door.

## A FISH STORY
### Luke 5:1–11

> 5:1 **Once while Jesus was standing beside the lake of Gennesaret, and the crowd was pressing in on him to hear the word of God, 2 he saw two boats there at the shore of the lake; the fishermen had gone out of them and were washing their nets. 3 He got into one of the boats, the one belonging to**

Simon, and asked him to put out a little way from the shore. Then he sat down and taught the crowds from the boat. ⁴ When he had finished speaking, he said to Simon, "Put out into the deep water and let down your nets for a catch." ⁵ Simon answered, "Master, we have worked all night long but have caught nothing. Yet if you say so, I will let down the nets." ⁶ When they had done this, they caught so many fish that their nets were beginning to break. ⁷ So they signaled their partners in the other boat to come and help them. And they came and filled both boats, so that they began to sink. ⁸ But when Simon Peter saw it, he fell down at Jesus' knees, saying, "Go away from me, Lord, for I am a sinful man!" ⁹ For he and all who were with him were amazed at the catch of fish that they had taken; ¹⁰ and so also were James and John, sons of Zebedee, who were partners with Simon. Then Jesus said to Simon, "Do not be afraid; from now on you will be catching people." ¹¹ When they had brought their boats to shore, they left everything and followed him.

As the story begins, Jesus has Simon the fisherman row him out from shore in order to find a better vantage point from which to preach to the gathered crowds (5:1–3). From that simple introduction, the story immediately escalates in wonder and drama. No reason is given for Jesus' instruction to the experienced fisherman: Did he spot a school of fish? The likelihood of so simple an explanation is lessened by the report that the whole night of fishing had been unproductive. Nevertheless, Simon does what he is told, calling Jesus by a title ("Master") found only on the lips of Jesus' disciples, and used only in Luke (8:24, 45; 9:33; 49; 17:13), in places where parallels in Mark and Matthew use either "teacher" or "rabbi." The word translated as "master" carries the meanings of commander, administrator, or supervisor—in other words, someone with authority, as the title itself and Simon's immediate obedience both convey (5:5). The catch was beyond belief, being so large that it threatened to sink not only Simon's own boat but also the second boat on which he had called for help.

Beginning in 5:8, the "fish story" that briefly gets our attention (5:6–7) slips out of focus. Simon suddenly acquires—without explanation—the second name "Peter" (a masculine form of the word for "rock" or "rocky ground"). His response to the great catch has none of the respectful obedience of the words he spoke earlier (5:5), but instead expresses fear and a desire to distance himself from Jesus. Although others share in Simon's amazement, Jesus' words are to him alone. They begin with the angels' refrain, "Do not be afraid" (5:10; see 1:13, 30; 2:10), and they end with the promise that he will be catching people—literally catching people *alive*.

The difference is an important one. While he has been catching fish in order to take them out of the environment where they live and to turn them into food for people to consume, his new catch is to be gathered together for life and not for death.

The response of Simon and the others (probably implying also James and John) strikes us as almost a formula for discipleship: "They left everything and followed him." But before the term "disciple" is too readily restricted to an elite group among Jesus' followers, thus separating us from its challenge, we should note that the same response is later attributed to the tax collector Levi (5:28), whose name does not appear on the list of the twelve "chosen" apostles in 6:14–15. Willingness to leave "everything" behind—one's family, possessions, status, economic security, and identity itself—in order to join in Jesus' ministry of the good news of God's reign characterizes all of Jesus' followers. It has implications for the nature and norms of the new community being formed around Jesus, which form the basis of the church.

## A MAN IS HEALED OF LEPROSY
## Luke 5:12–16

> 5:12  Once, when he was in one of the cities, there was a man covered with leprosy. When he saw Jesus, he bowed with his face to the ground and begged him, "Lord, if you choose, you can make me clean." [13] Then Jesus stretched out his hand, touched him, and said, "I do choose. Be made clean." Immediately the leprosy left him. [14] And he ordered him to tell no one. "Go," he said, "and show yourself to the priest, and, as Moses commanded, make an offering for your cleansing, for a testimony to them." [15] But now more than ever the word about Jesus spread abroad; many crowds would gather to hear him and to be cured of their diseases. [16] But he would withdraw to deserted places and pray.

In the next episode a man approaches Jesus. The man is suffering from a condition that is not necessarily Hansen's disease, which is what we know as "leprosy," but another condition whose symptoms are visible on the skin of the man's body. Like Simon earlier (5:8), he bows down in front of Jesus. But unlike Simon, who wanted to separate himself from Jesus, this man's words declare his confidence in Jesus' power to make him well, and hence no longer someone from whom people would want to keep their distance.

The story of the healing is poignant: It happens precisely when Jesus touches this person whom law and custom have prevented from being touched. He urges the man to complete the process of having his healing recognized by the religious authorities as the law prescribed (5:14), so that he could join once again in community with other people. In that step we see perhaps the clearest expression of the social dimension that is at least implicitly a part of all of the healing stories, just as there is a social aspect to all disease. In these stories the person with the disease has been relegated to the margins of the community or of society, whether because of attitudes toward his or her condition or because the condition itself restricts mobility and social interaction. As part of the healing process itself, that person is enabled to rejoin the community and to participate again in both the joys and demands of the common life.

The summary with which the story concludes carries both an affirmation and a warning. It affirms Jesus' growing renown as a teacher and a healer. But the mention of Jesus withdrawing to pray signals a major turning point at hand (see 1:10; 2:37; 3:21; 6:12; 9:18, 28–29; 11:1; 22:41). In this case, the time of prayer serves as an unspoken warning: Jesus will be using that time apart to prepare himself for the series of conflicts that is about to begin.

## A PARALYZED PERSON IS HEALED: A CONFLICT ABOUT FORGIVENESS
### Luke 5:17–26

5:17 **One day, while he was teaching, Pharisees and teachers of the law were sitting near by (they had come from every village of Galilee and Judea and from Jerusalem); and the power of the Lord was with him to heal. [18] Just then some men came, carrying a paralyzed man on a bed. They were trying to bring him in and lay him before Jesus; [19] but finding no way to bring him in because of the crowd, they went up on the roof and let him down with his bed through the tiles into the middle of the crowd in front of Jesus. [20] When he saw their faith, he said, "Friend, your sins are forgiven you." [21] Then the scribes and the Pharisees began to question, "Who is this who is speaking blasphemies? Who can forgive sins but God alone?" [22] When Jesus perceived their questionings, he answered them, "Why do you raise such questions in your hearts? [23] Which is easier, to say, 'Your sins are forgiven you,' or to say, 'Stand up and walk'? [24] But so that you may know that the Son of Man has authority on earth to forgive sins"—he said to the one who was paralyzed—"I say to you, stand up and take your bed and go to your home." [25] Immediately he stood up before them, took what he had been lying on, and went to his home, glorifying God. [26] Amazement seized all of them, and they glorified God and were filled with awe, saying, "We have seen strange things today."**

Up to this point in the narrative, Jesus has had no interaction with Jewish religious leaders. The only opposition he has encountered has been from the other townspeople of Nazareth. Thus, the arrival of the "Pharisees and teachers of the law" in the midst of the crowd that has gathered to hear Jesus' teaching and to witness healings signals danger only to the readers already familiar with the Gospel accounts. At the beginning of this episode, the religious leaders are simply some of the observers of an amazing effort on the part of a group of men to obtain help for another person who is paralyzed (5:17–19). It is important to keep in mind a certain anachronism in the prominent role played by Pharisees in these controversies and elsewhere in the Gospel. In Jesus' day the Pharisees were a fairly small and not very powerful group within Judaism. They were noted for their careful interpretation and meticulous observance of the law, not out of an egocentric attempt to build a positive balance on some heavenly spreadsheet of moral credits and debits, but so that God might find a people prepared to be God's agents in the realization of God's dominion of justice and peace. After the destruction of Jerusalem and of the temple in 70 C.E., when careful observance of the law was the principal way remaining to live out one's Jewish identity, the Pharisees rose to greater prominence. By the time the Gospel of Luke was written, the Pharisees had come to represent the dominant voice of Jewish religious leadership. For Luke's audience, their role was clear; in the time of Jesus, however, they were only one voice in the chorus of interpreters (and would-be reformers) of Judaism.

Within the purposes of this story, the author does not address the moral question of whether those carrying the person who was paralyzed should have dismantled the roof of the house where Jesus was teaching. Their action is accepted simply as evidence of their determination to get help for their friend, and it seems to be what is called "their faith" (5:20). That faith then triggers Jesus' words of forgiveness to the one who is paralyzed. Those words introduce problems in several areas. The first is the theological problem of the implied link between the person's condition and a need for forgiveness. Does the tradition underlying the Gospels, or even the church's memory of Jesus' own ministry, share the common assumption in the ancient world that disease is a consequence of sin? That conclusion appears to be supported by the text. Even though such an assumption may have been held by biblical authors (or even by Jesus), we cannot ignore what science has taught us about the physical causes of disease and of various physical disabilities. To ignore such knowledge, and to heap guilt on people who are suffering by implying that they have caused their own condition, is clearly inappropriate. On the other hand, modern medicine is only beginning to explore the connections between spiritual, emotional, or psychological health (or lack of it) and physical illness or well-being. Thus, if the paralyzed person felt a connection between the physical paralysis and his or her "sin," an effort to heal the latter without attention to the former might well be in vain. If indeed that was the person's understanding, Jesus' words of forgiveness (5:20b) and healing (5:24c) together might have enabled that person to be restored to health.

The healing story (5:18–20, 24c-26) is actually complete in and of itself. It is rather typical of healing stories found in the Gospels, with the identification of the person's condition, an account of efforts to reach Jesus, interaction between Jesus and the patient, evidence of the success of the healing (in this case, the person is able to walk), and the response of onlookers—a pattern very similar to that of any person's account of illness, treatment, and eventual recovery. The words of forgiveness might be seen as part of this core story—part of the "treatment." But they also introduce the story that occupies the middle of the passage (5:21–24b), Jesus' conflict with the religious leaders. That conflict appears at first to interrupt the healing story, but it ends up providing the key to the meaning of this particular healing story for Luke.

The controversy is provoked by the religious leaders who are concerned about "blasphemies." According to the Hebrew Bible, blasphemy involved abusing the name of God (Lev. 24:10–11, 14–16, 23) or attacking something belonging to God (2 Kings 19:4, 6, 22; Ezek. 35:1–2). Here, however, the issue is God's unique power to forgive. The words attributed to Jesus—"your sins are forgiven you"—are in the passive voice, leaving God as the implied subject who does the forgiving. The objection seems to center on who has the right to say what God is doing. According to the religious leaders, Jesus has no such right.

Jesus' response to their questions is a trick question of his own (5:23). On the one hand, declaring forgiveness is easier, because if one has misspoken, no one will know. On the other hand, if one says to someone who is paralyzed, "Stand up and walk," and does not have the power to heal that person, one's foolishness will be obvious immediately. But one cannot speak lightly on God's behalf either, and so the dilemma stands. It is resolved in the claim that evidence that the "Son of Man" does have authority to forgive sins (and not merely the authority to identify what God has done) lies in the effective healing by Jesus of the person who is paralyzed (5:24).

Luke clearly understands the title "Son of Man" to refer to Jesus: Proof of the authority of the former is in the power of the latter. It is important to be aware, though, that this connection we so easily take for granted rests on fuzzy beginnings. In both Hebrew and Aramaic there are idioms that can be literally translated into the phrase "the son of the human being." As is the case with idioms in many languages, however, a literal translation does little to convey the meaning. (Think, for example, of the English expression "to take a bath." Neither the common meaning of "bathe oneself in a tub" nor the more figurative meaning of "lose all one's wealth"—as in the sentence, "When the stock market fell, he really took a bath!"—is a literal rendering of the verb, "take," plus the object, "bath.")

What the words "the son of the human being" actually meant in Jesus' day is unclear. Some of the uses of this phrase outside the New Testament have the phrase functioning like an indefinite pronoun, meaning "whoever" or "anyone who" does something. Others carry the meaning of "human being," just as the phrase "a son of Israel" means "an Israelite." Still other examples find it working as a third-person reference to the speaker, just as we might say, "I tell you, *this kid* would never be caught doing anything that stupid!" In Daniel 7:13 the phrase (translated in the NRSV as "a human being") refers to a heavenly figure who will come as judge at the end-time. Throughout the book of Ezekiel the phrase (translated in the NRSV as "mortal") refers to the prophet under assignment from God. Several translators have suggested "the Human One" as a way to encompass the various meanings in a phrase that is still a title (as the Gospel writers clearly intend it to be), and that avoids the exclusively masculine gender of the traditional language.

Indeed, all of these uses find echoes in the Gospels. Jesus is the only character in the Gospels who is said to use the title; no other character uses it in any confessional sense to refer to Jesus. If we conclude from that evidence that we get this phrase from Jesus' own usage, the problem remains of what it meant, and how he might have used it. Did it express his expectation that God's judgment was at hand? Was it an oblique way to refer to his own authority or task on earth (such as in this passage, or in 19:10 and other places)? Did it have its beginning in a general recognition of human mortality, or of the likelihood that anyone (any prophet, perhaps) following a course like Jesus' could expect to suffer (9:22, 44b; 18:31–33)? Unfortunately, scholars' decisions about these various possibilities usually rest on prior assumptions about Jesus, his message, and his ministry.

In the Gospels the NRSV has followed the traditional wording of earlier translations, using "the Son of Man." In order to avoid confusion, I will follow the same convention. That familiar language should not mask the fact that the origins and meaning of this title are unknown. Our best course is simply to try to understand the various ways the Gospel writers use it, and to see what its rich and textured meaning adds to our picture of Jesus.

## FROM TAX AGENT TO DISCIPLE? A CONFLICT ABOUT TABLE COMMUNITY
## Luke 5:27–32

> 5:27 **After this he went out and saw a tax collector named Levi, sitting at the tax booth; and he said to him, "Follow me."** [28] **And he got up, left everything, and followed him.**
>
> [29] **Then Levi gave a great banquet for him in his house; and there was a large crowd of tax collectors and others sitting at the table with them.** [30] **The Pharisees and their scribes were complaining to his disciples, saying, "Why do you eat and drink with tax collectors and sinners?"** [31] **Jesus answered, "Those who are well have no need of a physician, but those who are sick;** [32] **I have come to call not the righteous but sinners to repentance."**

This story takes us from a private home to the semi-public setting of a tax collector's booth. The story of Levi unfolds with many gaps and inconsistencies. For example, no explanation is provided for Jesus' invitation to Levi or for Levi's immediate and unquestioning response. No sudden windfall of profits (like the miraculous catch of fish in 5:1–11) provides Levi with evidence of Jesus' power or authority. Nothing is said about Levi's self-understanding or self-image either before or after encountering Jesus. Jesus invites, and Levi gets up, leaves his post, and follows (5:27–28). As in the case of the fishermen who left their boats and fishing gear behind and followed Jesus, Levi too abandons his profession. In neither case does a vow of poverty seem to be the issue. In fact, Levi is said still to own a house and to have enough resources to host a banquet for many guests (5:29). In both cases, what is left behind is the earlier way of earning a living—the basic security of an income and a place in the social hierarchy that is familiar, regardless of whether it is prestigious or lowly.

Another gap in the story occurs in that no explanation is given for why Pharisees and their scribes not only happen to be aware of the guests at the banquet but even are in attendance themselves and can challenge Jesus on site (5:30). Jesus' response (5:31–32) accepts the Pharisees' assessment of the tax collectors and other guests at the party, and then claims that it is precisely because they are sinners that he has singled them out. If the previous story spoke of *forgiveness* freely given, with no initiative or response demanded from the one forgiven (for Jesus comments on "their faith," not on that of the paralyzed person), this story picks up the theme of *repentance* that has been part of the summary of John's message (3:3) and that will be carried forward into the church's proclamation in the name of the risen Christ (24:47).

## A QUESTION ABOUT FASTING, AN ANSWER ABOUT TIME
### Luke 5:33–39

5:33  **Then they said to him, "John's disciples, like the disciples of the Pharisees, frequently fast and pray, but your disciples eat and drink.** [34] **Jesus said to them, "You cannot make wedding guests fast while the bridegroom is with them, can you?** [35] **The days will come when the bridegroom will be taken away from them, and then they will fast in those days."** [36] **He also told them a parable: "No one tears a piece from a new garment and sews it on an old garment; otherwise the new will be torn, and the piece from the new will not match the old.** [37] **And no one puts new wine into old wineskins; otherwise the new wine will burst the skins and will be spilled, and the skins will be destroyed.** [38] **But new wine must be put into fresh wineskins.** [39] **And no one after drinking old wine desires new wine, but says, 'The old is good.'"**

With no change of scene, the Pharisees and their scribes continue questioning Jesus, shifting to what we might call the spiritual disciplines of prayer and fasting. Jesus' response does not talk about the value of such disciplines themselves, but instead talks about their timing. According to Jewish practice, the joyful celebration of a wedding takes precedence over any other obligations. Mourning, acts of penance, and religious vows of fasting or other abstinence are to be set aside in the presence of the bridal couple. Once they have gone on their way, other disciplines would resume. The controversy is thus resolved for Luke by the fact that Jesus' presence creates the same sort of interval in "normal" time as would be created by a wedding. Once Jesus was no longer among them, there would be time enough to resume usual religious practices (5:33–35). What is not clear is whether Luke thinks his church is living in a time when the "bridegroom" has been taken away, because Jesus has been crucified, or whether with the risen Christ the celebration continues. The mention of a time when fasting will be resumed makes the former seem to be the case.

The twin parables of the patch and the wine clarify the response to the Pharisees that has been attributed to Jesus. Both parables depend on common sense, just as the previous saying depends on one's recognition of how weddings come as a joyful interruption in life and business as usual. Common sense recognizes that no one would tear a piece out of a new garment in order to repair an old one, even though the old one still is worth saving. The new one would be left with a hole in it, and the patch would not work to fix the old one either. The two would not match to begin with, and in the days before fabrics were preshrunk, the new patch would soon pull away from the surrounding garment. Both the old and the new would be ruined (5:36). In the same way, to put new wine that is still fermenting into stiff old wineskins would result in the skins bursting, ruining them and spilling the wine. Again, both valuable commodities would be lost (5:37–38).

The common-sense wisdom of the parables reinforces Luke's double affirmation in the previous saying. Both the old and the new garments, and both the new wine and the old wineskins, are valuable. Similarly, traditional religious practices like fasting are valued and good too, in their appropriate time. Jesus does not put down the religious practices of the other groups. At the same time, though, Luke affirms that Jesus' presence supersedes that value: At stake is an even greater good.

The saying in 5:39 is an ironic reference to the strong appeal of the old—old wine, and, by implication, old habits and old ways—compared with the new. Unlike the saying in 5:35 that points to a time when fasting will be resumed, this saying suggests that Luke and his church participate in the radical newness and the break with business as usual that is associated with Jesus. " 'The old is good'—or at least good enough for me!" may be the refrain of those in Luke's community who are tempted to abandon the gospel for a safer and more predictable way of life, or to restrict the gospel to one of the other "orderly accounts" or "things about which [they] have been instructed" that Luke thinks it is time to leave behind.

## SABBATH WORK
## AND SABBATH HEALING
## Luke 6:1–11

6:1 **One sabbath while Jesus was going through the grainfields, his disciples plucked some heads of grain, rubbed them in their hands, and ate them.** 2 **But some of the Pharisees said, "Why are you doing what is not lawful on the sabbath?"** 3 **Jesus answered, "Have you not read what David did when** he and his companions were hungry? [4] He entered the house of God and took and ate the bread of the Presence, which it is not lawful for any but the priests to eat, and gave some to his companions?" [5] Then he said to them, "The Son of Man is lord of the sabbath."

[6] On another sabbath he entered the synagogue and taught, and there was a man there whose right hand was withered. [7] The scribes and the Pharisees watched him to see whether he would cure on the sabbath, so that they might find an accusation against him. [8] Even though he knew what they were thinking, he said to the man who had the withered hand, "Come and stand here." He got up and stood there. [9] Then Jesus said to them, "I ask you, is it lawful to do good or to do harm on the sabbath, to save life or to destroy it?" [10] After looking around at all of them, he said to him, "Stretch out your hand." He did so, and his hand was restored. [11] But they were filled with fury and discussed with one another what they might do to Jesus.

The growing tension between Jesus and the Pharisees (who appear to be following his every move) shifts its focus to questions about sabbath observance. According to the two stories, which may reflect the shape of controversies between the Christian church and the neighboring synagogue as much as any reminiscences of Jesus' time, the Pharisees ask about the limits on one's sabbath activity, while Jesus presses for a discussion of the purpose and intent of sabbath-keeping. In both stories, Jesus draws on principle and precedent in the Hebrew Bible to resolve the disputes.

The first dispute (6:1–5) probably comes from the context of disagreements between church and synagogue about various points of law, and not from Jesus' own interaction with the religious authorities of his day. The fact that Pharisees are again noted as the opponents is one clue to this context. So is the fact that the disciples' conduct and not Jesus' is at issue. There are also several inconsistencies in the story that make it seem like a literary creation and not a remembered incident. First, picking the heads of grain can only serve an immediate need, and that is always permissible on the sabbath. Such picking does not constitute harvesting, which is indeed prohibited on the sabbath. Second, what would have violated sabbath law was traveling on the sabbath, and not only is that activity on the part of the disciples not challenged, but apparently their accusers have been walking with them, and thus also "doing what is not lawful on the sabbath." Finally, the argument from scripture that offers a Davidic precedent does not fit the case (1 Sam. 21:1–6); the biblical example is not about sabbath law. It also represents a type of argument more typical of later disputes between church and synagogue than of other instances where Jesus is said to be addressing the demands of the law.

The concluding saying of the first story—"The Son of Man is Lord of the sabbath" (6:5)—is clearly the point of the passage. Again the key figure is the Son of Man, which serves only to provoke more questions. To say that this figure is sovereign over the sabbath is not to deny the importance of keeping the sabbath, but instead to locate the authority to define sabbath-keeping in a different place. Luke has omitted the first half of Mark's version of the saying: "The sabbath was made for humankind, and not humankind for the sabbath" (Mark 2:27), which already declares the purpose of the sabbath. Luke's conclusion centers not generally on humankind, but rather on Jesus. As Son of Man, Jesus is the reliable source for sabbath rules.

The second of the two stories focusing on sabbath law (6:6–11) establishes Jesus' authority to define by his deeds as well as his words the proper way to keep the sabbath. At the same time, it clarifies the underlying principle and meaning of sabbath-keeping. The setting of this story is a sabbath gathering in a synagogue. It is important to recall that there have been earlier accounts of Jesus' performing healings and exorcisms on the sabbath without any objections being raised (4:31–39). Although healing is clearly considered work and is therefore generally prohibited on the sabbath, healing or any type of work *is* permissible as long as it deals with a life-threatening condition (such as, presumably, demon possession or a high fever).

What at first appears to be at issue is whether this circumstance meets the criteria. Luke identifies the afflicted hand as the right one—a detail by which he suggests to a world where right-handedness is dominant that this man's ability to work and to earn a living would have been compromised. Since he could not have worked on the sabbath anyway, however, it would appear that nothing would be lost by waiting until sundown—the end of the sabbath—to heal the man's hand. The details of the man's condition do little to justify him as a candidate for a legitimate sabbath healing. Since scribes and Pharisees are said to be present, by this point in the narrative we have come to expect to find them keeping an eye on just such details.

Luke quickly shifts the argument to another level, which may indicate how debates between church and synagogue about proper sabbath observance were unfolding in Luke's community. Jesus' words and actions are deliberate. Calling the man forward, Jesus asks not about the *conditions* under which the sabbath is appropriately observed, but about the *purpose* of keeping the sabbath: "Is it lawful to do good or to do harm on the sabbath, to save life or to destroy it?" If the foundational commandment, which all specific sabbath laws are designed to implement, is "Observe the sabbath day and keep it holy" (Deut. 5:12), the answer to Jesus' question is obvious: In fact, no answer is needed or given. Note that Jesus is not said to wipe away sabbath law. Instead he affirms that the specific conditions under which the sabbath is appropriately observed, as well as any points of law, are to be tested against the overarching purpose for which the sabbath laws were derived—a much more radical proposal.

The rage of the opponents is clear in Luke's concluding comment (6:11), but he has tempered Mark's outright statement that they conspired to destroy Jesus (Mark 3:6). The townspeople of Nazareth remain the only ones in Luke's account to let anger move them to action. A hint of danger is sounded again, though—the first echo of what will become a more insistent theme as the Gospel unfolds.

## THE TWELVE ARE CHOSEN
## Luke 6:12–19

6:12 **Now during those days he went out to the mountain to pray; and he spent the night in prayer to God.** 13 **And when day came, he called his disciples and chose twelve of them, whom he also named apostles:** 14 **Simon, whom he named Peter, and his brother Andrew, and James, and John, and Philip, and Bartholomew,** 15 **and Matthew, and Thomas, and James son of Alphaeus, and Simon, who was called the Zealot,** 16 **and Judas son of James, and Judas Iscariot, who became a traitor.**

17 **He came down with them and stood on a level place, with a great crowd of his disciples and a great multitude of people from all Judea, Jerusalem, and the coast of Tyre and Sidon.** 18 **They had come to hear him and to be healed of their diseases; and those who were troubled with unclean spirits were cured.** 19 **And all in the crowd were trying to touch him, for power came out from him and healed all of them.**

The background for this scene is the previous collection of stories of Jesus' continuing power to heal and his authority to teach, and at the same time stories of many-sided objections raised to his work and to his lifestyle by the religious authorities. Against that background, Luke reports the establishment of the administrative structure that will make possible the ongoing life of this movement that Jesus is beginning. Jesus' withdrawal to a mountain top to pray again signals the importance of what follows. Out of the whole group of people who have "left everything and followed" Jesus, and who apparently are with him on the mountain, an inner circle of twelve are "chosen" and named "apostles," or "sent-ones." Luke's list includes the three who have left their nets (5:1–11): Simon (whom Jesus is now said to name "Peter," despite the fact that the double name "Simon Peter" has already been used in 5:8), James, and John. The list, however, does not include the tax agent Levi, who was also identified as a person who left everything and followed Jesus (5:28). The rest of the names on the list of the twelve appear here for the first time in Luke's Gospel. Two names differ from the parallel lists in Matthew 10:2–4 and Mark 3:16–19: "Simon, who was called the Zealot" is called "Simon the Cananaean" in both other lists; and "Judas son of James" appears as "Thaddaeus" in the others. The list of the twelve (or at least the eleven remaining after the death of Judas) that is found in Acts 1:13 also contains the names of Simon the Zealot and Judas son of James. A number of textual variants indicate that some of the Christian scribes who copied the manuscripts of Luke and Acts tried to harmonize the various lists, either among the Synoptic Gospels or within Luke's writings. When all of the evidence has been weighed, however, it appears that Luke was working with a list that differs at these two points from the lists of the other Gospels.

The Gospel says nothing about the authority or responsibilities of these apostles, or about the nature of the sending intended for them. At this point in Luke's narrative they are simply chosen: They and we must wait to learn what lies ahead.

This section of Luke's Gospel concludes with a summary statement (6:17–19) that also introduces the following section. The setting is no longer on a mountain with only the disciples, but on a level, more accessible, and more public place. Many disciples—not just the twelve—and a large crowd of others are present. The geographical origins of the people in the crowd point to the broad appeal of Jesus (including people from Tyre and Sidon, cities located near the modern border between Israel and Lebanon, which probably had many Gentile inhabitants). The three activities of teaching (or preaching), healing, and exorcism once again serve to define Jesus' ministry, even though in the section that began in 5:1–11 no stories explicitly about exorcisms have been related. Those activities have become for Luke a formal way of identifying Jesus, and like many such summaries in Luke's Gospel, this one functions to indicate a change of subject. It is as if the curtain is brought down on one act, then quickly raised to begin the next.

# 5. Training for Apostles
*Luke 6:20–9:6*

The mixed audience—"a great crowd of his disciples and a great multitude of people"—mentioned in the summary verses that provide the transition between this section and 6:17–19 sets the stage for the entire next segment of Luke's Gospel. Between the time of the choosing of twelve of the disciples to serve as apostles and their actual sending out on a missionary journey (9:1–6), Jesus' public ministry continues. Meanwhile, the disciples are often mentioned explicitly as observers of the events and hearers of the teachings that constitute that ministry, learning by example and apprenticeship about the ministry for which they have been chosen. Interspersed through the public events are occasions where the disciples are given more extensive explanations of teachings (e.g., 8:9–18) or witness additional examples of Jesus' power and authority (e.g., 8:22–25). In 6:17–9:6, Luke invites his own audience to overhear the apostles' education for ministry.

## THE "SERMON ON THE PLAIN"
## Luke 6:20–49

The title "Sermon on the Plain" is commonly used to identify the first unit of this ministerial curriculum, and it does indeed serve as a convenient label. It is important to remember, however, that what that label identifies is more like a collection of somewhat related teachings on a variety of themes, rather than a coherent argument or single "sermon" delivered at one time. In this overall design, as well as in much of its content, Luke's "sermon" resembles Matthew's even more famous "Sermon on the Mount" (Matt. 5:1–7:29). Luke's collection, however, is only about one-fourth as long as Matthew's. It includes teachings found in other parts of Matthew as well as in the Sermon on the Mount. Conversely, significant portions of Matthew's sermon are found at other points in Luke's narrative. None of the material in Luke's sermon is found in Mark, whereas Matthew has incorporated some material from Mark into his sermon—sayings that Luke records in other parts of the Gospel.

Both Matthew and Luke seem to exercise considerable freedom in constructing their collections of Jesus' teachings to meet their own literary and theological purposes. In other words, neither can be shown to be recording an actual event of preaching and teaching in Jesus' ministry. The fact that both present such collections of teachings fairly near the beginning of Jesus' public ministry, however, suggests that such a format and type of event is deeply carved into the community's ministry. These "sermons" corroborate and enlarge upon the summary statements and other specific accounts of Jesus' preaching and teaching, and thus they emphasize the importance of that aspect of his ministry.

Instead of speculating about why Luke did not include particular teachings found in Matthew's sermon or why he wove them into other parts of the Gospel narrative, it seems more helpful to work with the collection of teachings Luke does present, identifying points of emphasis and guiding themes of his sermon. Luke's collection can be divided into four sections: blessings and woes (6:20–26), relationships with enemies and benefactors (6:27–35), mercy and judgment (6:36–42), and personal integrity (6:43–49).

## Blessings and Woes (Luke 6:20–26)

6:20 **Then he looked up at his disciples and said:**
  **"Blessed are you who are poor,**
    **for yours is the kingdom of God.**
  21 **"Blessed are you who are hungry now,**
      **for you will be filled.**
  **"Blessed are you who weep now,**
      **for you will laugh.**
  22 **"Blessed are you when people hate you, and when they exclude you, revile you, and defame you on account of the Son of Man.** 23 **Rejoice in that day and leap for joy, for surely your reward is great in heaven; for that is what their ancestors did to the prophets.**
  24 **"But woe to you who are rich,**
      **for you have received your consolation.**
  25 **"Woe to you who are full now,**
      **for you will be hungry.**
  **"Woe to you who are laughing now,**
      **for you will mourn and weep.**

<sup>26</sup> **"Woe to you when all speak well of you, for that is what their ancestors did to the false prophets."**

Both Matthew and Luke begin their collections with a series of blessings or "beatitudes"—nine in Matthew, of which four are echoed in Luke. In addition, Luke mirrors each of his blessings with the corresponding woe, ending both lists with parallel references to "what their ancestors did to the prophets" (6:23b) or "to the false prophets" (6:26b). All except the last of Matthew's blessings are general statements in the third person (for example, "Blessed are those who mourn, for they will be comforted" [Matt. 6:4]), whereas Luke's are in the second person, directed to his immediate audience ("you will be filled," "you will laugh" [6:21]). The fact that both the blessings and the woes in Luke are in the second person suggests that the large audience described as present for the sermon (as well as Luke's own audience) included both some people who benefited from the status quo (and thus would hear the woes directed to them) and those who suffered from it (and thus heard a word of blessing).

The first two of Luke's blessings appear to differ significantly from the parallels in Matthew. In the first, Luke maintains that the realm of God belongs to "the poor," whereas Matthew refers to "the poor in spirit." Does Luke refer only to an economic condition, whereas Matthew leans toward a meaning parallel to "the meek" in Matthew 5:5? The distinction may be a modern one. Matthew's two blessings (Matt. 5:3, 5) appear to draw together references to the poor, the humble, and the meek that are found in such biblical texts as Isaiah 61:1; 66:2; and Psalm 37:11. The words used in the Septuagint of such texts to identify the groups referred to are very similar in meaning and virtually interchangeable. They refer to people who are economically destitute, who can claim no power in the prevailing economic system, and who reap no benefits from it. We might refer to them as "oppressed" or "marginalized." It is to such people that God's reign belongs. The blessing is part of the reversal of fortunes that characterizes God's project, as Luke has already made clear in the hymns and stories of the birth narratives and in the appropriation of the Jubilee text of Isaiah 61:1–2 in 4:18–19. To see the beatitude as rewarding an attitude (as Matthew seems to imply) or an economic condition for its own sake (as Luke seems to imply) is to miss the principal point.

Similarly, Luke's second beatitude ("Blessed are you who are hungry now") also finds its parallel in Matthew ("Blessed are those who hunger and thirst for righteousness"), sounding in Matthew as though ethics rather than physical need is at issue. Matthew, however, does not usually use the word "righteousness" to refer to human action, but to God's saving work. Specifically, he often links it to the reign of God (for example, Matt. 5:10). "Hunger" or yearning for salvation is often linked to physical hunger in the imagery of the Hebrew Bible, and the satisfaction of hunger is one of the signs of God's presence (Ps. 107:4–9, 35–37; 146:5–10; Isa. 32:6; 49:7–10; 65:13). In addition to echoing the motif of a reversal of fortune, this beatitude in both Luke and Matthew affirms that the basic human need for food is both a specific example and a symbol of all the human needs that are met in the establishment of God's reign.

The last two blessings in Luke's list elaborate on the pattern of reversal between present suffering and coming joy. If the first two blessings appear to address sufferings that are the consequences of political or economic systems or decisions, the third appears to refer to the universal human experience of sorrow or mourning (although tears too are more frequent companions of people who have been pushed to the margins of society than of those who reap its benefits). The final blessing addresses specifically those in the audience who are suffering "on account of the Son of Man," comparing people's abuse of them to what happened to prophets in the past, and connecting the coming reversal of fortunes ("Your reward is great in heaven") to the implied blessings the prophets now enjoy (6:22–23).

In each case, the blessing makes a statement of fact: one is blessed because of a future that is a sure part of God's reign. There is no note of threat or challenge in these blessings: Nowhere do they say, "Do this in order to guarantee a specific result." They announce a truth about the divine agenda rather than a mandate for human morality. In a similar way the list of woes is not one of behaviors to be avoided or changed in order to avert disaster. Instead, it states facts: People who are rich, well fed, laughing, and enjoying good reputations will also experience the alternative. They are not being punished for their actions; rather, they have enjoyed the blessings, and now the turn passes to others.

The pattern of reversal carried out in these blessings and woes has led a number of scholars to suggest that they might represent Jesus' sermon on Isaiah 61:1–2. In the episode set at Nazareth, which, according to Luke, centered on that Jubilee text, the "sermon" really addresses the fulfillment of the text, not its meaning. The blessings, in particular, expand on the theme of good news to the poor, and on such contrasts as prisoners being set free and blind people having their sight restored. The woes, then, would be a good reason to cause dismay in the townspeople who hear the privileged place in God's project (which they assume belongs to them) being attributed to others (4:25–27). In any event, the themes of this section of the teachings are not new to Luke's account, and once again they set the agenda for a major section of Luke's Gospel.

## Relationships with Enemies and Benefactors (Luke 6:27–35)

> 6:27 "But I say to you that listen, Love your enemies, do good to those who hate you, [28] bless those who curse you, pray for those who abuse you. [29] If anyone strikes you on the cheek, offer the other also; and from anyone who takes away your coat do not withhold even your shirt. [30] Give to everyone who begs from you; and if anyone takes away your goods, do not ask for them again. [31] Do to others as you would have them do to you.
>
> [32] "If you love those who love you, what credit is that to you? For even sinners love those who love them. [33] If you do good to those who do good to you, what credit is that to you? For even sinners do the same. [34] If you lend to those from whom you hope to receive, what credit is that to you? Even sinners lend to sinners, to receive as much again. [35] But love your enemies, do good, and lend, expecting nothing in return. Your reward will be great, and you will be children of the Most High; for he is kind to the ungrateful and the wicked."

The second block of teachings explores two types of relationships that common wisdom views as reciprocal. Enemies are usually treated with the same sort of hostility they have shown, and one does good to one's benefactors. The principal point of this section of teachings is that, on the contrary, the behavior of the other person should not determine one's own involvement in a relationship. A dramatic statement of that change in the conduct of relationships is in the general principle, "Love your enemies." Statements of that general principle (6:27, 35) frame a disparate collection of sayings about specific dimensions of the theme.

The intervening sayings fall into two general categories. The first develops the theme of one's response to mistreatment. The positive commands—"do good to those who hate you, bless those who curse you, pray for those who abuse you" (6:27b–28); and "Do to others as you would have them do to you" (6:31)—are in the plural and give general guidelines. The instructions on how to respond to being hit, robbed, or persistently begged for alms are in the singular, bringing the general principle to the specific interactions of daily life. The assumption underlying these sayings is that they are addressed to the "victims" and not the victimizers. In fact, nothing is said about changes mandated for those who abuse, hate, curse, hit, rob, or steal. The point is that those on the receiving end of such actions are not to remain victims whose responses are dictated by the initial encounter.

The second set of teachings (6:32–34) deals with the equally (if not actually more) difficult problem of relationships with benefactors. There the usual pattern of repaying one favor with another simply perpetuates relationships based on calculation and mutual advantage. Such relationships represent no more than business as usual, particularly in a society (like those in which both Jesus and Luke lived) defined by systems of "patronage." In a patronage system, a person's status in the society is determined by those who have to depend on that person, and by those, in turn, on whom that person must rely. Personal relationships in a patronage system are marked by calculations of debts and credits: Who owes what to whom? For example, if you help me, I will owe you my loyalty as well as material compensation. At best, you will have a "chip" you can call in for a future favor. At worst, the less powerful person becomes virtually a slave of the more powerful. Since both one's status in the society and one's economic debts and credits are strictly calculated, the same dynamic that determines social status also undergirds the system of financial indebtedness that was so destructive to small landowners in rural Palestine of Jesus' day and to poor city dwellers elsewhere in the Empire in Luke's day as well.

For Luke, an important aspect of the good news present in Jesus is that such calculation in both economics and social status is ended, and the patronage system in general is replaced by a social structure founded on generosity, respect, and equal treatment for everyone. In the sermon, these changes are expressed in the specific economic language of borrowing and lending and in the more abstract terms of loving and doing good. Later in Luke, that same dynamic will be developed in relationship to rules of etiquette and hospitality so central to the life of the early Christian communities (14:12–14). In contrast to the strictly calculated relationships of patronage and reciprocity, as the closing statement in 6:35 makes clear, the equivalent to loving one's enemies when one is among friends is the uncalculating generosity that mirrors the generosity of God.

## Mercy and Judgment (Luke 6:36–42)

6:36 **Be merciful, just as your Father is merciful.**
37 **"Do not judge, and you will not be judged; do not condemn, and you will not be condemned. Forgive, and you will be forgiven;** 38 **give, and it will be given to you. A good measure, pressed down, shaken together, running**

over, will be put into your lap; for the measure you give will be the measure you get back."

$^{39}$ He also told them a parable: "Can a blind person guide a blind person? Will not both fall into a pit? $^{40}$ A disciple is not above the teacher, but everyone who is fully qualified will be like the teacher. $^{41}$ Why do you see the speck in your neighbor's eye, but do not notice the log in your own eye? $^{42}$ Or how can you say to your neighbor, 'Friend, let me take out the speck in your eye,' when you yourself do not see the log in your own eye? You hypocrite, first take the log out of your own eye, and then you will see clearly to take the speck out of your neighbor's eye."

God's own nature sets the standard for the third cluster of teachings as well. In this case, God's mercy is the norm (6:36); and in the initial image, it does set a standard for a certain kind of reciprocity: What one gives, one can expect to receive (6:37–38). Mercy tempers judgment, both in the way one is regarded and in the way each person treats others. "Mercy" transforms calculated measurement into abundance and generosity.

Not only the divine model but also human weakness make mercy the necessary accompaniment of judgment (6:39–42). Luke draws together a "parable" and sayings found in various places in Matthew, which use exaggeration and obviously silly examples to make their point and Luke's: One blind person cannot serve as guide to another (presumably in territory unfamiliar to both of them), and someone whose eye is blocked by a log of wood cannot help another person whose eye is irritated by a speck of dust (6:39, 41–42). Only someone who has become like the "teacher"—in this case, like God—can begin to carry out the task of merciful judgment.

## Personal Integrity (Luke 6:43–49)

6:43 "No good tree bears bad fruit, nor again does a bad tree bear good fruit; $^{44}$ for each tree is known by its own fruit. Figs are not gathered from thorns, nor are grapes picked from a bramble bush. $^{45}$ The good person out of the good treasure of the heart produces good, and the evil person out of evil treasure produces evil; for it is out of the abundance of the heart that the mouth speaks.

$^{46}$ "Why do you call me 'Lord, Lord,' and do not do what I tell you? $^{47}$ I will show you what someone is like who comes to me, hears my words, and acts on them. $^{48}$ That one is like a man building a house, who dug deeply and laid the foundation on rock; when a flood arose, the river burst against that house but could not shake it, because it had been well built. $^{49}$ But the one who hears and does not act is like a man who built a house on the ground

**without a foundation. When the river burst against it, immediately it fell, and great was the ruin of that house."**

The concluding section of teachings in the "sermon" explores the integrity of action and speech (6:43–46) and listening and action (6:47–49). It is clear that the evidence of one's actions defines the words one speaks and makes clear how carefully one has been listening. The first point is made by two proverbs about plants that bear fruit. Both the quality of the fruit (6:43) and its type (6:44) depend on the quality and type of the plant from which it comes. Those proverbs are then applied to the direct connection between a person's conduct and the quality of his or her heart (6:45). That conduct is the actual message a person conveys (the "speech" one acts out), and it ought to be congruent with the words one speaks (6:46).

The second part of this section of teachings (6:47–49) uses a parable to establish the contrast between someone who acts on what he or she has learned from Jesus and someone "who hears and does not act." The parable depicts a contrast that would be easily recognized by people from areas where long droughts are interrupted by torrential rains that turn dry river beds into floodwaters. Houses that are anchored in bedrock can (sometimes, at least) survive the onslaught, while those resting on loose soil are destroyed with the first wave. The point is not to teach sound building strategies, but rather to make clear how life-encompassing Jesus' message is. What is needed to ground a person in Jesus' teachings is to move from learning as an intellectual or emotional achievement to learning embodied in action.

Clearly, the four sections of this collection of teachings do not fit together into a single argument or theme. They do, however, form an interesting introduction to the training program that the apostles are receiving. The blessings and woes recall what is emerging as the dominant theme in Luke's Gospel, namely, the sort of reversal of fortunes that constitutes "good news to the poor"—those who have been left on (or pushed to) the margins of the part of the society that has benefited from the status quo. That theme sets the stage for specific teachings about aspects of personal conduct and relationships that affect the quality of a person's life in general, and especially the quality of the ministry of those chosen as apostles. Their preparation for their work begins with hard lessons about personal interactions and accountability in their daily life, not with academic theories or training for leadership in public events. The very purpose of the gospel as "good news" depends on the coherence and integrity of the lives of those who bear its word of justice and liberation.

## JESUS' PROGRAM IS REVIEWED
### Luke 7:1–50

### The Centurion's Faith (Luke 7:1–10)

7:1 **After Jesus had finished all his sayings in the hearing of the people, he entered Capernaum.** [2] **A centurion there had a slave whom he valued highly, and who was ill and close to death.** [3] **When he heard about Jesus, he sent some Jewish elders to him, asking him to come and heal his slave.** [4] **When they came to Jesus, they appealed to him earnestly, saying, "He is worthy of having you do this for him,** [5] **for he loves our people, and it is he who built our synagogue for us."** [6] **And Jesus went with them, but when he was not far from the house, the centurion sent friends to say to him, "Lord, do not trouble yourself, for I am not worthy to have you come under my roof;** [7] **therefore I did not presume to come to you. But only speak the word, and let my servant be healed.** [8] **For I also am a man set under authority, with soldiers under me; and I say to one, 'Go,' and he goes, and to another, 'Come,' and he comes, and to my slave, 'Do this,' and the slave does it."** [9] **When Jesus heard this he was amazed at him, and turning to the crowd that followed him, he said, "I tell you, not even in Israel have I found such faith."** [10] **When those who had been sent returned to the house, they found the slave in good health.**

The observation that the sermon is finished and a change of scene from the open countryside to the town of Capernaum signal that a new phase in the narrative is beginning. In the stories collected in chapter 7, Luke reminds the disciples about the general shape of Jesus' ministry by developing once again the themes of his inaugural sermon at Nazareth (4:16–30), but this time playing them in a different key.

In the episode at Nazareth, Jesus cites the examples of Elijah and Elisha, whose ministry to Gentiles is used to warrant Jesus' own prophetic reading of Isaiah 61:1–2 (4:25–27). Luke 7 begins in a similar vein with one account describing Jesus' healing of a Gentile's slave (7:1–10), and the next (7:11–17) describing the raising from the dead of a widow's son—the latter being an account remarkably similar to stories of Elijah (1 Kings 17:17–24) and Elisha (2 Kings 4:32–37) referred to in 4:25–27.

The story in 7:1–10 is told also in Matthew 8:5–13 and John 4:46–53, but in each case with its own narrative context and theological and literary purpose. Luke's version of the story stars the centurion, but his is not a role to be coveted by a budding actor, for he never comes on stage. Instead, he is represented by some Jewish elders (7:3) and some friends (7:6–8), who convey his initial request for help, advocate on his behalf, and report to Jesus his words of confidence and respect, which Jesus calls "faith" (7:9). The story is the only one in Luke that tells of Jesus' healing someone at a distance.

The centurion is a Gentile in service to Rome, perhaps in particular serving Herod Antipas, tetrarch of Galilee, or Pontius Pilate, whose headquarters were at nearby Caesarea. He is portrayed as an admirable man, both for his generosity and respect shown to the Jews and for his efforts to obtain healing for his slave. We should note that nowhere does Luke question the institution of slavery, nor does he attribute such a concern to Jesus. One aspect of the centurion's praiseworthiness is his kindness toward and good treatment of his slave, but that compassion does not extend to setting the slave free. As is often the case in this Gospel and in Acts, Luke appears to take for granted many of the institutions and customs of his society (see also the discussions of 10:38–42 and 14:7–14), despite his determination to confront and change others (see the discussion of 6:27–35).

The description of the centurion is remarkably similar to that of Cornelius in Acts 10:1–2. Both are Gentiles in the service of Rome, and both are close to the Jewish community—perhaps to be understood as representatives of the group of "God-fearers" from whom many early Christians came. The baptism and welcome of Cornelius into the church in Acts is previewed here in this Roman soldier who seeks and obtains healing from Jesus without himself meeting Jesus, just as will all Christians of subsequent generations.

The drama of the story builds from the statement of the problem (7:2) to its resolution (7:10) as the depth of the centurion's faith is revealed. His initial request focuses on the need for Jesus to heal his slave (7:3). The centurion seems to perceive Jesus as an itinerant healer whose services might be used to help one of the marginalized people who regularly had to rely on such healers for their medical care. The Jewish elders, who in this story are friendly to Jesus, then testify to the centurion's generosity and love for the Jews, to make the case that he is "worthy" of Jesus' aid (7:4–5). Their testimony already suggests that the faith of this Gentile exceeds simple faith in Jesus' healing powers, but it also respects the theological foundations of the Jews themselves: He even built their synagogue for them.

The friends (possibly Gentiles, though their ethnic identity is not specified), who convey the man's own statement that he is "not worthy" to have Jesus enter his home, further clarify the nature of the centurion's faith. The centurion, himself a man of considerable authority (7:8), recognizes that Jesus' word is more powerful still. Just as the centurion's slaves and the soldiers under his command obey his word, so Jesus' word has authority over the forces causing the slave's disease. Those words evoke Jesus' affirmation that the centurion's faith even exceeds that of Israel (7:9), and the concluding statement bears evidence that his faith is well placed: Jesus' word alone, even without his physical presence, has power to heal. This Gentile is the first person said to experience Jesus' healing power when Jesus is not actually present with the person being healed.

The centurion's story also serves as a bridge between two other stories in the combined narrative of Luke-Acts. It links Luke's earlier reference to Gentiles who benefit before the Israelites from God's saving presence revealed in the prophets Elijah and Elisha (4:25–27), with the story of another centurion named Cornelius, which is told in Acts 10. The centurion's faith is an important building block in the preparation of the apostles for their ministry on Jesus' behalf. The authority of Jesus' word, which they will be commissioned to carry, is sufficient even in Jesus' absence to continue the ministry of teaching, healing, and exorcism with which they will be entrusted (9:1–6).

### The Widow's Son (Luke 7:11–17)

7:11  **Soon afterwards he went to a town called Nain, and his disciples and a large crowd went with him. [12] As he approached the gate of the town, a man who had died was being carried out. He was his mother's only son, and she was a widow; and with her was a large crowd from the town. [13] When the Lord saw her, he had compassion for her and said to her, "Do not weep." [14] Then he came forward and touched the bier, and the bearers stood still. And he said, "Young man, I say to you, rise!" [15] The dead man sat up and began to speak, and Jesus gave him to his mother. [16] Fear seized all of them; and they glorified God, saying, "A great prophet has risen among us!" and "God has looked favorably on his people!" [17] This word about him spread throughout Judea and all the surrounding country.**

The previous story echoes the Elijah and Elisha references in 4:25–27 by the introduction of the Gentile beneficiary of Jesus' healing, and it escalates the level of Jesus' healing power beyond what Luke has previously described by having him heal the slave at a distance. The story of the widow's son further heightens the picture of Jesus' power by telling not just of the healing of a Gentile, but of the resuscitation of someone who is already dead. This story echoes stories in which both Elijah and Elisha healed young men (1 Kings 17:17–24; 2 Kings 4:32–37). In the case of the Elijah story, not only is the general outline of the story the same, but the very wording of 7:15—"[he] gave him to his mother"—is exactly the same as the Greek text of 1 Kings 17:23. In both of these stories that begin chapter 7, Luke portrays Jesus as a prophet in the tradition of Elijah and Elisha, thereby giving his audience a framework for understanding Jesus' ministry as yet another step in God's saving presence with them. At the same time, he moves his audience to recognize ever greater dimensions of Jesus' power and authority as his ministry unfolds.

The beginning of the story of the widow's son seems to leap off the front page of a newspaper. Yet another mother left on her own to raise her children is on her way to bury a young son. We are not told the cause of death in this story, but our hearts recognize in him the many children whose deaths have come too soon, due to disease, or accidents, or the culture of violence. Stories of such deaths are so common that it takes an act of will to feel the horror and pain anymore. Then—suddenly—in Luke's story, the mood changes from one of death to one of life. It is a story that reaches beyond the private rejoicing of the mother to signal God's will for life that will not be thwarted.

The precise location of the village called Nain is uncertain, other than that Luke intends it to be somewhere in Galilee. The story set there is poignant in its details. Jesus and the disciples are interrupted at the gate of the town by a funeral procession. This particular procession of mourners accompanies a mother and her son's body to the usual place of burial outside of the town. The grief that greets any death is here compounded by the inappropriateness of this death: Although in Jesus' day parents frequently had to bury their infant children who fell victim to accidents or to childhood diseases, this son is an adult, and he has survived those threats. Children who survived to adulthood—then as now—usually buried their parents, and not the other way around. Furthermore, this mother is described as a widow and the dead man as her only son. With his death she is not only alone; she is also without the greater economic security that a man would have afforded her in that society, and without the social security of being someone's wife or mother.

This is the first instance in which the author refers to Jesus as "the Lord." Earlier in the Gospel that title is used of Jesus in the angel's announcement of the birth (2:11), and as a form of address that need not be seen as anything more than the respectful title, "sir" (5:8, 12; 6:46; 7:6). By identifying Jesus as "the Lord," Luke prepares his audience for the miracle that follows: Like God, who is also frequently referred to by that title in the scriptures of Luke's community and in the Gospel as well, Jesus will be seen to have authority over life and death.

Jesus' "compassion" initiates the drama, which Luke heightens by his use of direct discourse: We overhear his words and the response of the

crowd, even as we watch the action unfold. Jesus' words to the mother—
"Do not weep"—at first seem jarringly inappropriate (see also 8:52). Is he
denying her need to mourn? But those words and his hand placed on the
bier on which the corpse was carried stop the funeral procession in its
tracks. Jesus' next words—"Young man, I say to you, rise!"—turn the situation around. The one whom death had laid low and silenced sits up and
begins to speak, and the one whom death had taken away is given back to
his mother. Life and family are both restored. Nothing in the story suggests that this man will not eventually die again, for he is apparently restored to normal human life, and not to some "eternal" or "spiritual" condition (like Jesus after the resurrection, for example). But for a time, at
least, life triumphs, and the mother's grief can end.

The crowd's response of fear and praise identifies Jesus once again as a
prophet, and it affirms the event as evidence of God's care for God's people. What they have witnessed is not a private miracle that heals the grief
of one woman and buys a few more years of life for a young man. Rather,
it is part of the larger agenda of Jesus' ministry (7:17), which here is clearly
identified with God's saving purpose and power.

## Jesus, John, and the "Coming One" (Luke 7:18–35)

7:18 **The disciples of John reported all these things to him. So John summoned two of his disciples** [19] **and sent them to the Lord to ask, "Are you the
one who is to come, or are we to wait for another?"** [20] **When the men had
come to him, they said, "John the Baptist has sent us to you to ask, 'Are you
the one who is to come, or are we to wait for another?'"** [21] **Jesus had just
then cured many people of diseases, plagues, and evil spirits, and had given
sight to many who were blind.** [22] **And he answered them, "Go and tell John
what you have seen and heard: the blind receive their sight, the lame walk,
the lepers are cleansed, the deaf hear, the dead are raised, the poor have
good news brought to them.** [23] **And blessed is anyone who takes no offense
at me."**

[24] **When John's messengers had gone, Jesus began to speak to the crowds
about John: "What did you go out into the wilderness to look at? A reed
shaken by the wind?** [25] **What then did you go out to see? Someone dressed
in soft robes? Look, those who put on fine clothing and live in luxury are in
royal palaces.** [26] **What then did you go out to see? A prophet? Yes, I tell you,
and more than a prophet.** [27] **This is the one about whom it is written,**

> **'See, I am sending my messenger ahead of you,**
> **who will prepare your way before you.'**

²⁸ I tell you, among those born of women no one is greater than John; yet the least in the kingdom of God is greater than he." ²⁹ (And all the people who heard this, including the tax collectors, acknowledged the justice of God, because they had been baptized with John's baptism. ³⁰ But by refusing to be baptized by him, the Pharisees and the lawyers rejected God's purpose for themselves.)

³¹ "To what then will I compare the people of this generation, and what are they like? ³² They are like children sitting in the marketplace and calling to one another,

'We played the flute for you, and you did not dance;
we wailed, and you did not weep.'

³³ For John the Baptist has come eating no bread and drinking no wine, and you say, 'He has a demon'; ³⁴ the Son of Man has come eating and drinking, and you say, 'Look, a glutton and a drunkard, a friend of tax collectors and sinners!' ³⁵ Nevertheless, wisdom is vindicated by all her children."

The summary ending the previous story alerts Luke's audience to another shift in the narrative. No setting is given for what follows, and the cast of characters emerges only gradually. Luke has already reported John's imprisonment by Herod (3:19–20), apparently under circumstances that would have allowed him to remain in contact with his followers. Exactly what should be understood as included in "all these things" that they reported to him about Jesus is not clear, but the two preceding healing stories seem to be on that list. Despite such stories, and despite the kinship of Jesus and John that Luke identifies in the story of the visit of Mary to Elizabeth (1:39–56), John's question about Jesus is fundamental: "Are you the one who is to come, or are we to wait for another?"

In Jesus' day, the "coming one" could have referred to any one of several figures associated with events of God's final redeeming acts in human history, but it was especially linked to the prophet Elijah, whose return was eagerly awaited. The first three chapters of Luke's Gospel portray John as destined from before his birth to be the herald of someone even greater who was to follow him. The question posed by this passage is about the relationship between Jesus as the one of whom John was herald, and the "coming one" for whom John and others longed.

The implication is that John knew he was to prepare the way for Jesus, although that is not stated explicitly. In addition, Luke has just depicted Jesus as duplicating the role of Elijah in the episode of the raising of the widow's son (7:11–17), of which, presumably, John has just been told. It would appear, then, that Jesus is doubly portrayed by Luke as the "expected one" to whom John has been pointing, and as the new Elijah—the "coming one."

With all that narrative buildup pointing to John's knowledge of Jesus, the uncertainty reflected in the question seems out of place: How could he not know? The response to John's query is equally problematic, for it does not appear to answer John's question. Instead, it begins in Luke with a summary of Jesus' continuing ministry of healing and exorcism, which the disciples are sent back to report. Luke then joins Matthew in summarizing that identifying ministry of Jesus by means of a collage of sayings drawn from Isaiah (Isa. 6:10; 31:5–6; 29:18–19; 42:18; 43:8; 61:1–2). The response ends with a benediction that itself incorporates a challenge not to take offense at Jesus (7:23).

Two possibilities appear on the surface. The first is that the episode, which is part of the special source of traditions about Jesus shared by Matthew and Luke, reports an actual incident in Jesus' life (see also Matt. 11:2–6). If that is the case, then it would suggest that John may not have been as certain about Jesus' identity as the Gospel writers themselves suggest that he was. It would also conform to evidence found elsewhere that healing, exorcism, and the proclamation of good news to the poor characterized Jesus' ministry. Whether or not Jesus himself used the texts from Isaiah to give shape to that ministry, the early church clearly did, for themes and motifs from those texts abound in all three of the Synoptic Gospels.

The second possible explanation is that the story, in substance as well as in its present language, is the product of the early church, reflecting a time when there may have been interreligious jealousy between followers of John who saw him as the prophet of the end-time, and Christians who reserved all such roles for Jesus. In that case, this story would put John in his place by depicting his initial ignorance about Jesus, and by not even indicating how he responded to the report. Was he offended, as many others had been and would be in the future, by the generosity and inclusiveness of Jesus' ministry and of the community gathered around him? The readers are left to imagine. Furthermore, the collage of verses from Isaiah has clearly come to define the essence of Jesus' public ministry, even forming the heart of what Luke presents as Jesus' inaugural sermon (4:16–30; see also 6:20–26). According to that explanation, the story both defines Jesus in a way that the audience of the Gospel would clearly recognize, and it implies that John remained unaware of Jesus' identity.

The following verses, which follow the preceding ones in Matthew also (Matt. 11:7–19), provide a solution to the puzzle in the form of a different theological assessment of John and of his relationship to Jesus and his ministry. The results are surprising.

John's earlier *question* about Jesus leads to Jesus' *affirmation* about John in the form of a series of rhetorical questions to the crowds (7:24–26).

Reeds grow in abundance on the shores of the Jordan River and the Dead Sea, and at the various springs that create oases in the arid wilderness. Both the wind and the moving of the water often cause the stands of reeds to shudder. So common a sight surely would not have led people to make a special trip into the wilderness! On the other hand, one also would not travel into the wilderness in search of something that is not found there. The wilderness is not the habitat of the economic elite, whose status is literally worn on their backs in the form of elegant clothing.

What might draw one into the wilderness is the longing to hear the voice of a prophet, for the wilderness is the home of such prophets as Elijah. The people of Jesus' day were awaiting not just any prophetic word spoken into their world, but the word of the prophet who would herald the events of the end-time. John is thus further affirmed by Jesus, using the language of Malachi 3:1, as more than *a* prophet, but rather *the* prophet who prepares the way for God's chosen one who will inaugurate that final time of salvation. In other words, John himself is the "coming one."

The texts from Isaiah cited to summarize Jesus' identity make clear that he is not the "coming one," but rather he already participates in the end-time to which the "coming one" was to point. The comforting word to John in prison is that there is no other for whom to wait, but instead, his most precious longing has been more than realized: He is the "coming one," and the "greater one" he has proclaimed has already come as well.

John's place at the hinge joining everyday reality and the reign of God is elaborated on by a statement of comparison (7:28). John is indeed at the pinnacle of the old order (see also 16:16), but even he is surpassed by everyone who participates in God's reign. Receiving John's baptism (3:3) is the single crucial factor for all the people in the crowd to whom these words are addressed, whatever might be their status according to the usual canons of moral worth—whether they were "sinners" or religious leaders. Their response to John expresses their acceptance or rejection of God's purpose for their lives and for the whole world, and God, in turn, is "justified" by them (7:29–30).

In other words, although Jesus and John stand on different sides of the dividing line marking the onset of God's reign, they share a common agenda from God, and they are similarly rejected by "this generation." The parable about the children in the marketplace (7:31–32) paints a poignant picture of groups of children, each bent on their own game: Some want to play funeral while the others want to play wedding, and then they switch games. In the end, they never manage to play together at all. In a similar way, John's asceticism causes people to doubt his sanity, and the merrymaking enjoyed by "the Son of Man" (here clearly a reference to Jesus himself) causes them to question his morality. Neither the repentance proclaimed by John nor the good news proclaimed by Jesus gets a favorable hearing.

The concluding proverb (7:35) introduces the subject of "wisdom," or perhaps better put, "Wisdom" spelled with a capital letter. The reference is not to human intelligence or even to the reservoirs of insight, common sense, and knowledge of the world that constitute folk lore or "folk wisdom" (which seems to be the simple meaning of the word intended in 2:52, referring to the growth of the child Jesus, and in 11:31, referring to "the wisdom of Solomon"). Instead, in this passage "Wisdom" refers to the divine principle or active agent by which God has crafted the creation, and according to which God sustains the world (see Proverbs 8, for example). Wisdom or "Sophia" loves truth and righteousness and longs for people who will embrace these same values. In so doing they take Wisdom herself into their lives, and they become her children. Unlike the frustrated and contrary children of the parable, and unlike those of their contemporaries who dismiss both John and Jesus, Wisdom's "children" welcome both the repentance and the joy appropriate to God's purpose and reign, each in its season. Just as God is said to be justified or vindicated by all who receive John's baptism (7:29), so also is Wisdom justified by her children.

With the introduction of the cantankerous children and those who reject the ministries of both Jesus and John, a crucial piece of the picture painted in Luke 7 falls into place. Such factors as the parallels to the Elijah and Elisha stories mentioned in 4:25–27; the question about Jesus' identity; the collage of passages from Isaiah to characterize Jesus' ministry; the emphasis on God's purpose, God's reign, and God's timetable of salvation; and finally the theme of rejection all echo Luke's account of Jesus' ministry at Nazareth (4:16–30). Luke seems to be deliberately replaying in a different key that episode in which the agenda of Jesus' subsequent ministry is introduced, just as the account of Jesus' Galilean ministry is drawing to a close. The one major theme from that episode that has not yet been sounded in Luke 7 is the theme of "release" or "forgiveness." It is on that theme that the plot of the final episode of the chapter turns.

## The Anointing Woman (Luke 7:36–50)

> 7:36 **One of the Pharisees asked Jesus to eat with him, and he went into the Pharisee's house and took his place at the table.** [37] **And a woman in the city, who was a sinner, having learned that he was eating in the Pharisee's house,**

brought an alabaster jar of ointment. [38] She stood behind him at his feet, weeping, and began to bathe his feet with her tears and to dry them with her hair. Then she continued kissing his feet and anointing them with the ointment. [39] Now when the Pharisee who had invited him saw it, he said to himself, "If this man were a prophet, he would have known who and what kind of woman this is who is touching him—that she is a sinner." [40] Jesus spoke up and said to him, "Simon, I have something to say to you." "Teacher," he replied, "Speak." [41] "A certain creditor had two debtors; one owed five hundred denarii, and the other fifty. [42] When they could not pay, he canceled the debts for both of them. Now which of them will love him more?" [43] Simon answered, "I suppose the one for whom he canceled the greater debt." And Jesus said to him, "You have judged rightly." [44] Then turning toward the woman, he said to Simon, "Do you see this woman? I entered your house; you gave me no water for my feet, but she has bathed my feet with her tears and dried them with her hair. [45] You gave me no kiss, but from the time I came in she has not stopped kissing my feet. [46] You did not anoint my head with oil, but she has anointed my feet with ointment. [47] Therefore, I tell you, her sins, which were many, have been forgiven; hence she has shown great love. But the one to whom little is forgiven, loves little." [48] Then he said to her, "Your sins are forgiven." [49] But those who were at the table with him began to say among themselves, "Who is this who even forgives sins?" [50] And he said to the woman, "Your faith has saved you; go in peace."

The scene shifts to the home of a Pharisee on the occasion of a dinner party. Perhaps Luke intends his audience to think of the host as one of those who earlier had refused John's baptism and by so doing "rejected God's purpose for themselves" (7:30). On the other hand, this appears to be a rather formal meal at which the guests "recline" at the table, and a host honors a guest by such an invitation. This particular Pharisee, then, begins as a positive character in the story, apparently favorable to Jesus.

The identification of the host as a Pharisee and the setting of the story of Jesus' anointing by a woman even during Jesus' ministry in Galilee already set this story apart from the anointing stories in the other three Gospels (Matt. 26:6–13; Mark 14:3–9; John 12:1–8). As Luke's story unfolds, several other crucial differences emerge as well. For instance, in Matthew, Mark, and John the themes of love and forgiveness are absent. Instead, one or more of the disciples object to the woman's action as wasteful, and maintain that it would have been better for her to honor Jesus by selling the ointment and giving the money to the poor. However, since in all three cases the anointing is set shortly before the account of Jesus' arrest and trials, the anointing is justified as a prophetic act anointing Jesus for burial even before his death. In contrast, the story of the anointing is set much earlier in Luke's narrative, and no such justification is given.

Only in Luke are we given a picture of the depth of the woman's emotion, which might explain why she approaches Jesus as she does. Also, in Luke's story the woman washes and anoints Jesus' feet, while in Matthew and Mark Jesus' head is anointed, in an action that amounts to the woman's formal confession of him as the Christ (which in Greek means "anointed"). John speaks of the woman anointing Jesus' feet and wiping them with her hair, but there is no mention of tears or of her washing Jesus' feet.

Whether Luke is building here on an independent tradition about Jesus being anointed by a woman, or whether he has adapted his story from the version found in Mark is impossible finally to determine. In any event, the result is so completely different that Luke's story must be explored on its own, without attempting to harmonize it with the stories in the other Gospels.

The story in Luke is set in motion by the arrival of a woman from the city, who has deliberately sought out Jesus. Her presence at the dinner itself would not have been all that shocking, since at such dinner parties poor people of the neighborhood would have been free to come into the courtyard to share in food that might remain after the guests had eaten. The practice solved several needs at once: Needy people received food, leftover food that might otherwise have spoiled was not wasted, and the host had an opportunity to perform a meritorious act of charity above and beyond the required tithe that would already have been given (see Deut. 14:22–29).

What introduces a note of tension is the woman's identification as a sinner, her approach to Jesus while he was at table eating, her evident emotion, and the specific nature of her actions. Nothing is said about the nature of the woman's sin. A woman would have been called a sinner if she were known as a liar, a thief, a cheat, or any other type of sinner in her own right, or she might simply have been the wife of a man who was known to be immoral or the practitioner of any one of a number of professions looked down upon as the breeding ground of dishonesty. Tradition has viewed this woman as a prostitute, but the only clues in the text that point to that are her unbound hair (see Num. 5:18) and the fact that she has with her a jar of ointment, which might have been used in massage or other activities associated with her trade.

The woman in Luke's story is unnamed. Only in John's version of the anointing is the woman identified by name. In that Gospel she is Mary of Bethany, sister of Martha and Lazarus. That name, the mention of Mary Magdalene in the list of women who accompanied Jesus in Luke 8:2, and the assumption that both Mary Magdalene and this woman "sinner" were prostitutes have led to the mistaken identification of this woman as Mary Magdalene. In fact, her name as well as her specific sin are not identified.

The woman's position "behind [Jesus] at his feet" is easy to picture in the case of a formal dinner at which the guests "reclined." The low tables would have been arranged in a horseshoe shape, with the fourth side of the oblong or square open to allow servants access to the tables. The guests would be reclining on cushions, propped on their left elbows, using their right hands to reach the food that was on the table. Their feet would be curled behind them, pointing away from the tables. The guests would be barefoot, having removed their sandals upon entering the room, and presumably having been provided with a basin and towel with which to wash their feet.

In the case of highly honored guests, a servant would be assigned to wash the guest's feet. Usually only the lowliest of the servants would be assigned such a menial task. In extreme cases, the host might perform it himself, in order to demonstrate his respect for and devotion to the guest. The woman in this story, in effect, takes on the role of such a host, for she does not act under orders as a servant would, but moved by her own emotion (whether that emotion is sadness or joy is not made clear until later in the story). She goes even beyond such a measure of honor, however, for instead of a basin of water and a towel, the woman's own tears and hair provide the gentle cleansing, and she kisses ("kisses fervently" is the literal meaning) Jesus' feet and anoints them with precious ointment (7:38). The action is sensuous, and the scene is intimate and tender.

The relationship between Jesus and the unnamed woman stands in sharp contrast to the dialogue between Jesus and the Pharisee, whose name is given as Simon. That dialogue moves into the foreground of the story. Simon's judgmental thoughts are revealed as a direct quotation (7:39). The woman and Jesus are condemned at once—she as a sinner, and he for letting her touch him. The host is now firmly linked to the rejecters of God's purpose in the previous episode, for his thoughts debate Jesus' connection to the prophets to whom Jesus' own words referred (7:26). Although Simon's words deny that Jesus could be a prophet, the fact that Jesus is portrayed as replying to his unspoken thoughts demonstrates that Simon is mistaken.

Jesus' response to his host (7:41–42) appears at first not to reply to the host's thought. Instead, their conversation seems to fit the social conventions of such dinner parties, which would include lively conversation, story telling, and the sharing of riddles or philosophical puzzles. Indeed, Simon's reply (7:43) treats the question posed by Jesus like a riddle or parlor game, and the reply masks the economic and theological wisdom that informs the question.

Jesus' question features a situation common in both first-century Palestine and the Hellenistic world in general, namely, that of two debtors and their creditor. Heavy tax burdens imposed both by Rome and by local officials, patterns of tenant farming and absentee landholding, reliance on seasonal income from agriculture, periodic crop failures and poor yields, and a host of other factors meant that virtually everyone understood the dynamics of debtors and creditors. If the denarius was the usual day's wage for a laborer, both debts in the example were substantial—the lesser worth about two months' wages, and the greater those of about a year and a half. For anyone to be that far in debt probably meant that landholdings and any other marketable property had already been sold. To be unable to repay either amount would leave a debtor in danger of becoming a debt slave, along with other members of his family. For *either* amount to be forgiven would have meant freedom in place of slavery for the debtor. In *both* cases the gratitude or "love" would have been absolute, not relatively less or more.

Jesus' reply to Simon—"You have judged rightly"—plays along with the parlor game only long enough to turn it around to make the theological point. The woman's actions that have provoked Simon's judgment of her and of Jesus are contrasted with Simon's own failure to provide basic hospitality to Jesus (7:44–46), and those same actions are cited as expressions of great love. The tears with which she washed Jesus' feet are now identified as tears of gratitude for forgiveness already experienced—abundant and overflowing love. Simon's own self-assessment as morally upright and less in need of forgiveness than the woman he calls a sinner, in turn, accounts for his lack of love (7:47).

A little reflection, though, makes clear the irony of this reading: Love (or gratitude) is not quantifiable. Simon's response that misses the economic point of the parable—that forgiveness for either debtor is a gift of freedom and life, and therefore both will love the forgiving creditor—also misses the larger theological point. He and the woman are in exactly the same situation of "debt" or sin, for which the only possible solution is forgiveness. The relatively large or small "amount" at stake is meaningful only in theory, only in a riddle or a parlor game.

The focus of the story shifts briefly back to the woman. Jesus' words to her (7:48) underline the point that Simon seems not yet to have recognized: Her sins are already "forgiven." The word in Greek has the same root as the noun in 4:18, "to proclaim *release* to captives." It speaks not of a measured doling out of only the amount of pardon necessary to cover a specific quantity of sins, but rather of a letting go: Her sins, whether many or few, have fallen away, as from open hands.

All hands are not opened to participate in the freedom this woman has come to know, for Jesus' dinner companions question his credentials for making such a pronouncement (7:49). Similar questions about Jesus' authority and identity will follow from characters in other stories (for example 8:25; 9:9), but for Luke himself the question is rhetorical: Jesus is the one anointed not only by this woman's love, but also by the Holy Spirit, for just such a ministry.

Jesus sends the woman on her way with a blessing (7:50). That blessing speaks of her "faith" that has saved her or made her well, while the story until then has spoken only of her love and of the release of her sins declared by Jesus. What seems at first to be a pious but inappropriate ending to the story turns out to be making a crucial point. What is called "faith" is not a doctrinal confession about Jesus or even personal loyalty to him, but rather the woman's participation in the rhythms of receiving release or forgiveness in Jesus' presence and responding with equally lavish and uncalculating love. Those rhythms embody the good news of healing and liberation at the heart of Jesus' ministry.

## FROM FOLLOWERS TO FAMILY
## Luke 8:1–21

### Men and Women Follow Jesus (Luke 8:1–3)

8:1 **Soon afterwards he went on through cities and villages, proclaiming and bringing the good news of the kingdom of God. The twelve were with him,** 2 **as well as some women who had been cured of evil spirits and infirmities: Mary, called Magdalene, from whom seven demons had gone out,** 3 **and Joanna, the wife of Herod's steward Chuza, and Susanna, and many others, who provided for them out of their resources.**

The scene shifts following the story of the woman's love and forgiveness. Luke prepares his audience for a change of subject by the brief summary of Jesus' proclamation of the reign of God (8:1). Such summary statements are never throwaway lines for Luke—a mere opening and closing of the curtain to indicate a new scene. In this case the summary statement is the occasion to introduce some of Jesus' co-workers and traveling companions, the twelve and several particular women, among the "many others" who were with him (8:1–3). We are told the women's names—itself an unusual detail, given women's usual anonymity and virtual invisibility in the writings of the ancient world. Of the women named, Mary Magdalene has a prominent role in the narratives of Jesus' death, burial, and resurrection in all four Gospels (Matt. 27:56, 61; 28:1; Mark 15:40, 47; 16:1; Luke 23:49, 55 [though in both cases only by implication]; 24:10; John 19:25; 20:1–2, 11–18), and Joanna is mentioned again in that context in Luke 24:10 (and included by implication in 23:49, 55). Susanna is mentioned nowhere else in the Gospels.

We are told that "evil spirits" and "demons" had afflicted these women, and that Jesus had healed them. Recall that in the understanding of the Gospel writers and their communities such spirits were seen in the physical and emotional pain that people suffered; they did not cause the people they "possessed" to sin or to be morally evil. In fact the only hint that we get about the moral character of these women is their faithful accompaniment of Jesus. Apparently, at least some of them were women of means, but instead of hiding in the comfort wealth could provide or supporting the mission of Jesus from the safety of their homes, they are said to be traveling with him.

Many scholars have attempted to reconstruct the circumstances of Jesus' mission, in order to figure out under what circumstances the women might have traveled along. Should we envision precursors of such missionary couples as Prisca and Aquila? Would the women have traveled together, in pairs or teams separate from the men? Was there any scandal perceived in this traveling crowd that included both women and men? It is unfortunate that we do not have enough information to reconstruct the movement with any confidence. Even though women are not featured in any of the leadership roles attributed in the Gospels to the twelve, women are clearly portrayed as present with Jesus from the beginning of his journey. Their eventual marginalization in the leadership of the church seems to reflect the customs and social world of the emerging Christian communities rather than any exclusionary policy of Jesus.

## Parables That Hide and Reveal (Luke 8:4–18)

8:4 **When a great crowd gathered and people from town after town came to him, he said in a parable:** 5 **"A sower went out to sow his seed; and as he** sowed, some fell on the path and was trampled on, and the birds of the air ate it up. [6] Some fell on the rock; and as it grew up, it withered for lack of moisture. [7] Some fell among thorns, and the thorns grew with it and choked it. [8] Some fell into good soil, and when it grew, it produced a hundredfold." As he said this, he called out, "Let anyone with ears to hear listen!"

[9] Then his disciples asked him what this parable meant. [10] He said, "To you it has been given to know the secrets of the kingdom of God; but to others I speak in parables, so that

'looking they may not perceive,
 and listening they may not understand.'

[11] "Now the parable is this: The seed is the word of God. [12] The ones on the path are those who have heard; then the devil comes and takes away the word from their hearts, so that they may not believe and be saved. [13] The ones on the rock are those who, when they hear the word, receive it with joy. But these have no root; they believe only for a while and in a time of testing fall away. [14] As for what fell among the thorns, these are the ones who hear; but as they go on their way, they are choked by the cares and riches and pleasures of life, and their fruit does not mature. [15] But as for that in the good soil, these are the ones who, when they hear the word, hold it fast in an honest and good heart, and bear fruit with patient endurance.

[16] "No one after lighting a lamp hides it under a jar, or puts it under a bed, but puts it on a lampstand, so that those who enter may see the light. [17] For nothing is hidden that will not be disclosed, nor is anything secret that will not become known and come to light. [18] Then pay attention to how you listen; for to those who have, more will be given; and from those who do not have, even what they seem to have will be taken away."

The disciples form a circle close to Jesus and are enveloped by a crowd, to whom Jesus tells the parable usually called (following Matt. 13:18) the "parable of the sower" (8:5–8). In fact, the parable is more about the fate of the seed than about the sower's action. A comparison of Luke's version of that parable with its parallels in Matt. 13:3–9 and Mark 4:3–9 shows the artistry of Luke's editorial pen. Every word is essential to unfold the story of the freely broadcast seed that is subsequently plowed under (a sequence appropriate to the arid and shallow Palestinian soil). People would always pack down a path through the field, and some seed would thus be exposed to the ever-scavenging birds. Other seed would fall on the thin soil that hides some of the many rocks in that region. (A tale is told even today in Israel/Palestine, that after the creation, God summoned two angels and gave each a sack of rocks. One angel scattered the rocks all over the world. The other dumped the entire sackful on the land lying just west of the Jordan River.) As happens to every gardener, hearty weeds would choke out some of the young plants. The prospect for the harvest looks dim until the final statement of the parable: The seed that fell on good soil yielded a hundredfold—a yield that would bring the farmer great joy.

In all three Gospels the parable ends with a challenge to pay attention. That challenge also hints that not everyone will understand what is basically a simple story. Except for the unusual yield from the seed that falls on good soil, the parable describes the normal experience of Galilean farmers and their families, who would have constituted a major portion of the crowd that is posited as the audience. Where does the problem lie?

The parable has not been called a parable of God's reign, but the response of Jesus to the disciples (not the smaller group of twelve) makes that connection. The parable is related to "the secrets of the kingdom of God" (8:10), which the disciples are to know, but are communicated to "others" only in parables. All three Synoptic Gospels state that Jesus speaks in parables "so that 'looking they may not perceive, and listening they may not understand.'" The quotation (more accurately, paraphrase) is of Isaiah 6:9–10, where the prophet declares that the people who have persistently disregarded the word of God made known through the prophet will not suddenly perceive and understand and therefore repent at the last minute. Matthew quotes the entire oracle (Matt. 13:13–15), whereas Mark 4:12 and Luke 8:10 present only summaries. Luke, in whose Gospel the call to repent and the message of divine forgiveness are so prominent, stops short of the full reason given in Mark, "so that they may not turn again and be forgiven."

Even in Luke's gentler form, the explanation is troubling. Why should the disciples be given an explanation, while "others" are intended not to understand? There is no suggestion of any merit among the disciples—greater intelligence or faithfulness, for example—nor of any greater misdeed among the others. The saying goes beyond the truism that at any gathering some people catch on to what is happening while others do not: In this case, some are *not supposed to* catch on. There is a hint of divine predestination that simply defies human comprehension, but even that explanation is not made explicit.

All three Synoptic Gospels have included this saying, which they recognize as part of the teachings attributed to Jesus. Whether Jesus himself actually spoke of intending that only an inner circle would understand about God's reign, or whether it was the early church that at some point in its history and in the midst of some particularly sensitive dispute drew such a conclusion, is impossible to determine.

All three Synoptic Gospels also relate similar interpretations of the parable to the disciples (Matt. 13:18–23; Mark 4:13–20; Luke 8:11–15). Mark and Luke begin by equating the seed that is sown with the word of God. If that point were maintained, the parable would be a simple allegory of the proclamation of God's reign. In an "allegory," or a code in story form, each action, character, and detail in the story stands for something else in the "real" world that lies behind the story. Once the code is "cracked," the meaning of the story becomes self-evident. For instance, in this case, the seed would be the word, and the various types of soil would represent various types of human recipients of that word. Some falls on human "soil" that is inhospitable (for a variety of reasons), but that which falls on "fertile ground" yields an abundant harvest.

However, the allegory does not work that way, for quickly the image shifts, and the "seed" is not the word of God, but rather the persons who receive that word, and the different growing conditions represent the circumstances or quality of their lives. In Luke's version, the seed on the path represents those vulnerable to the devil's theft of the word from their hearts. The seed that fell on rocky soil represents those whose initial enthusiasm cannot stand up to a test or trial (perhaps a time of suffering). The seed among the weeds represents persons consumed by cares, or wealth, or pleasure. "But as for that in the good soil, these are the ones who, when they hear the word, hold it fast in an honest and good heart, and bear fruit with patient endurance" (8:15).

The way Jesus explains it, the moral to the story seems to be that the disciples ought to be tending to the circumstances of their lives so that they might be fruitful seed. Once again, however, the larger plot of this section of the Gospel turns in a different direction. In place of that obvious moral, Luke again follows Mark in returning to the issue of hiddenness and secrecy that was raised in the earlier saying (8:10; Mark 4:11–12). This time the saying (introduced by the parable of the lamp and the lampstand) does not justify secrecy, but affirms that what was hidden will be revealed (8:16–17; see also 11:33–36). By implication, we learn that the disciples who have received the plain explanation of what others know only in the parables are given the task of "enlightening" the others.

The final warning (8:18) echoes the earlier recognition that listening and understanding should, but do not necessarily, go together: The disciples must pay attention to how they listen. At this point, the confusing double allegory of the interpretation of the parable (in which the "seed" is both the word of God and the recipients of that word) is resolved. It is the disciples who have been given knowledge of God's reign (God's sovereign "word"). More than an intellectual grasp, that knowledge has become part of the persons they are and of the ministry in which some of them are about to engage (9:1–6). The very circumstances and commitments that characterize their lives will determine whether that word will become a reality in their midst. In the imagery of the parable, they are the "seed" that is God's word, and the quality of "soil"—the quality of life— in which they are planted will be reflected in the "harvest," and that quality will determine whether it will bring the bounty of God's reign or a barren field.

The parable, its interpretation, and the accompanying sayings convey the promise and joy of God's reign, the hundredfold yield. But the promise and joy are wrapped in stern warnings. The "theological education" that these disciples (and especially the chosen twelve) are receiving in the company of Jesus is no academic exercise or ecclesiastical requirement. Instead, everything is hanging in the balance in it: "To those who have, more will be given; and from those who do not have, even what they seem to have will be taken away."

## Kinship with Jesus (Luke 8:19–21)

8:19 **Then his mother and his brothers came to him, but they could not reach him because of the crowd.** [20] **And he was told, "Your mother and your brothers are standing outside, wanting to see you."** [21] **But he said to them, "My mother and my brothers are those who hear the word of God and do it."**

There is no indication of a change of scene or passage of time, so, according to Luke's narrative, we are to imagine that just as he finishes his warning to the disciples (8:18), Jesus is informed that his mother and brothers want to see him. We are not told whether he honors their specific request. Instead, he continues his teaching on the word of God, offering a new definition of family. Not simply hearing the word of God (presumably not even listening with understanding), but *hearing and doing* it is what makes people Jesus' family. Whether the members of his biological family meet those criteria is not the issue. Rather, with those criteria the boundaries of that most intimate human community are opened up. What matters is not genealogy, but embodying the word of God in one's life and actions.

The saying echoes the concluding teachings of the sermon on the plain (6:46–49): Just as hearing Jesus' words and doing them are inextricably bound together, so are hearing God's word and doing it. The issue now, however, is not only the quality of the disciple's ministry (6:43–49;

8:1–18), but the identification of those on whom Jesus will be able to count in times of crisis. The implicit question posed to the people who have been accompanying Jesus (8:1–3) is whether they are ready to make the move from followers to family.

## JESUS AND POWER
## Luke 8:22–56

Luke introduces a new section of his narrative by indicating a different time frame ("one day") that marks the beginning of Jesus' travels across the lake of Gennesaret to the eastern shore (the country of the Gerasenes), then back to the western shore. The journey encompasses four stories of Jesus' power over death, disease, demons, and what we would call the forces of nature. Luke has drawn these stories from Mark 4:35–5:43, with only a few changes in detail.

### Power over the Storm (Luke 8:22–25)

8:22  **One day he got into a boat with his disciples, and he said to them, "Let us go across to the other side of the lake." So they put out, 23 and while they were sailing he fell asleep. A windstorm swept down on the lake, and the boat was filling with water, and they were in danger. 24 They went to him and woke him up, shouting, "Master, Master, we are perishing!" And he woke up and rebuked the wind and the raging waves; they ceased, and there was a calm. 25 He said to them, "Where is your faith?" They were afraid and amazed, and said to one another, "Who then is this, that he commands even the winds and the water, and they obey him?"**

The first of the stories is set in the boat during their crossing of the lake. Only Jesus and the disciples are present—a fact that sets this apart from most stories about Jesus' deeds of power like healings and exorcisms. The story as it occurs in all of the Gospels is, however, precisely about Jesus' power (8:24) and about his identity (8:25b).

On one level, the story is not unusual at all. The lake of Gennesaret—what Mark calls the "Sea of Galilee"—is a large but relatively shallow lake, on the western side of which is a spine of hills. Pigeon Pass cuts through the hills, opening a channel for the wind to blow from the Mediterranean. Sudden gusts whip the waters of the lake into huge waves that come up very quickly, catching even experienced sailors unawares. When the winds die down, the water becomes calm again.

It is possible that this story goes back to a reminiscence of one time when just such a sudden storm (literally, "a 'whirlwind' or 'hurricane' of wind," 8:23) overtook Jesus and the disciples, and as soon as Jesus reassured them that they would be safe, the storm ceased. With our modern understanding of natural law, such a possibility is interesting to consider: Is the story really about a "miracle" in which Jesus overpowers what is natural, or is it a reinterpretation of a perfectly natural occurrence, attributing it (incorrectly) to Jesus?

The very question, however, is foreign to the writers and audiences of the Gospels. Those people would not have thought in terms of natural law and "miracle" in the way we mean those terms. They would have understood manifestations like a sudden storm to have come from the workings of various "powers" (sometimes seen as individual beings such as demons, and in other cases powers that remain without a specific form) that could only be managed or controlled by greater powers. Luke in particular has already made the point that Jesus is empowered by the Holy Spirit or by God (4:14, 36 and 5:17, for example). Here his power resembles God's own power over the seas (see, for example, Ps. 29:3–4; 65:7; 89:9; 104:6–7; 107:23–32). Just as in the stories of exorcisms, when Jesus "rebukes" the demons and they obey, Jesus' rebuke is understood to be what triumphs over the threat posed by the waves and whatever evil might lurk in them: He is the one whom even the winds and the water obey (8:25b).

Within the story of the stilling of the storm, the issue of Jesus' identity is raised, not as an affirmation by the disciples, but as a question: "Who then is this, that he commands even the winds and the water, and they obey him?" The disciples' response of fear and amazement prompts Jesus' question about their faith. That reaction by the disciples, along with such details as Jesus and the disciples being by themselves, and Jesus having been asleep (a common metaphor for death) and awakening, suggest some resemblance between this story and various stories of Jesus' appearances to the disciples after the resurrection (Matt. 28:16–20; Luke 24:13–35, 36–43; John 20:19–25, 26–29; 21:1–13).

While the very early church may well have shaped this story to speak of the presence and power of the resurrected Christ with them in their ministry (and Mark retains many of the details that support that role for the story in the life and theology of the church), Luke has minimized those details. In his narrative, it is a story of what happened when Jesus' closest followers were confronted with new aspects of Jesus' being and power. The question of Jesus' identity is one that Herod raises (9:9) and that the disciples are forced to answer a bit later in the narrative (9:18–22). It is a question that always leads to issues of power: Who has power, how is it expressed, and to what purposes is it used?

## Power over Demons (Luke 8:26–39)

8:26 **Then they arrived at the country of the Gerasenes, which is opposite Galilee.** [27] **As he stepped out on land, a man of the city who had demons met him. For a long time he had worn no clothes, and he did not live in a house but in the tombs.** [28] **When he saw Jesus, he fell down before him and shouted at the top of his voice, "What have you to do with me, Jesus, Son of the Most High God? I beg you, do not torment me"**—[29] **for Jesus had commanded the unclean spirit to come out of the man. (For many times it had seized him; he was kept under guard and bound with chains and shackles, but he would break the bonds and be driven by the demon into the wilds.)** [30] **Jesus then asked him, "What is your name?" He said, "Legion"; for many demons had entered him.** [31] **They begged him not to order them to go back into the abyss.**

[32] **Now there on the hillside a large herd of swine was feeding; and the demons begged Jesus to let them enter these. So he gave them permission.** [33] **Then the demons came out of the man and entered the swine, and the herd rushed down the steep bank into the lake and was drowned.**

[34] **When the swineherds saw what had happened, they ran off and told it in the city and in the country.** [35] **Then people came out to see what had happened, and when they came to Jesus, they found the man from whom the demons had gone sitting at the feet of Jesus, clothed and in his right mind. And they were afraid.** [36] **Those who had seen it told them how the one who had been possessed by demons had been healed.** [37] **Then all the people of the surrounding country of the Gerasenes asked Jesus to leave them; for they were seized with great fear. So he got into the boat and returned.** [38] **The man from whom the demons had gone begged that he might be with him; but Jesus sent him away, saying,** [39] **"Return to your home, and declare how much God has done for you." So he went away, proclaiming throughout the city how much Jesus had done for him.**

The boat trip leaves Jesus and the disciples on the eastern shore of the lake, where there were a number of cities and villages inhabited by Gentiles. According to Luke, this is Jesus' only foray into Gentile territory, and the only instance of his ministry taking place outside the boundaries of the community of the Jews, or God-fearers like the centurion whose servant was healed (7:1–10). Various manuscripts give different names for the city where this incident is set, and the "correct" one where an incident in Jesus' life may have taken place is impossible to determine.

But historical realism in any sense is clearly not the point of this story.

Even if one were to accept demon possession as a way to name the disintegration of someone's personality that we recognize as mental illness, and even if we were to recognize exorcism as a way to speak about healing, this story is marked by such grotesque and fantastic descriptions that it is like a caricature drawn in primary colors. Even though Luke has eliminated some of the details found in Mark, enough remain to identify the story as a symbolic statement of the power of Jesus, and not a report of a medical case needing only interpretation into modern clinical categories.

At the beginning of the story the man is living outside the boundaries of human society. Even harsh attempts by his society to control him—guards, chains, and shackles (8:29b)—are unsuccessful, and he returns to "the wilds" beyond the boundaries of civilization. He lives naked among the dead (8:27b) instead of clothed and as a part of living human society.

Just as happened in the earlier exorcism story (4:31–37), the demons, speaking through the man, recognize Jesus and the threat he represents to their power. Although they themselves know Jesus' identity, they have no name, but only a number: A Roman *legio* was composed of about six thousand soldiers and an equal number of support-troops. To residents of the Roman Empire, the Roman legion symbolized the occupying forces whose power was overwhelming and whose presence meant the loss of control over every dimension of their own society. What better name for the demons that were wreaking such havoc on this man's life?

The demons negotiate with Jesus. Instead of being sent into the abyss—the place of the dead in the underworld, to which the tombs lead and from which evil was said to originate—they ask to be sent into a herd of pigs. Jewish hearers would recognize the pigs as unclean animals particularly fit for takeover by demons, but the story is set in Gentile territory, where raising pigs represented an economic enterprise (see also 15:15). In what may be ridicule of the legions' military exploits, the pigs are said to rush (in formation?) down the steep bank into the lake to their own destruction.

The Gospel writers do not say what the swineherds reported, but apparently their story made as big a splash as the pigs, for people came to see for themselves. The story says nothing about the people's reaction to the economic loss represented in the destruction of the herd of pigs; nor does the story address the issue of the morality of destroying the animals. Instead, the focus shifts to the man who has been "healed" (or "saved") and is now "clothed and in his right mind" (8:35–36) and to the response of the townspeople.

The people's response is fear (8:35, 37), which leads them to ask Jesus to leave the area. The basis for their fear is not identified. Perhaps we are intended to see it as recognition of the tremendous power exercised over the demons, and the awe that great power inspires. On one level, fear seems to be the opposite of what should be evoked, since the man who before had evoked their strenuous efforts to subdue and control him, is now quiet and no threat at all. Would not joy be the more appropriate response, and a celebration welcoming him back to their community from the "far country" of his mental and physical exile (15:11–32)? Could he have been judged less threatening in chains and shackles—controlled— than healed and whole, but free?

Given the play on words present in the name "legion," one would need to ask if the Gospel writers are not also engaging in political allegory when they speak about the people's fear. Would not any power that could order the legions' destruction inspire as much terror as the legions themselves? Might the Gospel writers be chiding the people for the ways they manage life under Roman control, such that they are finally less fearful with the evil present and somehow worked around or pushed to the margins of their daily lives, than they would be to find the evil power banished, and freedom and wholeness restored?

The response of the healed man himself is to want to accompany Jesus, but instead, he is sent home to "declare how much God has done for you" (8:39). The concluding sentence tells us that he did not get the message quite right, attributing his healing to Jesus rather than to God. On one level, Luke's audience might see the two actors—Jesus and God—as the same, for the power at work in Jesus clearly was the power of God. In another sense, though, the difference is significant, for it suggests linking the healing to Jesus' person—perhaps as itinerant healer or wonder-worker— rather than to the presence of God's reign in Jesus' ministry. Perhaps that is why the healed man does not leave behind the remnants of his old life and follow Jesus, as others have done. On the other hand, he is instructed to tell his story, in contrast to others who are explicitly forbidden to tell anyone what has happened (see, for example, the command in 8:56). For this man, who is described as having lived outside of human community during the time of his illness, the opportunity to tell his story and communicate with his neighbors and family members, might be seen as the completion of his healing and his restoration to full humanity.

## Power over Illness and Death (Luke 8:40–56)

8:40 **Now when Jesus returned, the crowd welcomed him, for they were all waiting for him. 41 Just then there came a man named Jairus, a leader of the** synagogue. He fell at Jesus' feet and begged him to come to his house, [42] for he had an only daughter, about twelve years old, who was dying.

As he went, the crowds pressed in on him. [43] Now there was a woman who had been suffering from hemorrhages for twelve years; and though she had spent all she had on physicians, no one could cure her. [44] She came up behind him and touched the fringe of his clothes, and immediately her hemorrhage stopped. [45] Then Jesus asked, "Who touched me?" When all denied it, Peter said, "Master, the crowds surround you and press in on you." [46] But Jesus said, "Someone touched me; for I noticed that power had gone out from me." [47] When the woman saw that she could not remain hidden, she came trembling; and falling down before him, she declared in the presence of all the people why she had touched him, and how she had been immediately healed. [48] He said to her, "Daughter, your faith has made you well; go in peace."

[49] While he was still speaking, someone came from the leader's house to say, "Your daughter is dead; do not trouble the teacher any longer." [50] When Jesus heard this, he replied, "Do not fear. Only believe, and she will be saved." [51] When he came to the house, he did not allow anyone to enter with him, except Peter, John, and James, and the child's father and mother. [52] They were all weeping and wailing for her; but he said, "Do not weep; for she is not dead but sleeping." [53] And they laughed at him, knowing that she was dead. [54] But he took her by the hand and called out, "Child, get up!" [55] Her spirit returned, and she got up at once. Then he directed them to give her something to eat. [56] Her parents were astounded; but he ordered them to tell no one what had happened.

The narrative moves forward by means of a geographical observation: Jesus has returned to the side of the lake where the earlier incidents were set. Luke suggests a rapidly moving story, for there is no indication of any delay between Jesus' arrival welcomed by the crowd (8:40), and the approach of Jairus (8:41) whose plea to Jesus sets in motion the two healing stories that follow. The stories of the healings of Jairus's daughter and of the woman with the hemorrhages are unusual on several counts. First, they both focus on Jesus' ministry with women. Second, they are presented as a "sandwich," in which the first story is begun, the second interrupts it, then the first is completed. Third, the middle story presents an ambiguous picture of Jesus' role in the healing.

The first three Gospels contain many stories that begin as accounts of healings or exorcisms, and then, on the basis of some detail of the setting or of Jesus' action, turn into stories of Jesus' conflict with various groups of authorities. There are also a number of collections of healing stories, where one leads into the next in rapid succession. This pattern of the interweaving of two healing stories—the "sandwich" design—is unique to this passage.

Some interpreters point to its uniqueness as a basis for concluding that the story therefore reports an actual incident in Jesus' life, when he was interrupted on the way to complete one task, took care of the interruption, then continued on his way. Others suggest that the early church might have interwoven the two accounts. They point out that the interruption serves the dramatic need for a delay during which the condition of Jairus's daughter deteriorates. They note also the number of parallels between the stories—twelve years as the little girl's age and the duration of the woman's illness; the use of the word "daughter" in both stories; the little girl's being just at the threshold of puberty, and the woman's illness that would have made her unable to bear children; the stark contrast between the solicitous family and community caring for the little girl, and the woman who appears without companion or advocate; and the contrast between the woman's speech following her healing and the command of silence at the close of the other story. Such echoing back and forth between the stories suggests the work of storytellers accenting the stories to make them work together into a coherent whole. However, we have no way of judging whether this (or any other) specific incident actually happened as it is described. A more productive line of questioning to pursue is how this passage in its current form functions in Luke's Gospel.

The accounts in Mark (Mark 5:21–43) and Luke are very similar, and we need note only a few differences in detail. Matthew (Matt. 9:18–26), however, has shortened the stories significantly, eliminating many details in a way that emphasizes Jesus' role in the healings and takes the spotlight off the other characters. In Mark and Luke those very details give the stories life and beckon us to become involved with this dramatic moment in their accounts of Jesus' ministry.

Even though in all three Synoptic Gospels the two healing stories are interwoven, each of them deserves to be looked at on its own as well as in conjunction with the other. The framing story begins with abundant detail introducing the situation and its characters (8:41–42). We learn Jairus's name—itself an unusual detail. Apparently, at some point in the telling of the story, that name would have been recognized by the community who told it. Jairus is described as a leader of the synagogue, and by this time in Luke's narrative that detail sets us up to expect opposition to Jesus. Instead, this man falls at Jesus' feet and begs Jesus' help for his only daughter, who is dying. In the economics of health care delivery in the ancient world, a man of Jairus's station would normally go to one of the established medical centers or to a physician for help. Itinerant healers like Jesus represented the primary health care system for the destitute—those who did not have the money, or the leisure, or the confidence in the system to take advantage of more established resources. Jairus's desperation because of his beloved daughter's critical condition apparently has made him willing to do anything to get help for her, including humbling himself by pleading for Jesus to use his healing powers on her behalf.

Following the episode with the woman in the crowd, and right on the heels of Jesus' declaration to that "daughter" that her "faith" has made her well (8:48), Jairus receives the message that his daughter has died. Jesus urges Jairus to have the faith that the woman has exhibited (8:50). Apparently, however, Jairus and his wife and the inner core of the group of disciples (Peter, John, and James) are not able to accept Jesus' reassurance. Like the widow whose son has died (7:13), her family and the other mourners are told not to weep, but rather to "believe" (8:50). Instead, they laugh the bitter laugh of disbelief (8:53).

It is not clear whether Luke intends us to understand that she really is dead and that Jesus raises her from the dead, or rather that she is not dead (perhaps comatose) and is subsequently healed by Jesus. Jesus' own words assure that she is not dead, and his words generally are to be trusted. On the other hand, Luke marks her healing by noting that "her spirit [or breath] returned" (8:55), which suggests that she had been no longer the integrated, enlivened body that is the basis for human life: In other words, she was dead.

In any event, as evidence that she is now not only alive, but also on the road to wellness, Jesus tells her family to give her some food (8:55). What the story does not tell us directly, but what the daughter's age clearly implies, is that now that she is well she will soon be ready to be given in marriage. Thus she is not only restored to her life in her present family, but she will soon take her new place in another household as someone's wife and subsequently as mother. This story thus has implications beyond the specifics of the little girl's individual life. Implicitly, the story also holds out a social promise of well-being for the family and household structures that are the heart of the social and economic system of the Roman Empire. For the moment, however, the family and the three disciples who have witnessed the event are told to tell no one what has taken place.

The story in the middle (8:43–48) has a different feeling about it. The woman who is ill moves onto the stage by herself. The effect is ambiguous. We are struck by her independence and initiative. On the other hand, however, we note the contrast with the surrounding story, where a beloved daughter of a prominent family is surrounded in her illness by a family ready to do anything to get help for her.

The story provides no basis for drawing any conclusions about whether the woman actually has a family at home. Levitical laws relating to her condition (Lev. 15:19–30) would probably not have had a direct effect on her family life. The concerns about purity at the heart of those laws affected people who needed to have access to the temple, and this story is set far from the temple, in Galilee. Furthermore, the same laws that identify what makes someone impure provide for the remedy or proper ritual for purification: The woman's condition is no cause for punishment or condemnation; it simply sets up a situation that would have to be taken care of in the course of normal family life.

Whether the existence of such purity laws would have affected the woman's self-image or attitude toward life in general is impossible to say. In any event, that question is not an explicit factor in Luke's story. We should not therefore conclude on the basis of the Levitical laws that the woman's presence in the crowd would have put her in jeopardy for "contaminating" those she touched. Luke's story does not suggest that she has taken any particular risk by moving about in public or by approaching Jesus. In fact, none of the versions of the story mention the Levitical purity laws as a factor in the way the story unfolds.

On the other hand, though, two details about the woman's circumstances are clearly implied by her condition. First, for twelve years she would have been unable to become pregnant and thus to participate in what her society (and probably Luke's as well) would have seen as her principal role in the family and the economy, bearing children. That fact might have had an effect on a woman's marriage, particularly if she had not already borne children, but this story itself says nothing about any such circumstances. Apparently Luke would have his readers assume that she lived in normal circumstances—that is, within a family and a household. Second, after twelve years of even mild but constant bleeding, she would have been physically weakened.

The story itself tells us further that the formal system for medical care—the "physicians"—had "bled" her economically as well (8:43). She may have shared Jairus's sense of desperation in coming to Jesus for help, but she also had become part of the population whose lack of financial resources made them dependent on itinerant healers when the techniques of folk medicine routinely practiced in the family were not effective.

Whether she may have had other family members who might have gone to her aid, in the narrative she is the one who takes the step necessary to obtain healing. In contrast to the ineffectiveness of traditional medical care, Luke tells us that the woman's cure by Jesus is swift and simple. Even the "fringe" of his garment (perhaps the fringe of his prayer shawl) mediates healing power, and her condition is healed (8:44). The bleeding stops, but the story continues.

Jesus' power may be tremendous, but as Mark and Luke tell the story, he has not controlled its use. The power has been tapped by a determined touch in the midst of the pressing crowd. Jesus is said to have felt something identified as "power" flowing out of him, but not to know who touched him in this special way (8:45–46). What happens next is puzzling, and its lack of flow with the narrative is like a "speed bump" in the road that slows us and compels our attention. We have been told that Jesus did not know who had touched him, and presumably the woman could have slipped away, returned to her home, performed the appropriate rituals of purification required in the law, then presented herself to the proper authorities who could certify her healing. Instead, she recognizes that she cannot remain hidden. Like Jairus when he approached Jesus, she falls down before him. Instead of asking for help, she "declared" what she had done and what had happened to her (8:47).

Several details highlight the importance of her action. First, the word translated "declared" is one of a family of Greek words that convey the meaning of public announcement or "proclamation": The woman preached to the crowds. Luke tells us two things about the importance of her preaching. First, up to this point in the narrative, he has mentioned the "crowds" who were pressing around Jesus (8:40, 42, 45). Suddenly her preaching is in the presence of all the "people" (8:47). It is clear that the cast of characters has not changed, but now they are referred to by a word Luke sometimes uses for Israel as the people of the promise (for example, 1:10, 17, 68, 77; 7:16; 24:19) and for people to whom Jesus preaches or teaches (for example, 6:17; 7:1, 29; 18:43; 20:1, 9, 45; 21:38). It is the Greek word underlying the English word "laity." The formless (and perhaps somewhat threatening) "crowds" take shape as a "people" in response to the woman's proclamation.

We know little of the content of the preaching itself. We read only that she said "why she had touched him, and how she had been immediately healed." The "why" is not explained, and the narrative itself offers nothing beyond her desperate need for healing and the implication that she thinks that need can be met by Jesus, to account for her touch. Yet Jesus' benediction (8:48) refers to her "faith." Furthermore, he says that faith has made her well (the same word that is often translated "save").

Luke clearly implies that more has happened than simply the cure of her physical illness. That cure itself would have enabled her to return to full participation in family life, including, presumably, again being able to bear children. But even the social dimension of the healing is eclipsed in importance for Luke by the importance of her telling her story. By calling that articulation of her story "proclamation," Luke links it to the proclamation of the gospel (a word with the same root in Greek) that is his principal agenda. In the logic of the narrative itself, what is called "faith" is not simply her enacted belief that Jesus could heal her, nor is it any creed, or in particular a "christological" confession that conveys a correct statement of Jesus' identity. Rather her faith is the proclamation—speaking "the whole truth," as Mark 5:33 calls what she does—that reads her life in terms of the gospel, and that does so out loud. Church tradition even has named this woman "Veronica"—"she who speaks the truth."

This unnamed woman plays no further role in Luke's (or any other) Gospel account, but what she has done is crucial. Her "preaching" represents the first time a human being makes the connection between Jesus' work as a healer and the larger project that defines his life and ministry (4:18–19): She proclaims how she has been set free from her illness. With that change, in contrast to the earlier physical "cure" in which the bleeding stopped (8:44), the woman is "made well" or, literally, "saved."

Having "faith" or "believing" (the verb has the same root in Greek) and being "saved" are linked twice in this double story. In the case of Jairus's daughter, they are linked in the form of a promise: "Do not fear. Only believe, and she will be saved" (8:50). In Jesus' parting words to the woman, having faith and being saved are linked as an accomplished fact, which is expressed in a benediction (8:48). In neither case, though, does that connection lead to a formula for achieving a personal or private salvation, whether from immediate physical ills or in some eternal hereafter. Rather, in these stories, whatever the human need or assumption about Jesus' power that may account for people's coming to Jesus, "faith" draws them beyond that moment. By their "faith" they participate in a project whose effects stretch far beyond them. A mood of mourning is transformed into the occasion for celebration, and threatening crowds become a people with an identity and a purpose. Where illness and death held sway, life now reigns in all its fullness.

## THE TWELVE TRY THEIR WINGS
### Luke 9:1–6

9:1 **Then Jesus called the twelve together and gave them power and authority over all demons and to cure diseases, 2 and he sent them out to**

**proclaim the kingdom of God and to heal. [3] He said to them, "Take nothing for your journey, no staff, nor bag, nor bread, nor money—not even an extra tunic. [4] Whatever house you enter, stay there, and leave from there. [5] Wherever they do not welcome you, as you are leaving that town shake the dust off your feet as a testimony against them." [6] They departed and went through the villages, bringing the good news and curing diseases everywhere.**

The twelve Jesus had chosen to be apostles—"sent ones"—in 6:13–16 have now completed their time of preparation for the task (6:17–8:56). In a "commencement ceremony" they are vested with power and authority and are sent out to continue what they have learned in their time of apprenticeship to Jesus: A ministry marked by exorcisms, healings, and the proclamation of God's reign. Like many rites of passage in our own experience, this one leaves us with as many questions as clues about its meaning.

First, the testimony of the various Gospels is ambiguous, and we cannot be certain that Jesus actually sent out followers on their own missions during his lifetime. The Gospel of John tells of no such mission. The Synoptic Gospels all include stories of Jesus' sending out of the twelve, and Luke speaks also of a second missionary campaign by a larger number (10:1–20). A comparison of details of the various stories suggests that both Mark and the other source shared by Matthew and Luke contained such an account, which the two Gospel writers then edited in different ways.

But the stories all incorporate aspects of the church's later missionary activity, when leaders indeed went out to carry the gospel message beyond the boundaries of Jesus' own ministry. For example, according to the various accounts, the missionaries are to go on their journeys without any baggage that would allow them to carry their security with them. Although the stories differ in details, it appears that the missionaries are to carry no weapons, no extra clothing, and no money, but instead are to accept the hospitality of any who receive them along the way (9:3–4). When they are not received, they are to move on to the next place leaving behind a testimony against those who have rejected them (9:5).

Both Paul's own letters (for example, Rom. 16:1–2; 1 Cor. 16:5–11; 2 Cor. 12:14–18; Phil. 2:19–30; Philem. 22) and Luke's accounts of the missionary journeys of the apostles in the book of Acts (for example, Acts 9:10–31; 15:30–36; 16:13–15; 17:10–15; 18:5–11, 22–28; 21:7–8; 28:7–10) sketch a similar style of missionary life, in which hospitality extended even to strangers was the hallmark of Christian communities. Whether any of the early missionaries went totally without provisions is not clear. Some—

including Paul—appear, on the contrary, to have combined their missionary journeys with business trips during which they practiced their various trades and carried out commercial ventures.

In their general outline, though, the Gospel accounts of the sending out of disciples on their journeys may reflect the experience of the early church. Its missionaries too were prepared by being steeped in the accounts of Jesus' life and teachings. They were then sent out to continue Jesus' work of preaching and healing, with faith and confidence in God's accompaniment and providence on their way.

# 6. Who Is This Man?
## Luke 9:7–50

The question about Jesus' identity that was introduced at the end of the story of the stilling of the storm (8:25) becomes the focus of the section of the Gospel that follows the sending out of the apostles. Herod, the crowds, and the disciples reflect on that question within the narrative itself, and Luke provides his own answers in the stories about the feeding of the huge crowd of people (9:10–17) and the transfiguration of Jesus (9:28–36). Those narratives and the following ones on true and false authority (9:37–50) draw together the implications of the Galilean ministry and set the stage for the account of Jesus' long journey to Jerusalem that begins in 9:51.

## HEROD'S CONFUSION
## Luke 9:7–9

9:7 **Now Herod the ruler heard about all that had taken place, and he was perplexed, because it was said by some that John had been raised from the dead,** [8] **by some that Elijah had appeared, and by others that one of the ancient prophets had arisen.** [9] **Herod said, "John I beheaded; but who is this about whom I hear such things?" And he tried to see him.**

The shadow of Herod Antipas, tetrarch of Galilee, has already fallen over Luke's narrative. He was introduced in Luke's elaborate dating of the ministry of John the Baptist (3:1) and identified as having been "rebuked by him because of Herodias, his brother's wife, and because of all the evil things that Herod had done," and as having "added to them all by shutting up John in prison" (3:19–20). Joanna, the wife of Herod's steward Chuza, was identified as one of the women who supported and accompanied Jesus (8:3). Whether Herod knew it or not, Jesus' ministry had touched Herod's own household. Following this episode, he appears twice more—once as the source of a threat to kill Jesus (13:31), and again in the passion narrative (23:6–12, 15).

This glimpse of Herod (9:7–9) carries less overt hostility than those that precede and follow it, but his anxiety is ominous: Anxious rulers always bode ill for those in their power. In this case, he acknowledges already having beheaded John, but rumors about Jesus cause Herod to associate him with the Baptist, or else with Elijah or another prophet. Those links are not simply Herod's musing about the religious eccentricities of the people in his charge. They show his assessment of whether Jesus has become the focus of the people's longing for divine action that will include their political liberation. On Herod's lips, "Who is this about whom I hear such things?" is a question that carries a threat—an ominous theme that is repeated with increasing clarity on the road to Jerusalem. When does the moment come to take action to stop this movement that Jesus started before it gets out of hand?

## THE FIVE THOUSAND ARE FED
## Luke 9:10–17

> 9:10 **On their return the apostles told Jesus all they had done. He took them with him and withdrew privately to a city called Bethsaida. ¹¹ When the crowds found out about it, they followed him; and he welcomed them, and spoke to them about the kingdom of God, and healed those who needed to be cured.**
> ¹² **The day was drawing to a close, and the twelve came to him and said, "Send the crowd away, so that they may go into the surrounding villages and countryside, to lodge and get provisions; for we are here in a deserted place." ¹³ But he said to them, "You give them something to eat." They said, "We have no more than five loaves and two fish—unless we are to go and buy food for all these people." ¹⁴ For there were about five thousand men. And he said to his disciples, "Make them sit down in groups of about fifty each." ¹⁵ They did so and made them all sit down. ¹⁶ And taking the five loaves and the two fish, he looked up to heaven, and blessed and broke them, and gave them to the disciples to set before the crowd. ¹⁷ And all ate and were filled. What was left over was gathered up, twelve baskets of broken pieces.**

On their return from their mission, the twelve are called simply "the apostles," and their return is mentioned almost as an aside (9:10). The arrival of crowds interrupts their planned retreat in Bethsaida, and Jesus resumes his usual ministry—proclamation of the reign of God and healing. The approaching sunset ushers in the drama that unfolds from logic, to illogic, to a liturgical resolution. The account of the feeding of the crowd is the only such account in Luke (in contrast to Mark and Matthew who each relate two such stories, one in Jewish territory and one among the Gentiles, Matt. 14:13–21; 15:32–39; Mark 6:30–44; 8:1–10).

Luke's story is set "in a deserted place" in the region of Bethsaida. Although the actual location of Bethsaida is not known, the narrative implies that it is a small fishing village near the lake of Gennesaret. Such localities would have lacked facilities to accommodate large numbers of visitors. Since day's end meant the time for the principal meal of the day, and time also for people to seek shelter for the night, the suggestion of the twelve makes sense (9:12): The crowd should secure hospitality in the surrounding region before daylight failed.

Jesus' instruction that the twelve should give them food focuses the episode on the first and most immediate of their needs (nothing more is said about the people's need for lodging). The available supplies are meager—five loaves and two fish. With a crowd of five thousand men (and presumably women and children), logic suggests that grocery shopping is in order (9:13b–14a). The disciples' comment about buying food is ironic, perhaps even sarcastic, for they are not near any large marketplaces, and obtaining that much food in a remote fishing village would hardly have been possible. The menu itself is appropriate to a peasant community in first-century Palestine, for bread would have been the mainstay of the diet, and in fishing villages the day's catch that remained unsold would have been incorporated into a family's own meal. Quickly, however, the narrative moves away from a logical story of an event in the everyday life of Jesus and the twelve, to a highly symbolic narrative whose setting is the life of Luke's church. Clearly, this is no ordinary picnic supper.

The numbers, first of all, are symbolic. The number five is a number signifying completeness in Jewish writings: five books of Moses, five books of Wisdom, five divisions in the book of Psalms, for example. The five loaves thus signify a similar holy fullness: There will be bread enough for the meal that is about to take place. Two fish are also enough—a kind of completeness of the species, like the animals who boarded the ark to survive the flood (Gen. 6:19–20). If the two fish are not enough by themselves to feed the crowd, at least they can begin the process of reproduction that in time will result in enough fish to feed all who are hungry (Luke 6:21).

If the numbers of loaves and fish convey the assurance that the food would suffice, the number in the crowd conveys a similar sense of completeness. The number ten was seen as a "perfect" number in both Jewish and Gentile lore. Five thousand—five times ten, times ten, times ten—should not be understood as an actual estimate of the size of the crowd, but as a number signifying that "everyone" was present. In Luke's account, "everyone" means that the whole church is present, prepared to receive the holy supper.

Symbolic numbers are joined by symbolic actions of blessing, breaking, and giving. The disciples divide the crowd into dining groups of fifty (again a symbolic number; see Leviticus 25). In language that foreshadows the liturgical rhythms of the last supper (22:19–20), Jesus takes the loaves and fish, blesses them, breaks them, and gives them to the "disciples." More hands are needed than only the twelve to whom the original instruction to feed the people was given, for the disciples, in turn, distribute the food to the crowd. All of the followers, and not just an elite group of leaders, share in the serving.

Not only does the food suffice, but "twelve baskets" of pieces remain (9:17). Again, the language is symbolic. If the meal was sufficient for the whole church, what remained would feed Israel—a basket for each of the twelve tribes. The "baskets" are the small baskets that Jews would fasten to their belts so that they could carry food on journeys through Gentile or Samaritan territory. Thus they could be assured of having food that had been properly prepared, and on which the tithe-offerings had been made (Deut. 14:22–29). For Luke, the point of the twelve baskets full of pieces is important. The bounty of God's reign will suffice for all people, for Jews and Gentiles alike.

Luke has been clear from the beginning of the Gospel that the identity of God's chosen people has not simply passed from Israel to the church. Rather, the salvation that Luke identifies as having come through Jesus is for "all flesh" (3:6). The numbers symbolic of completeness and wholeness, and the abundant feast that follows Jesus' taking, blessing, breaking, and giving of the food, are the first part of Luke's answer to the question of Jesus' meaning and identity at this crucial turning point of the Gospel.

## PETER'S CONFESSION
## Luke 9:18–27

9:18 Once when Jesus was praying alone, with only the disciples near him, he asked them, "Who do the crowds say that I am?" [19] They answered, "John the Baptist; but others, Elijah; and still others, that one of the ancient prophets has arisen." [20] He said to them, "But who do you say that I am?" Peter answered, "The Messiah of God."

[21] He sternly ordered and commanded them not to tell anyone, [22] saying, "The Son of Man must undergo great suffering, and be rejected by the elders, chief priests, and scribes, and be killed, and on the third day be raised."

[23] Then he said to them all, "If any want to become my followers, let them deny themselves and take up their cross daily and follow me. [24] For those who want to save their life will lose it, and those who lose their life for my sake will save it. [25] What does it profit them if they gain the whole world, but lose or forfeit themselves? [26] Those who are ashamed of me and of my words, of them the Son of Man will be ashamed when he comes in his glory and the glory of the Father and of the holy angels. [27] But truly I tell you, there are some standing here who will not taste death before they see the kingdom of God."

In contrast to the huge crowd that has shared in the supper, the next episode finds Jesus and the disciples alone in an undisclosed location. Jesus has been praying, a detail that alerts Luke's readers that a crucial moment is at hand (see, for example, 3:21; 5:16; 6:12; 9:28–29; 11:1; 22:41). Jesus first asks the disciples how his identity is being perceived by the crowds. The disciples' response echoes Herod's earlier summary of the gossip about Jesus (9:7–8). The follow-up question about the disciples' own perception leads to Peter's confession that Jesus is "the Messiah of God" (9:20).

Luke obviously would affirm that identification as a correct statement about Jesus. Within the narrative, however, Peter's words win no praise or commendation (such as they receive in Matthew's version of the story—quite obviously standing as Matthew's own judgment about his confession, Matt. 16:17–19). Instead, Luke follows Mark in having Jesus first command the disciples not to tell anyone, and then pronounce the first formal prediction of his passion (9:21–22; Mark 8:30–31).

The command to tell no one about Jesus' power to heal or about his identity as Messiah has long been recognized as a characteristic of Mark's Gospel: For Mark, Jesus is always the crucified Messiah, and until he is known in that way, his identity must remain a secret. Whether the "messianic secret" is only a point of Mark's theology, or whether it has roots in Jesus' own reluctance to risk the political vulnerability of being identified prematurely in his messianic role, is impossible to say. Both explanations are plausible—the first as Mark's determination to correct those in the church who may have wanted to avoid recognizing themselves as disciples of the crucified one (emphasizing instead only his power and glory, and the triumph of the resurrection), and the second as a reflection of the political danger in Jesus' day for anyone who was acclaimed as Messiah. In any event, the commandments to keep silent about Jesus' power and identity became firmly rooted in the accounts of Jesus' life, and they figure in Luke's and Matthew's Gospels as well as in Mark's.

By immediately following the command to keep silent with the prediction of the suffering, rejection, death, and resurrection of the Son of Man, Luke leaves open the question of whether the command came from Jesus or from Mark. For Luke, the important point is that, while Peter is correct in his identification of Jesus, he is in need of instruction as to its correct meaning.

The prediction of Jesus' suffering, death, and resurrection clearly owes its form to the church that has summarized details of the passion narrative itself (including the list of religious leaders opposed to Jesus). Whether the prediction records a core formula from Jesus himself is harder to say. If one believes that Jesus knew everything that would befall him and thus could have predicted the exact manner of his death, there is no problem. Such an assumption, however, contradicts the church's affirmation of Jesus' full humanity, as well as the picture of the human Jesus presented by the writers of the Synoptic Gospels. If one affirms Jesus' humanity, and therefore assumes that Jesus (like all other people) could not have known his fate or the precise circumstances of his death, it is still possible that he might have been remembered to have predicted his premature death. He would not have needed special foreknowledge to recognize that if he persisted in his proclamation of God's reign and his ministry of liberation for persons pushed to the margins of society, and if he was acclaimed as a leader by many of them, representatives of public order (both political and religious) would soon be ranged against him. To continue on this road could well lead to death for him and even for his followers. Such a simple and general statement, remembered through the lens of the horrifying events of Jesus' final week, could easily be refined into a formal passion prediction like the one in 9:22, the general predictions in 9:44 and 17:25, or even the very detailed one in 18:31–33.

That the passion predictions are principally theological statements and not historical reports is clear from the way these formal predictions, like other summaries of Jesus' passion, are linked to divine necessity (for example, 9:22; 13:33; 17:25; 24:6–7) or to the fulfillment of scripture (for example, 18:31–33; 24:44–46. Luke says nothing about why God might require such a fate for Jesus—nothing, for example, about his death being necessary to atone for human sin. It is important, therefore, to reflect on Luke's understanding of the meaning of Jesus' death without importing into the discussion Christian doctrines that arose elsewhere in the tradition. Luke's appeal to God's plan of salvation known in scripture or to the "necessity" of Jesus' death allows him to avoid lodging human blame for the event either with the Jewish leaders or with Rome. In that way, Luke is able to both continue to affirm that Jew and Gentile alike have a place in God's unfolding project (3:6) and to avoid supporting attitudes of suspicion and distrust between the church and the imperial authorities.

Two additional factors must be taken into account in the interpretation of the passion summaries. First, Luke's use of the Son of Man title in all but the last of the passion summaries (24:44–46) further complicates the task of their interpretation. Although that title is used only by Jesus, it is not clear whether the use here referred only to him or in a more general way to the fate of any human being engaged in a ministry like his. Second, in contrast to the variety in the details concerning the passion, the summaries say little about the resurrection. In each case there is simply a statement that Jesus will "be raised" (9:22) or "rise" (18:33; 24:7, 46) on the third day. Note the difference between the passive voice in 9:22 and the active voice in the other statements. The fact that Mark consistently speaks of Jesus "rising" from the dead (for example, Mark 8:31; 9:31; 10:34) and Matthew consistently says he "was raised" (Matt. 16:21; 17:23; 20:19), indicates that both expressions were acceptable to the early church. The passive voice emphasizes that it was God acting in Jesus who effected the resurrection. By using that form in the first of the passion summaries, Luke prepares his readers to hear the others also as affirmations that Jesus' resurrection is God's victory—the triumph of God's sovereign power.

Luke has omitted from the episode of Peter's confession the harsh conclusion of Mark's version of the dialogue between Jesus and Peter found in Mark 8:32–33. As a result, in Luke this episode is educational and not polemical. Instead of emphasizing the error or even danger of Peter's words, Luke stresses the correct understanding that his readers are to acquire. Jesus himself provides the definitive interpretation of the title "Messiah" or "anointed one" and thus another answer within the Gospel narrative to the question "Who is this?"

Whether the episode itself is a product of the church's reflection on Jesus or whether it goes back to a remembered event in Jesus' life is unknown. The account has obviously been heavily shaped by the theological concerns of the Gospel writers, but the core question has a ring of historical plausibility about it. Even with the clarity of hindsight, the picture presented in the Synoptic Gospels of the early period of Jesus' ministry is ambiguous. It would not be hard to imagine that Jesus might have checked with his disciples—perhaps even several times—about what the people were saying who were coming out to hear his message and to be healed. That he might even have asked the disciples themselves what they saw happening in their midst, and how they understood his role and their movement, seems equally likely.

Whether Jesus knew from the beginning what his fate was to be and how his life would unfold, or whether he was clear from the beginning of his ministry (or even from childhood) about his call from God or his relationship to God, is impossible to say. Such accounts as the stories of Jesus' birth and childhood (Luke 1 and 2), of his baptism and testing in the wilderness (3:21–22; 4:1–13), and of his transfiguration (9:28–36) may reflect moments of insight or clarification for Jesus himself. Modern attempts to discuss such questions are entangled in a basically psychological and individualistic model for thinking about vocation and identity, which does not allow for the more communal perspective of the worlds of the Gospel writers and of Jesus. In the communal model, even such personal matters as vocation and identity were known when and as the community affirmed them. Who it was that the crowds and the disciples said Jesus was affected who he in fact could be. (A similar dynamic exists today in the "free" churches, where a person's "call" to the ministry must be recognized by the community in which the person will serve. Until that affirmation comes, any inner sense of call that a person might have is not seen as definitive.)

Conversely, who Jesus was affected who his disciples would be: The identity and fate of a disciple mirrored the identity and fate of the one followed. Thus the prediction of Jesus' own fate is followed by teachings about discipleship that mirror that fate, including suffering and death, as well as the triumph of the resurrection. Both the saying about taking up the cross and the saying about losing and finding life occur again in Luke 14:27 and 17:33. The double occurrence in Luke (and also in Matthew; the two sayings occur in Matt. 10:38–39 and in 16:24–25, where they are parallel to Mark 8:34–35 and Luke 9:23–24) suggests that forms of the sayings were carried in at least two sources of the Synoptic traditions, and a saying similar to that about finding and losing life is found also in John 12:25. Such multiple occurrences of a saying or other tradition testify to its importance in the collection of traditions about Jesus. In Luke 9:23–27 those sayings form the core of a set of teachings about the meaning and nature of discipleship.

In Jesus' day, the cross was an instrument of Roman political execution. A person would take it up only once, as a consequence of an administrative verdict about one's involvement in treasonous or other criminal acts: One would carry it only once, to one's own place of execution. Both Mark's version of the saying (Mark 8:34) and the other occurrences of the saying in Matthew and Luke (Matt. 10:38; Luke 14:27) reflect such an origin of the saying. In 9:23, however, Luke has added the word "daily" to the saying, making taking up one's cross a metaphor for any burden involved in following Jesus. It is still a strong saying, however, for it involves a readiness to renounce one's own life and self.

"Denying" one's self does not mean giving up pleasures or comforts (denying something to one's self), but rather saying of one's self what Peter will say of Jesus, "I do not know him" (22:57). In any context where honor and prestige are primary values, status depends on a person's competing to be known and recognized. To set aside such goals for the sake of Jesus (and, by implication, for the sake of the program he represents) is to negate the competitive and hierarchical social order of the dominant society. The saying is aimed at those who want to be held—or who hold themselves—in high esteem, not at persons whose value and dignity as human beings is already threatened. Furthermore, the saying does not celebrate self-denial as a value for its own sake, but rather, in the name and for the cause of Jesus. As the teachings and stories of Luke's Gospel have already made clear, persons on the margins of society, for whom honor and dignity as well as material well-being are distant dreams, find in that same cause an affirmation of life in its fullness.

The first saying is mirrored in the second (9:24), in the apparently self-contradictory truth that when people act to protect their life, they will lose it, and those who even lose their life as a consequence of their discipleship will save it. The saying does not make death itself something good to be sought, nor is it an encouragement to seek martyrdom in the cause of the gospel. Rather, it addresses the likelihood that this particular discipleship will have death as a consequence, in a social, political, and economic context whose values the gospel contradicts. Profit, according to the terms of that day's dominant society, can come only at the cost of one's heart, as defined by this new way of Jesus (9:25). The way of the gospel in any age is not the dominant society's "Easy Street."

The key to the teachings on discipleship comes in their ultimate or "eschatological" consequences (9:26–27). To be "ashamed" of Jesus does not refer to an emotional sense of embarrassment. Instead it means to dishonor Jesus, as one might dishonor or disrespect someone considered to be one's social inferior. It is the opposite of the way one would treat a superior or a member of one's own family. The sayings thus refer to the fundamental realignment of family structure in which the community of Jesus' followers become sisters and brothers to one another. They have this new relationship as a gift from God, and not because they have chosen to join together in a new religious fraternity or sorority. They are siblings because Jesus and the God whom Jesus represents have claimed Jesus' followers as their family.

The assurance that a short time remains before they see God's reign (9:27) adapts Mark's version of the saying in this same passage. In Mark, Jesus assures his hearers that God's reign will have *come* before some who are present with Jesus die. Jesus' words in Luke contain, instead, the assurance that some will *see* that reign. Luke apparently recognizes that the coming of that reign in all its splendor is an event that belongs to God's future and not necessarily to the lifetimes of people in his church. Luke is clear that God's reign is glimpsed (though not fully realized) in the life and ministry of Jesus, and in that fact his audience would find comfort.

The question about Jesus' identity is thus not only related to how his followers and others perceive him, but it also determines the nature and quality of life for his followers. The contradictory picture of Jesus who is the "messiah of God" but who also will face suffering, rejection, and death, is mirrored in the saying that the two goals of preserving or securing one's life and finding salvation are incompatible. What to human standards appears as a contradiction, God's wisdom holds together.

## THE TRANSFIGURATION
## Luke 9:28–36

9:28 Now about eight days after these sayings Jesus took with him Peter and John and James, and went up on the mountain to pray. ²⁹ And while he was praying, the appearance of his face changed, and his clothes became dazzling white. ³⁰ Suddenly they saw two men, Moses and Elijah, talking to him. ³¹ They appeared in glory and were speaking of his departure, which he was about to accomplish at Jerusalem. ³² Now Peter and his companions were weighed down with sleep; but since they had stayed awake, they saw his glory and the two men who stood with him. ³³ Just as they were leaving him, Peter said to Jesus, "Master, it is good for us to be here; let us make three dwellings, one for you, one for Moses, and one for Elijah"—not knowing what he said. ³⁴ While he was saying this, a cloud came and overshadowed them; and they were terrified as they entered the cloud. ³⁵ Then from the

**cloud came a voice that said, "This is my Son, my Chosen; listen to him!"**
**³⁶ When the voice had spoken, Jesus was found alone. And they kept silent**
**and in those days told no one any of the things they had seen.**

God's own voice provides the definitive word on the question of Jesus'
identity: "This is my Son, my Chosen" (9:35). The voice speaks in the account of Jesus' "transfiguration"—the apparently temporary transformation of his appearance from that of an ordinary person to that of an exalted or heavenly being. This account is closely linked to the preceding
one by the observation that it occurred eight days (a week) later. The relatively greater importance of the second episode is signaled by the fact
that not just any disciples, but Peter, James, and John—the same three selected to witness the healing or raising of Jairus's daughter (8:51)—
accompany Jesus. Not only is Jesus once again at prayer, but the location
is on a mountain, a traditional site for holy encounters.

The account of Jesus' transfiguration is presented as referring to an experience of the disciples during Jesus' lifetime. Some scholars have interpreted the account as the story of an appearance of the resurrected Jesus
mistakenly set in the context of the earlier period of Jesus' ministry. However, several details make that seem like an inappropriate way to understand the story. First, Jesus and the disciples ascend the mountain together, whereas in the resurrection appearance stories, Jesus suddenly
appears or is revealed to the disciples who have gathered without him.
Second, resurrection appearance stories often include some commission
*from* Jesus to the disciples (for example, 24:46–48), but not heavenly words
*about* Jesus. Finally, in the transfiguration the change in Jesus' appearance
is only temporary, rather than an example of his new heavenly presence
that both *is* Jesus and yet is not immediately recognizable (24:13–35,
38–43).

In fact, the closest parallel to this story is not found among the resurrection appearance stories, but is the story of Jesus' baptism (3:21–22).
That story also features a heavenly voice that announces Jesus' identity,
but to Jesus himself at the outset of his ministry: "You are my Son, the
Beloved; with you I am well pleased." What began as a word *to* Jesus (a
sort of "call" to a new vocation) now comes at the end of his ministry in
Galilee as a heavenly word *about* Jesus. That word is said to be witnessed
by the inner core of his followers. Through it they learn that Jesus is the
Chosen One of God, and they are to listen to him.

Jesus himself is described as taking on heavenly qualities in his dazzling
clothes and transformed face (like the face of Moses on Sinai, Exod.

34:29–35). With him are Moses and Elijah, also heavenly figures who "appeared in glory." They were the two biblical characters in whose likeness the long-awaited prophet of the end-time was expected to come. Luke adds several details to Mark's version of the story. For example, he explains that the sleepy disciples stayed awake to witness these things (9:32): They were not dreaming.

Luke also summarizes the conversation between Jesus and the heavenly figures about the events that lie ahead (9:31). The word translated as "departure" is the Greek word *exodos*. It is usually interpreted here as referring to Jesus' death that will take place when he gets to Jerusalem, or perhaps to the complete event of his death, resurrection, and ascension in which he "departs" into heaven. While such readings are possible, another seems more likely. In the Greek translation of the accounts of Israel's journey from Egypt to the promised land, the moment of *exodos* was the departure from Egypt that began the journey that was completed only with their arrival at the Jordan River. In Luke's Gospel, the account of the transfiguration finds Jesus also at the point of beginning a long journey, which finds its end point or completion in Jerusalem (9:51–19:27). The journey of the Israelites described in Exodus, Leviticus, and Numbers (and summarized in Deuteronomy), like Jesus' impending journey, uses an ill-defined itinerary as a framework within which to present accounts of God's saving work, as well as extended blocks of instruction to the travelers (but really to the subsequent audience or readers of the accounts). In addition to those points of similarity between the two journeys, a number of details of the transfiguration account recall Moses' vision on Sinai (for example, the location on a mountain, the change in Jesus' and Moses' faces, and the presence of Moses as a character in both accounts). Taken together, these factors make it appear that Luke intended to refer here to the heavenly clarification of Jesus' identity at the moment of his "departure" toward Jerusalem.

Peter's suggestion that they set up three "dwellings" or "tents" may also evoke memories of the accounts of Israel's *exodos*. The word translated as "dwellings" is the word used in the Septuagint for the "booths" that are symbols of the Feast of Tabernacles (Lev. 23:33–43). Despite its origins as a harvest festival, by Jesus' day (and certainly in Luke's day after the destruction of the temple in Jerusalem), the Feast of Tabernacles was a festival of pilgrimage celebrating Israel's wanderings through the wilderness to freedom.

With or without that connection to the journey that followed the *exodos*, Peter's suggestion also reflects the poignant human longing somehow to mark the places and preserve the moments where one has encountered God. Jesus, Moses, and Elijah would be honored and protected in these dwellings. In addition, there would be a clear marker to which Peter and the others could return to experience again the power and splendor of such a moment.

The mystery and ineffability of the moment is heightened in the description of the cloud that encompassed them. The disciples and the very moment itself are isolated, frozen in time and space by their inability to see their surroundings or each other. Terror overtakes them as they find themselves alone with a voice from within the cloud (9:34–35). The voice answers the question that has been a red thread through this section of the Gospel: "Who is this?" The divine voice at once identifies Jesus and establishes their relationship to him: He is their "master" (9:33; the parallel in Mark 9:5 calls him "rabbi"), and they are to heed him during the days they still have to share together.

The scene ends as abruptly as it began, with Jesus alone with them again, and no further word spoken concerning what has transpired. The meaning is clear for Luke's audience: Prior questions within the narrative have been resolved with the answer about Jesus' identity that Luke and his church have known all along. Whatever else might be said about him, Jesus is the Son of God, acknowledged by angels (1:32, 35) and by God's own voice (3:22; 9:35).

## TRUE AND FALSE AUTHORITY
## Luke 9:37–50

### The Demons Know
### the Difference (Luke 9:37–43a)

> 9:37 **On the next day, when they had come down from the mountain, a great crowd met him. 38 Just then a man from the crowd shouted, "Teacher, I beg you to look at my son; he is my only child. 39 Suddenly a spirit seizes him, and all at once he shrieks. It convulses him until he foams at the mouth; it mauls him and will scarcely leave him. 40 I begged your disciples to cast it out, but they could not." 41 Jesus answered, "You faithless and perverse generation, how much longer must I be with you and bear with you? Bring your son here." 42 While he was coming, the demon dashed him to the ground in convulsions. But Jesus rebuked the unclean spirit, healed the boy, and gave him back to his father. 43 And all were astounded at the greatness of God.**

Once again the reference to a brief passage of time links the story of the transfiguration to what follows. This time the action resumes on the following day, when Jesus and the three disciples land with a thud at the base of the mountain in the midst of a clamoring crowd. Even in the Gospel, we are provided only a fleeting glimpse of moments with God.

The contrast between divine presence and daily reality is accentuated by the arrival of a man whose son suffers from convulsive seizures attributed to the presence of an alien spirit (9:38–39, 42a). To make matters worse, Jesus' disciples—presumably including the remaining nine, who had been given "power and authority over all demons" (9:1)—have been unable to help the boy (9:40). With what in Luke's Gospel is a rare outburst of irritation and frustration (9:41), Jesus does what the disciples have proven unable to do (9:42b). In a witness from the underside—from the demon that possessed the boy—Jesus' identity is affirmed once again, not by a title, but in the power the demon must acknowledge. For its part, the crowd recognizes not a power belonging to Jesus, but the very greatness of God (9:43a).

## Hard Words about Discipleship (Luke 9:43b–48)

9:43b **While everyone was amazed at all that he was doing, he said to his disciples,** 44 **"Let these words sink into your ears: The Son of Man is going to be betrayed into human hands."** 45 **But they did not understand this saying; its meaning was concealed from them, so that they could not perceive it. And they were afraid to ask him about this saying.**

46 **An argument arose among them as to which one of them was the greatest.** 47 **But Jesus, aware of their inner thoughts, took a little child and put it by his side,** 48 **and said to them, "Whoever welcomes this child in my name welcomes me, and whoever welcomes me welcomes the one who sent me; for the least among all of you is the greatest."**

The disciples lack not only the power to control the demon but also comprehension of the nature of this Jesus whom they are following: They just don't get it. How could someone who can command demons fall prey to human power (9:43b–45)? Beginning with the return of the apostles (9:10), Luke's narrative has unfolded in a counterpoint of glory and suffering, power and weakness, divine presence and human desolation. Both poles of each pair of opposites encompass Jesus and the disciples alike. Finally, action grinds to a halt in the disciples' fear even to ask the meaning of Jesus' words.

The depth of their confusion becomes even clearer when, in the wake of their failure, they quarrel over who is greatest (9:46). It is a debate that recurs in the context of the last supper (22:24) apparently representing a

problem Luke encounters in many guises in the church for which he
writes. The question reflects the disciples' continued captivity to the
norms of their society—in fact, of any society where honor is allocated as
a scarce commodity. In such an economy of scarcity, honor for one means
dishonor for another. Each person's place in the hierarchies of power and
prestige is both fixed and relative to others' places: I gain only if (and to
the extent that) you lose.

The response attributed to Jesus (9:47–48) addresses the argument
concerning their relative status by contradicting the premises of a society
structured on the basis of honor, power and merit. In such a society, children are on the bottom of every hierarchy—physically least powerful, economically dependent, and politically nonpersons. While the disciples hag-
gle among themselves, Jesus places himself in the position of a child. To
welcome a child in Jesus' name—to receive the child as an honored guest
who is one's peer or one's superior (which the disciples would be little inclined to do)—is to receive Jesus (which they would compete to do) and
even to receive God (which none could even imagine). Just as attempting
to save life is the way to lose it and losing life for Jesus' sake is the way to
salvation (9:24), so also the least is the greatest (9:48b).

## A Stranger in the Family (Luke 9:49–50)

> 9:49 **John answered, "Master, we saw someone casting out demons in your
> name, and we tried to stop him, because he does not follow with us."** [50] **But
> Jesus said to him, "Do not stop him; for whoever is not against you is for
> you."**

The argument about prestige and place is really basically an argument
about the newly defined family of Jesus' followers (8:19–21)—those to
whom honor, respect, and acceptance are to be accorded. The disciples' final conversation with Jesus before the journey to Jerusalem begins (9:49–
50) makes it clear that the disciples still do not understand how completely
their prior assumptions have been confronted and transformed in their relationship with Jesus. What the disciples have been unable to do—cast out
demons in Jesus' name—someone is accomplishing who is not officially one
of their number. By their criteria, such activity is not permitted because, for
them, membership in their group is still limited. Jesus' response instead sets
absolutely minimal criteria to define those engaged in their work, which is
finally God's sovereign project of good news and liberation: Anyone not
against them is for them. For the moment, that will be enough of a test to
carry them into their journey toward Jerusalem.

# 3. "Making the Path While Walking": The Road to Jerusalem

*Luke 9:51–19:28*

# 7. Tough Teachings for Daily Life
## Luke 9:51–11:36

Jesus' ministry in Galilee comes to an abrupt halt, as Luke begins the narrative of Jesus' journey toward Jerusalem (9:51–19:27). All three Synoptic Gospels tell of Jesus making only a single trip to the holy city, so in that basic sense all of them contain a "travel narrative." Only Luke, though, uses the journey from Galilee to provide a framework for an extensive collection of teachings, interspersed with a few stories about events along the way.

The journey provides only the barest outline. There are few indications of their actual geographical progress, and even those are simply reminders that they are on the way, rather than indicators of the route they are traveling (9:51–53, 56–57; 10:38; 13:31, 33; 17:11), and few reminders of the city that is their goal (9:53; 13:22, 33–34; 17:11; 18:31; 19:11). In that sense, Luke's travel narrative resembles the account of Israel's wanderings in the wilderness, especially as that journey is condensed and reviewed in Deuteronomy. There too the actual route takes a backseat to the instruction provided to the people along the way. In Luke's case, the immediate beneficiaries of the instruction are those who have been following Jesus since his beginnings in Galilee, and the extended audience includes the church for which Luke is writing.

The teachings themselves are only loosely related to one another by topic or theme. A small amount of the material found in the travel narrative has been taken from Mark, and some is found only in Luke. By far the largest amount comes from the special source shared by Luke and Matthew, though Matthew has incorporated it into different places in the Gospel narrative. Attempts to identify the structure of the travel account seem arbitrary at best. In general, the teachings all focus on the demands entailed in following Jesus. That "discipleship" involves major changes in behavior and understanding, putting aside the common wisdom of any

society governed by human norms, and adopting the project identified as
the reign of God. The teachings collected in this section of the Gospel are
designed to prepare the disciples to respond to coming events in Jerusalem
and to prepare the church to continue the ministry of Jesus after the events
of his passion and resurrection.

## A SAMARITAN STOPOVER:
## A BAD BEGINNING
### Luke 9:51–56

9:51 **When the days drew near for him to be taken up, he set his face to go
to Jerusalem.** [52] **And he sent messengers ahead of him. On their way they entered a village of the Samaritans to make ready for him;** [53] **but they did not
receive him, because his face was set toward Jerusalem.** [54] **When his disciples James and John saw it, they said, "Lord, do you want us to command
fire to come down from heaven and consume them?"** [55] **But he turned and
rebuked them.** [56] **Then they went on to another village.**

The journey begins with an affirmation of Jesus' determination to go to
Jerusalem, but also with a double hint of divine purpose undergirding the
trip. The first indication is that the time is being "fulfilled" or "completed"
(a better translation than "drew near") for him to be "taken up." Luke suggests here, as in other references to the "necessity" of his passion (for example, 9:22; 13:33; 17:25; 24:6–7), that the approaching events are part of God's
will or plan. Here the specific event in focus appears to be Jesus' ascension at
the very end of the passion and resurrection accounts (24:50–53). The second hint of divine purpose is in the description of Jesus' "setting his face" toward Jerusalem. The language echoes Isaiah 50:7, where the servant of God
sets his face "like flint," never to waver despite opposition to his task. Whatever obstacles impede the journey and however bleak the ending promises to
be, Jesus' commitment to God's will, which he proclaimed in the wilderness
(4:1–13) and confirmed by his ministry in Galilee, will stand firm.

Jesus' journey to Jerusalem begins with a detour through Samaria.
While the route from Galilee to Jerusalem through the highlands of
Samaria might seem on the one hand to be the most direct route, it is also
a route most Jews would avoid. Galilean pilgrims en route to Jerusalem
were known to encounter a hostile reception there, in a territory occupied
by a people who shared a common ancestry with the Jews, but who now
were their hated enemies.

The hatred between the two peoples dated at least to the Assyrian conquest of the eighth century B.C.E. What historical events one believes underlie that hatred depends on whose reports one reads. The Samaritans claimed to have maintained the worship of the God of Israel in their land, whereas the other Israelites became corrupted during their extended times in exile. The Jewish version of the same events (which is the one most familiar to Christian readers, since the Jewish point of view came to dominate in the period following the exiles' return) has their ancestors remaining faithful by accepting God's judgment against them, whereas the Samaritans consorted with their pagan captors and became corrupt in both ethics and religious practice. Charges and countercharges continued and even grew in intensity during the intervening centuries. To the Jews, the Samaritans came to symbolize corruption and uncleanness, and Jews avoided all contact with them (see John 4:9).

Luke sees the basis for a new twist in the relationship between Jews and Samaritans in the life of the church. In this passage, Jesus does not accede to the plan of James and John, the volatile "sons of thunder," who want to call down fire from heaven upon the inhabitants of the villages where they are not welcomed, in an act reminiscent of the prophet Elijah (2 Kings 1:1–12). Instead, Jesus apparently follows his own earlier instructions to the twelve (9:5), which are repeated in 10:10–12, that when they are not received in any village or household, they should simply move on. Later in the Gospel, Samaritans twice serve as positive role models for Christian behavior (10:29–37; 17:11–19), and twice in Acts a mission to the Samaritans is explicitly mentioned (1:8; 8:5–25). Clearly, old animosities cannot define life in the new community gathered around Jesus.

Several interesting narrative parallels exist between this story and that of Jesus' preaching in Nazareth that inaugurated his Galilean ministry. In both accounts there is an allusion to the prophet Elijah. In 4:25–27, Elijah and Elisha serve as positive models whom Jesus will emulate, whereas in 9:54–55 that prophet's fiercer side is rejected. Both accounts introduce major sections of the Gospel with stories of Jesus' rejection by the townspeople of a village, and in that way serve as foreshadowings of Jesus' rejection by the religious and political leadership as well as by the people of Jerusalem at the journey's end. Both here and in 4:30, Jesus' rejection serves to propel his mission to new places, as indeed his rejection in Jerusalem propels the gospel "to all nations," even "to the ends of the earth" (24:47; Acts 1:8).

## HARDER WORDS
## ABOUT DISCIPLESHIP
### Luke 9:57–62

> 9:57  As they were going along the road, someone said to him, "I will follow you wherever you go." [58] And Jesus said to him, "Foxes have holes, and birds of the air have nests; but the Son of Man has nowhere to lay his head." [59] To another he said, "Follow me." But he said, "Lord, first let me go and bury my father." [60] But Jesus said to him, "Let the dead bury their own dead; but as for you, go and proclaim the kingdom of God." [61] Another said, "I will follow you, Lord; but let me first say farewell to those at my home." [62] Jesus said to him, "No one who puts a hand to the plow and looks back is fit for the kingdom of God."

Gone are the simpler days when disciples were invited to follow Jesus and dropped everything to follow him (5:10–11, 27–28). The journey to Jerusalem begins with three people who express a desire to follow Jesus, but who are rebuffed. It costs something to follow Jesus now, and those who would join the movement need to be aware of how high that cost is.

All three responses address basic concerns for security and identity. The first announces a lifestyle of homelessness. Even wild birds and animals have places of shelter, in contrast to the "Son of Man" (9:58). This verse is an important window into Luke's use of that enigmatic term. First, it seems to refer to Jesus himself: Do they recognize his radical social rootlessness, which by becoming disciples they too will share? However, the term also encompasses Jesus' followers. It is not a title—or a fate—reserved to Jesus, but neither does it refer to "anyone," or humankind in general. Instead, it echoes the use of the term in Ezekiel, where God calls the prophet by that term (NRSV translates the term as "mortal") when giving Ezekiel a new prophetic commission to carry out (see, for example, Ezek. 2:1; 3:1, 4, 10, 25; 4:1; 5:1; 6:1 and many more). Likewise, those who would follow Jesus are sent out under God's commission, and their fate too will be to live without even the basic security of a dwelling place.

The second inquirer wants to delay following Jesus. His reason is a legitimate one, not only in terms of human emotion and sense of responsibility for one's family, but especially in that society where burying one's parents was a solemn obligation from which no one was exempt. Even priests serving in the temple were obliged to incur the ritual impurity brought on by contact with a corpse in the case of their own parents. Nothing is said about the age or health of the parent in this case, so it is not clear whether the delay envisioned is brief or long, and the length of time does not appear to be the issue.

Jesus' response denies the legitimacy of any such cultural obligations—and emotional ties—to one's biological family. The wording is harsh, implying that those who are not following Jesus are already among "the dead," so they might as well handle the burial chores. Family ties, like the security of a home, are superseded by the demands of following Jesus (see also 8:19–21; 18:29–30).

The third would-be follower asks only for a delay long enough to say good-bye to his family. Elijah granted Elisha permission for just such a leave-taking before the younger man took up his prophetic ministry (1 Kings 19:19–21). Here that request too is denied. The lines are drawn with stark clarity: One is either with Jesus one hundred percent, or one is against him (11:23). In this new phase of Jesus' ministry, discipleship is not something to be taken lightly or entered into casually. Almost with every step, the stakes get higher.

## "LAMBS" AND "WOLVES": MORE MISSIONARIES SENT OUT
## Luke 10:1–24

### The Missionaries' Mandate (Luke 10:1–16)

10:1 **After this the Lord appointed seventy others and sent them on ahead of him in pairs to every town and place where he himself intended to go. ² He said to them, "The harvest is plentiful, but the laborers are few; therefore ask the Lord of the harvest to send out laborers into his harvest. ³ Go on your way. See, I am sending you out like lambs into the midst of wolves. ⁴ Carry no purse, no bag, no sandals; and greet no one on the road. ⁵ Whatever house you enter, first say, 'Peace to this house!' ⁶ And if anyone is there who shares in peace, your peace will rest on that person; but if not, it will return to you. ⁷ Remain in the same house, eating and drinking whatever they provide, for the laborer deserves to be paid. Do not move about from house to house. ⁸ Whenever you enter a town and its people welcome you, eat what is set before you; ⁹ cure the sick who are there, and say to them, 'The kingdom of God has come near to you.' ¹⁰ But whenever you enter a town and they do not welcome you, go out into its streets and say, ¹¹ 'Even the dust of your town that clings to our feet, we wipe off in protest against you. Yet know this: the kingdom of God has come near.' ¹² I tell you, on that day it will be more tolerable for Sodom than for that town.**

**¹³ "Woe to you, Chorazin! Woe to you, Bethsaida! For if the deeds of power done in you had been done in Tyre and Sidon, they would have repented long ago, sitting in sackcloth and ashes. ¹⁴ But at the judgment it will be more tolerable for Tyre and Sidon than for you. ¹⁵ And you, Capernaum,**

will you be exalted to heaven?
No, you will be brought down to Hades.
[16] "Whoever listens to you listens to me, and whoever rejects you rejects me, and whoever rejects me rejects the one who sent me."

Only Luke has this second account of Jesus' sending out of disciples. It appears to be an elaboration of 9:1–6, with the basic story amplified by a number of loosely related sayings. These emissaries—sent out two by two, like the twelve in 9:1–6 (see also Acts 8:14; 13:2 15:32, 40; Rom. 16:7)—are given no specific destination of their own. On the contrary, they are to be a group of advance-teams traveling ahead of Jesus.

How ought we to understand the identity and task of these missionaries? Traditional interpretations of the passage have seen it as the foundation of the Gentile mission, since seventy is the number of the Gentile nations (Gen. 10:2–20). The instruction that the missionaries are to eat whatever is put in front of them (10:7–8) might support such a reading, for concern about food laws was a big issue among Jewish Christians in the early years when the church began to include substantial numbers of Gentile members (see the account of Peter's vision in Acts 10:9–16). On the other hand, some manuscripts of Luke note the number of missionaries as seventy-two, and if that were the original reading, it would not function as easily as a number symbolic of the Gentiles. Furthermore, seventy itself is also the number of the elders chosen by Moses to assist him in leading Israel (Exod. 24:1; Num. 11:16–25), so it is not necessarily a number linked to Gentiles. These ambiguities, added to the fact that the missionaries are not sent out of Israel, but rather to the same places where Jesus himself intended to go, leave the significance of this account uncertain. Perhaps it is Luke's attempt to look even beyond Jerusalem to a time when the mission—Jesus as proclaimed in the gospel—would encompass the whole known universe. Perhaps, instead, it is merely an escalation of the earlier story, where both threats to their work and the success of their mission are heightened (10:17–20, contrasted with 9:40–41).

Like the twelve sent out earlier, these missionaries are to travel without baggage or supplies. They are defenseless "lambs" in a potentially threatening environment of "wolves." They are to depend on the hospitality of the people to whose homes they come, and they are not to dally on the road, presumably engaging in idle chatter (10:4). The households and villages that receive them are to be blessed (10:6, 8–9). Those that do not are simply to be abandoned (10:6, 10–11). The judgment and punishment of such places are not for the missionaries to execute, but are in the hands of God (10:12–15).

The missionaries' task includes proclaiming the reign of God and healing (10:9), and also, apparently, looking for co-workers to help in the "harvest" (10:2). While the harvest often serves as a metaphor for God's judgment at the end of time (see, for example, 3:17), here it functions as a
metaphor for an urgent task that must be completed without delay, or else
all will be lost. The missionaries are to focus their attention on individual
households, in contrast, for example, to mass meetings for teaching or
preaching. In exchange for their missionary labor (10:5–7; see also 1 Cor.
9:14; 1 Tim. 5:18), they are to be provided for as members of those households. They are neither to shop around for the best living arrangements
(10:7b) nor to adapt their message to the warmth of the hospitality. On
the contrary, the message is always the same: "The kingdom of God has
come near to you" (10:9, 11). Whether that word is good or bad news depends on the response of the people to whom the word comes.

The woes proclaimed against inhospitable towns (10:12–15) are to be
pronounced in public—in the streets (10:10). They begin with the warning that even Sodom, on which fire and brimstone rained down (Gen.
19:24–28), fared better than they will fare when they come under judgment for their rejection of the missionaries. Chorazin has not been mentioned previously in Luke, but Bethsaida (9:10–17) and Capernaum (4:23;
7:1) have been identified as places that have witnessed Jesus' "deeds of
power." Instead of being privileged for having witnessed those deeds, the
people of those villages now face closer scrutiny. Their lack of hospitality
despite what they have witnessed will lead to a harsher judgment than that
against even Tyre and Sidon, for even such notorious pagan cities as Tyre
and Sidon would have repented in the face of such evidence as the others
have witnessed. The warning to people in Luke's church not to presume
on their Christian history is clear. Not what they have witnessed, but how
they have received strangers bearing the gospel, will determine their ultimate fate.

The concluding saying to the missionaries (10:16) replays in a slightly
different key the saying in 9:48. There, in the context of an internal squab-
ble among the disciples over who is greatest, Jesus tells the disciples to
welcome a child (a person without power or honor in that society) with
the honor they would willingly accord to Jesus. To receive a child in that
way is to welcome Jesus himself, and even the one who sent Jesus, namely
God. In contrast to the earlier passage, in 10:16 the disciples who have become missionaries stand in the place of the child. By implication, they too
are to be without honor and power in the world's terms, but in the value
system of the gospel there is another side to the story. To heed or reject

these missionaries is to heed or reject Jesus and the one in whose authority Jesus is sent. One's hospitality toward the missionaries has eternal consequences!

## Signs of Success (Luke 10:17–20)

**10:17 The seventy returned with joy, saying, "Lord, in your name even the demons submit to us!"** [18] **He said to them, "I watched Satan fall from heaven like a flash of lightning.** [19] **See, I have given you authority to tread on snakes and scorpions, and over all the power of the enemy; and nothing will hurt you.** [20] **Nevertheless, do not rejoice at this, that the spirits submit to you, but rejoice that your names are written in heaven."**

This time the missionaries can report success where earlier there had been failure (9:40). Jesus' reply to their triumphant announcement both assures them that their present victory will continue into the future (10:17, 19) and sets their mission in heavenly perspective. Earlier, Luke has called "Satan" simply "the devil" (4:2–13; 8:12), but from here on he uses the name Satan (11:18; 13:16; 22:3, 31). Luke draws on the traditional affirmation that Satan once dwelt in heaven (Job 1:6; 2:1; John 12:31; Rev. 12:7) but has fallen from that place of power. The picture is dramatic. The tenses of the verbs in Greek express action that continues over time: "I *was watching* Satan *falling* from heaven like a flash of lightning" (emphasis added). As Jesus watches, Satan explodes high in a burst of light like a Roman candle, and the cascade of sparks spills slowly toward earth. Satan can no more be restored to the former place of power than one could reassemble a Roman candle that has already been fired. For Satan, the show is over.

Satan's fall and the image of the disciples' authority to tread on snakes and scorpions without being harmed (Ps. 91:13) together announce the defeat of the powers of evil in the ministry of the seventy. As splendid as such power is, the real ground for their rejoicing is not power but life: Their names "written in heaven" (10:20). Their authority is never something they own or for which they can take credit. Instead, like Jesus' own authority, it points beyond them to God as the source of all authority, and indeed of life itself.

## Thanksgivings and Blessings (Luke 10:21–24)

**10:21 At that same hour Jesus rejoiced in the Holy Spirit and said, "I thank you, Father, Lord of heaven and earth, because you have hidden these things**

from the wise and the intelligent and have revealed them to infants; yes, Father, for such was your gracious will. [22] All things have been handed over
to me by my Father; and no one knows who the Son is except the Father, or
who the Father is except the Son and anyone to whom the Son chooses to
reveal him."
[23] Then turning to the disciples, Jesus said to them privately, "Blessed are
the eyes that see what you see! [24] For I tell you that many prophets and kings
desired to see what you see, but did not see it, and to hear what you hear,
but did not hear it."

The account of the mission of the seventy ends in a liturgical fragment
consisting of thanksgivings and blessings. The presentation of Jesus'
prayer and the mention of the Holy Spirit signal the importance of this
moment in the Gospel. The language already looks toward Jesus' words
to the disciples at the last supper before his arrest, when he hands over to
them the reign that God entrusted to him (22:29–30). In language that
also echoes both the style and content of the Gospel of John (see, for example, John 3:31–36; 5:19–38; 17:2–9), Jesus affirms his position as medi-
ator between God and the disciples (10:22). Jesus' affirmation of this role
places him in the tradition of Wisdom or *Sophia* as an expression of God's
own reality ( Job 28:12–28; Prov. 8:22–36), which is taken up and adapted
in the hymn to the Word or *Logos* in John 1:1–18.

Jesus' thanksgiving to God and affirmation of the seventy continues the
theme of reversal that has marked Luke's Gospel from the beginning: Not
to the wise and intelligent, but to mere infants have these things been revealed (10:21). For this reason—God's surprising and revelatory grace,
and not their own merits—Jesus calls the disciples "blessed" (10:23). The
very moment of vision and insight marks a boundary: What their ancestors have merely longed for, the disciples have witnessed. The spectacu-
lar fall of Satan, marking the defeat of evil not only in Jesus' presence
(4:13) but also in those who carry forward the story in Jesus' absence, signals the start of a new day.

## ETERNAL LIFE AND NEIGHBOR LOVE
Luke 10:25–37

10:25 Just then a lawyer stood up to test Jesus. "Teacher," he said, "what
must I do to inherit eternal life?" [26] He said to him, "What is written in the
law? What do you read there?" [27] He answered, "You shall love the Lord
your God with all your heart, and with all your soul, and with all your

strength, and with all your mind; and your neighbor as yourself." [28] And he said to him, "You have given the right answer; do this, and you will live."

[29] But wanting to justify himself, he asked Jesus, "And who is my neighbor?" [30] Jesus replied, "A man was going down from Jerusalem to Jericho, and fell into the hands of robbers, who stripped him, beat him, and went away, leaving him half dead. [31] Now by chance a priest was going down that road; and when he saw him, he passed by on the other side. [32] So likewise a Levite, when he came to the place and saw him, passed by on the other side. [33] But a Samaritan while traveling came near him; and when he saw him, he was moved with pity. [34] He went to him and bandaged his wounds, having poured oil and wine on them. Then he put him on his own animal, brought him to an inn, and took care of him. [35] The next day he took out two denarii, gave them to the innkeeper, and said, 'Take care of him; and when I come back, I will repay you whatever more you spend.' [36] Which of these three, do you think, was a neighbor to the man who fell into the hands of the robbers?" [37] He said, "The one who showed him mercy." Jesus said to him, "Go and do likewise."

The awe-filled moment shared by Jesus and the disciples is all too quickly interrupted: A lawyer—a professional "wise and intelligent" person (10:21)—intends to test Jesus (10:25). The test question is what one must do to inherit eternal life. One might surmise from the question that the lawyer is a Pharisee whose theology included belief in the resurrection of the dead. The test may have been to see whether Jesus shared that perspective, or rather was a Sadducee (the aristocratic party connected to the temple, which did not believe in the resurrection).

The exchange of questions and answers that ensues (10:26–37) fits what we know about the way various points of religious law were debated among the Pharisees, who were the principal forerunners of rabbinic Judaism. Unlike similar dialogues recorded in Matthew 22:34–40 and Mark 12:28–31, where Jesus answers a question about the first or greatest commandment in the law by citing Deuteronomy 6:5 and Leviticus 19:18, in Luke it is the lawyer who cites those verses. The two commandments to love God with one's whole being, and to love one's neighbor as oneself, represent the heart of the Jewish law. The fact that in Luke it is the Jewish legal expert who makes that connection makes it clear that Luke himself did not understand Jesus to be the source of that affirmation. Rather, he drew it from his Jewish background. In fact, the following story is told about a famous rabbi who lived around the time of Jesus. A Gentile challenged the rabbi that if he could recite the entire Torah or "Law" while standing on one foot, the Gentile would convert to Judaism. The rabbi stood on one foot and said, "You shall love the Lord your God with all your heart, and with all your mind, and with all your strength; and you shall love your neighbor as yourself. That is the whole law. The rest is commentary." The rabbi then put his foot down, and his challenger was converted.

The lawyer in Luke's story receives Jesus' praise for his response (10:28), but he then appears to get caught in belaboring the "commentary" on his own answer (10:29). By saying that the lawyer wanted "to justify himself," Luke implies that he was seeking a definition of "neighbor" that would set clear limits on who was to be loved as he loved himself. Does the term include only family? More distant relations? People with whom he shares particular social connections? People within a specific geographical area? The question fits not only the personal concern of someone trying to live a righteous life, but also the context of Luke's church with its expanding ethnic and geographical boundaries. Just how far does our responsibility extend? By way of an answer, Luke presents a parable.

This parable is found only in Luke. That fact, plus the fact that the preceding dialogue in Luke is significantly different from its parallels in Matthew and Mark, lead most interpreters to conclude that it is part of Luke's special material about Jesus. Some details in Matthew's version of the dialogue (Matt. 22:34–40) echo Luke's and differ from the version in Mark 12:28–31, on which Matthew principally depends (for example, the identification of the questioner as a lawyer, his address to Jesus as "Teacher," the reference to "the law," and the lack of the introductory affirmation, "Hear, O Israel: the Lord our God, the Lord is one" [Mark 12:29]). Such details lead other interpreters to suggest that Luke's version of the dialogue, possibly with the parable attached, were part of the other source shared by both Matthew and Luke. Matthew, then, may have chosen basically to follow Mark in not presenting the parable because of the greater sensitivity in Matthew's Jewish Christian audience to animosity between Samaritans and Jews.

Wherever it came from, the parable presents a number of problems. In its present context, it serves as an example story that illustrates *how* a neighbor acts. That, however, represents a shift from the question to which it allegedly responds, "*Who* is my neighbor" whom I am to love as I love myself? Jesus' concluding question to the lawyer about who proved a neighbor to the injured man (10:36) yields the obvious answer (10:37): Being a neighbor entails doing acts of mercy. But that was not the question. At issue is recognizing the man in the ditch as someone to love. How does the parable engage that discussion for the lawyer and for others in Jesus' audience?

There are six characters or groups of characters in the story. Three play active roles: the priest, the Levite, and the Samaritan. Three others are in the background: the wounded man, the robbers, and the innkeeper. The lawyer would have viewed all six in a negative light. The priest and Levite were associated with the temple. While these religious leaders would have been persons generally respected in their society, the Pharisees often were in tension with the temple and its cult. The Pharisees concentrated their efforts on a careful interpretation of Torah that would make its precepts and requirements understandable and observable by the laity, and not only by the priestly classes. The Pharisees were motivated by the belief that an entire people prepared by living lives of purity and obedience to Torah would be truly pleasing to God.

The Pharisee's scorn for the Samaritan would be obvious, and the underlying ethnic animosity would be increased by the fact that such a traveler—like the wounded man—was probably a merchant or trader. Traders were notoriously dishonest, and their itinerant lifestyle and constant interaction with all sorts of people made it impossible for them to observe even the most basic laws concerning food preparation and purity. For that same reason the wounded man also would not have evoked the lawyer's empathy. Particularly as the man lay naked and perhaps dead, he would have represented someone to be avoided as a likely source of contamination. Only basic human empathy—"compassion"—could have led a "respectable" person to turn a caring hand toward the victim. Innkeepers too were a despised group. Their lives centered around places of public accommodation where transients like traders could be found. Only people with no family in the area and no social or economic claims on anyone's hospitality would ever stay in inns, and decent people would avoid them at all cost. Not only the Pharisee in the story, but also many (if not most) in Jesus' audience, would probably have shared in the general distaste and discomfort at the scene and cast of characters so far.

That left only the robbers. In first century Palestine, they would probably not have been simply muggers or highwaymen, but rather some of the roving terrorists staging their own form of protest against various types of official and unofficial exploitation of the poor. They would assault well-to-do travelers in the countryside, relieving them of their wealth and often leaving them with a persuasive reminder not to collaborate with the exploiters. A lawyer would have reason to be frightened of such robbers, as well as a general distaste for their threat to the public order. Others in Jesus' audience, however, may well have seen the robbers as the only sympathetic characters in the story. Some might even have engaged in such activity themselves. But the robbers get no active role in the parable: Their act is done, and only the human consequences remain to confront and to confound.

How Luke's own audience might have perceived the characters is harder to discern. Ethnic Jews would probably have caught the irony of the Samaritan's role as the positive example, and others might have picked up the story of the continuing animosity between Jews and Samaritans. Temple officials would have been an anachronism, symbolic only of professional religious leaders (perhaps even confused for Luke's audience with the successors to the Pharisees who, by then, were playing that role in the synagogues). In the context of Luke's city, robbers would probably not have been seen as likely freedom fighters, but simply as criminals who posed a threat to everyone alike. Human empathy for the victim (perhaps the blend of empathy, curiosity, and horror with which modern readers of the story drive past a car accident or a crime scene) may have been all that remained. For them as for us—and for Jesus' audience as well—the drama of the story rather than its cast of characters conveys its meaning and confronts the question: "Who is my neighbor?"

The story begins with the assault having happened, the robbers already off the stage, and the victim of the crime lying half dead. In perfect symmetry, the actions of the priest and Levite unfold: Each approaches, sees, and passes by on the other side. No explanation is given. Since both are said to be traveling *from* Jerusalem, concerns about ritual purity needed for temple service, or about the urgency of their public responsibility, provide no excuse. Did they suspect a setup, where the robbers still lurked to jump on anyone foolish enough to stop? Were they simply disgusted at the condition of the man's beaten body? Nothing is said: They simply pass by.

Since stories usually unfold in patterns of three, we expect another to arrive and resolve the tension. Who will it be who can clean away the fetid atmosphere that pervades the story? The third character is surprising, first because of his ethnic identity. A Samaritan on that road would already have been in hostile territory, even without the threat of more robbers. He too would have been affected by the same regulations concerning touching a corpse that the priest and Levite would have recognized, as well as the same commandment to love his neighbor.

The Samaritan too approaches, sees, and is "moved with pity" (10:33). The parallels among the actions of the three characters are thus broken, and the story stretches out in a carefully detailed account of the Samaritan's action—everything from first aid through long-term convalescence

(10:34–35). The lawyer summarizes the Samaritan's actions as showing "mercy" (10:37), to which Jesus responds, "Go and do likewise."

"Compassion" (10:33—a better translation than "pity") and "mercy" are the only clues given to how the parable really responds to the lawyer's follow-up question, "Who is my neighbor?" If that question implies the desire for a list of external criteria related to the neighbor for whom one is to care, the answer provides internal criteria for the care-giver. The question "Who is my neighbor?" is changed into "Who am I in this relationship of neighboring?" A person who is loved as one loves one's self cannot be the *object* of one's action, because a fundamental human drive is to be the *subject*—the one doing the action and making the decisions—of one's own life.

The neighbor, then, is someone with whom one feels empathy and identifies as another human being. No one can simply *have* a neighbor; one must also *be* a neighbor. Neighboring is a two-way street. The parable changes in a fundamental way how the question about neighbors is usually framed. The Gospel records no one's response to this story—neither the lawyer's nor the onlookers'. The story simply stands as yet another challenge to the transformation of daily life and business as usual, which lies at the heart of the practice of discipleship.

## MARY AND MARTHA
### Luke 10:38–42

> 10:38 **Now as they went on their way, he entered a certain village, where a woman named Martha welcomed him into her home.** [39] **She had a sister named Mary, who sat at the Lord's feet and listened to what he was saying.** [40] **But Martha was distracted by her many tasks; so she came to him and asked, "Lord, do you not care that my sister has left me to do all the work by myself? Tell her then to help me."** [41] **But the Lord answered her, "Martha, Martha, you are worried and distracted by many things;** [42] **there is need of only one thing. Mary has chosen the better part, which will not be taken away from her."**

The narrative continues with a note about a change of location, but the name of the village to which they have come is not given. The introduction of the characters as Martha and her sister Mary lead persons familiar with the Gospel of John to understand them to be the sisters of Lazarus, who lived in Bethany (John 11:1–12:8). Luke does not provide that additional information, but it seems likely that the same women are meant.

The only detail speaking against it is that in Luke Martha is said to welcome Jesus into "her" home (10:38), which would be an unusual way for Luke to describe it if he knew of the existence of her brother Lazarus. On the other hand, both women are named in two Gospels that appear to come from different sources of traditions about Jesus. That fact testifies to the prominence of these women in the Christian tradition, especially given the many women who remain unnamed or identified only by a husband's or a father's name.

In both Luke and John, Martha appears as the more active and outspoken sister, while Mary seems to hang back in the shadows. In John, both sisters eventually get starring roles—Martha in making the first formal confession of Jesus as "the Messiah, the Son of God, the one coming into the world" (11:27), and Mary in anointing Jesus (12:1–8). In Luke, however, Mary is the one praised for having "chosen the better part," while Martha receives only condescending criticism for her hard work (10: 41–42).

This story stands in an interesting parallelism with the preceding one. In the previous story, the respectable lawyer, who is concerned with the definition and delimitation of details of the law, learns from a most unlikely person to focus on what he himself should know is the heart of the law: He is told to "go and do." In this story, Martha, who excels in "doing"—in the traditional woman's task of providing for her household—learns from her own sister a different model: Jesus tells her to sit and listen. In the first story, the lawyer is left on his own to draw his conclusion, whereas in this one, Jesus gives the answer to the problem that Martha has identified. Both stories introduce radically fresh perspectives: A Samaritan models the compassionate ways of God that redefine "neighbor," and a woman is praised for not fulfilling her prescribed social role.

Despite what seems to be the point Luke is making, however, the story of Mary and Martha is a sad one for women. Martha, who welcomes Jesus and expends considerable energy in providing hospitality for him and those traveling with him, is called "distracted" and "worried." She is blamed for doing what she would have been expected to do in her society. Furthermore, she is portrayed as whining to the man Jesus about her sister's failure to help her, instead of resolving the matter herself, woman to woman. Instead of receiving a blessing as someone who welcomes Jesus and his followers (9:48; 10:8–9), she receives a scolding.

Mary fares no better. She gets to sit at Jesus' feet and listen to his teaching, just as the male disciples do, and she is praised by Jesus for it. But she is a silent learner. She poses no questions to Jesus, and she does not interact with him as the male disciples do. Unlike male disciples who are described as learning from Jesus, and who then are charged to carry the message on to others, Mary gets no commission to preach, no speaking part whatsoever. Whatever may have been Jesus' relationship with women followers (8:2–3), Luke allots them carefully circumscribed roles. For them, the lifestyle of discipleship—at least in Luke's church—promises few real changes.

## LESSONS ON PRAYER
## Luke 11:1–13

### The "Lord's Prayer" (Luke 11:1–4)

> 11:1 **He was praying in a certain place, and after he had finished, one of his disciples said to him, "Lord, teach us to pray, as John taught his disciples."** [2] **He said to them, "When you pray, say:**
> **Father, hallowed be your name.**
> **Your kingdom come.**
> [3] **Give us each day our daily bread.**
> [4] **And forgive us our sins,**
> **for we ourselves forgive everyone indebted to us.**
> **And do not bring us to the time of trial."**

Jesus' own time of prayer becomes the occasion for a request from one of the disciples that Jesus teach them to pray. The example of John the Baptist suggests that the disciple was asking for a prayer that would be characteristic of their particular community. The "Lord's Prayer" has played just such a role in the life of the church, and this episode in the Gospel serves to explain its origin with Jesus himself.

The prayer itself is found in two forms in the Gospels. The version in Matthew 6:9–13, with its carefully crafted poetry and liturgical rhythms, and with the addition of a concluding doxology ("For the kingdom and the power and the glory are yours forever"), is the one most commonly used in the contemporary church. Luke's version may actually have been used in his church, or its simpler and less-polished form may represent his attempt to preserve a form of the prayer carried in the source he shared with Matthew.

Luke's prayer consists of two petitions that focus attention on God (11:2), and three petitions that address human need (11:3–4). The two focused on God essentially affirm God's sovereignty. The prayer for God's reign to come expresses the human longing mirrored in God's own intention that has been proclaimed from the very beginning of Luke's Gospel. For God's "name"—God's very being—to be made holy would mean simply the realization of God's divine nature. Together, these petitions affirm the victory of the divine will over projects and relationships designed for less worthy purposes.

The petitions that express human need pray for bread, for forgiveness, and for an escape from "the time of trial." All three are in the plural, expressing not the private piety of an individual, but the hope of a community. The first and third of these "we" petitions are as simple in form as they are puzzling in content.

The word modifying "bread," which the NRSV translates in the traditional way as "daily," occurs only in this petition of the Lord's Prayer in both Luke and Matthew (11:3; Matt. 6:11), so what it really means is not clear. In addition to "daily bread," some of the meanings that are suggested are "bread necessary for existence," "bread for today," "bread for tomorrow," or "bread for the future." However one resolves the specific reading of this adjective (which blends the verb "to be" and a preposition whose meanings convey proximity or direction toward), it is clear that the meaning has something to do with the food necessary to sustain life. Matthew's prayer is that this bread be given as a onetime event (as can be seen by the reference to "this day," and by his use of a verb tense that indicates a onetime, completed action). Luke's prayer, on the other hand, asks that the bread be given "each day," over and over again (the verb tense emphasizes repeated or continued action). Particularly in Luke's form, it is a prayer most appropriate to persons living in a time and place of frequent famines, undependable harvests, and economic exploitation of the poor, such as was the case for Jesus and his followers, and for many in Luke's church as well. The petition resonates even more clearly as a prayer of discipleship in a community whose ministry was to be carried out in utter dependence on the hospitality of communities and households to which they came.

The third "we" petition asks simply that those praying not be brought to the "time of trial" (11:4c). This is usually understood to refer to a final judgment at the end of time. Because none can avoid facing that trial, the petition is usually understood as a prayer to withstand the trial, or to receive a favorable verdict in the divine courtroom. Luke, and even the source on which he drew, may, however, have had something much more human and immediate in mind. The petition may have been intended as a prayer that the community be spared the accusations and trials before various secular and religious authorities, in which some Christians were being required to witness to their faith even to the point of martyrdom (12:11–12).

In contrast to the two apparently (but deceptively) simple petitions, the petition for forgiveness (11:4a and b) is complex in both form and wording. Matthew and Luke differ in their wording of the initial clause of the petition, with Matthew's version praying for forgiveness of "debts," and Luke's for forgiveness of "sins." The difficulty is resolved if the prayer indeed goes back to Jesus and thus would have been expressed not in Greek, but in Aramaic or possibly in Hebrew. In each of those Semitic languages there is a single word that means both monetary "debts" and moral "trespasses" or "sins." Matthew preserves the meaning of "debts" in both halves of the petition in the prayer ("And forgive us our debts, as we also have forgiven our debtors"), and reflects the other meaning in a verse of elaboration that follows the prayer (Matt. 6:14). Luke retains both meanings within the prayer itself: "And forgive us our sins, for we ourselves forgive everyone indebted to us."

The petition for forgiveness is the only petition in the prayer that includes an action by those who are praying. How one should understand the human and divine actions being related is another point of difficulty in the prayer. One might logically expect that our forgiving of others' offenses against us would be mandated because God has forgiven us on a much grander scale: If God is willing to forgive us for everything that separates us from God, surely we should forgive those relatively minor offenses other people commit against us. Neither version of the prayer, however, offers such an argument from the greater to the lesser. Matthew's prayer suggests a parity in manner or scope—that God should forgive us in the way, or to the extent, that we forgive others: "Forgive us . . . *as* we also have forgiven" (Matt. 6:12). Luke suggests a relationship of effect and cause: "Forgive us . . . [*because*] we ourselves forgive . . ." (11:4a and b). Both readings on the surface seem to make human behavior and not God's grace the standard for forgiveness.

The problematic points in the second "we" petition are resolved when one recognizes the centrality of Jubilee images in the prayer as a whole, and particularly in this petition for forgiveness (see the discussion of 4:18). The Jubilee envisioned at the near boundary of God's reign, according to Isaiah 61:1, begins with an affirmation of God's sovereignty (here, the prayer that God's reign come). That Jubilee also includes "good news to the poor" (here reflected in the petition for bread as the physical basis to sustain life), and "release" or "forgiveness," both of monetary debts and of other expressions of captivity or enslavement. Human beings participate in this divine Jubilee as both forgivers and forgiven (see also Matt. 18:23–35). What is at stake is a wholly new basis for human interaction—the polar opposite of the systems of debt and obligation, patronage and merit, honor and shame, that characterize life under various human institutions and authorities. In the realm of God, those old rules are canceled, and all things are made new. It is a prayer to be both spoken and lived.

### Demand and Supply (Luke 11:5–13)

11:5 **And he said to them, "Suppose one of you has a friend, and you go to him at midnight and say to him, 'Friend, lend me three loaves of bread; 6 for a friend of mine has arrived, and I have nothing to set before him.' 7 And he answers from within, 'Do not bother me; the door has already been locked, and my children are with me in bed; I cannot get up and give you anything.' 8 I tell you, even though he will not get up and give him anything because he is his friend, at least because of his persistence he will get up and give him whatever he needs.**

9 **"So I say to you, Ask, and it will be given you; search, and you will find; knock, and the door will be opened for you. 10 For everyone who asks receives, and everyone who searches finds, and for everyone who knocks, the door will be opened. 11 Is there anyone among you who, if your child asks for a fish, will give a snake instead of a fish? 12 Or if the child asks for an egg, will give a scorpion? 13 If you then, who are evil, know how to give good gifts to your children, how much more will the heavenly Father give the Holy Spirit to those who ask him!"**

The lesson on prayer continues beyond the content of the prayer itself to emphasize the importance of persistence and determination in praying (11:5–8) and to assure the disciples of God's response to their prayer (11:9–13). The first point is made by means of a brief story. The story features three characters, all linked together in a chain of friendship. It blends the unlikely—a traveler arriving at midnight—and the assumed—obligations of hospitality among friends. Hospitality required that any guest arriving at one's home be offered something to eat. Bread was at the heart of the diet of rich and poor alike in first-century Palestine, and for a person of modest means, there would be little else but a few fruits and vegetables. Thus, the arrival of a guest required bread.

In the absence of supermarkets open around the clock, even the city dwellers to whom Luke wrote would have understood the seriousness of the problem being posed. For an audience familiar with the situation in a

Palestinian village of the first century, however, the point would have been even clearer. Providing the day's supply of bread for one's family was a project of considerable labor. Several hours of grinding would be needed to prepare the flour, and that part of the task would usually have been done late in the day. On the following morning the prepared dough would be brought to the village baker to be baked. Without preservatives, the bread would have had to be baked fresh each day, or at most every other day. Thus, to be caught without bread when a guest arrived at midnight would leave the host likely to be unable to meet the demands of hospitality.

In the story, the friend who has been embarrassed in that way awakens another friend in search of the needed bread. That friend, having locked up the house for the night, does not want to disturb the whole family who would have been asleep in their one-room dwelling. That excuse holds up even against the heavy demands of their shared friendship, but it crumbles in the face of the "persistence" of the friend to whom the traveler had originally come.

The image that comes to mind is of the friend standing in the street pounding relentlessly on the door and shouting to the one in the house. One can imagine that between them they manage to wake up the whole town, never mind disturbing the family! The second friend gives the first friend the bread just to get him to go away. It has all the makings of a comedy skit. But the word translated "persistence" would be better translated "shamelessness." With that reading, the meaning of the parable shifts. In a culture where criteria of honor and shame governed every aspect of life (including what one friend might expect from another), the middle friend's behavior is in fact "shameless" (in the way he violated the boundaries of his friend's privacy and disrupted the peace of the town). He sacrifices his own proper "shame" in order to obtain the help needed to care for his guest. The friend who at first refuses to help is won over by his neighbor's willingness to risk his own vulnerability for the sake of the traveler's need.

In the first passage, one might conclude that it was simply stubbornness that carried the day—or, in this case, the night. As a teaching about prayer, then, the story would suggest that one has only to badger God in order to get what one wants. With the reading of "shamelessness," however, the story suggests that the key to getting a response is being willing to set aside one's own prestige and security in pursuit of a request. The latter reading is consistent with Luke's confrontation and reversal of systems of honor and shame elsewhere in the Gospel, and thus it is probably closer to the meaning Luke intends.

The teachings on prayer continue with a double assurance that one's requests will be met (11:9–10). Both of the assurances consist of three modes of petition—ask, search, and knock—each followed by the appropriate affirmative response—receive, find, and the door will be opened. Does this sixfold affirmation pertain to any request one might make? Lest one turn the assurances into a recipe for greed, the teachings conclude with a word about the appropriate request to make in one's prayer (11:11–13). The section begins with the observation that not even a human parent would give a child something harmful when the child asks for food. A simple argument from the lesser to the greater (if a flawed or even "evil" human being gives good things, how much more will God give good things) is the way the parallel in Matthew 7:9–11 reads. Luke, however, specifies that the Holy Spirit is the superlatively good thing that God will give to those who ask. Luke thus reinforces the connection between prayer and the Holy Spirit as the experience of God's presence and God's blessing.

## SPIRITS AND POWER
## Luke 11:14–28

11:14 Now he was casting out a demon that was mute; when the demon had gone out, the one who had been mute spoke, and the crowds were amazed. 15 But some of them said, "He casts out demons by Beelzebul, the ruler of the demons." 16 Others, to test him, kept demanding from him a sign from heaven. 17 But he knew what they were thinking and said to them, "Every kingdom divided against itself becomes a desert, and house falls on house. 18 If Satan also is divided against himself, how will his kingdom stand?—for you say that I cast out the demons by Beelzebul. 19 Now if I cast out the demons by Beelzebul, by whom do your exorcists cast them out? Therefore they will be your judges. 20 But if it is by the finger of God that I cast out the demons, then the kingdom of God has come to you. 21 When a strong man, fully armed, guards his castle, his property is safe. 22 But when one stronger than he attacks him and overpowers him, he takes away his armor in which he trusted and divides his plunder. 23 Whoever is not with me is against me, and whoever does not gather with me scatters.

24 "When the unclean spirit has gone out of a person, it wanders through waterless regions looking for a resting place, but not finding any, it says, 'I will return to my house from which I came.' 25 When it comes, it finds it swept and put in order. 26 Then it goes and brings seven other spirits more evil than itself, and they enter and live there; and the last state of that person is worse than the first."

²⁷ **While he was saying this, a woman in the crowd raised her voice and said to him, "Blessed is the womb that bore you and the breasts that nursed you!"** ²⁸ **But he said, "Blessed rather are those who hear the word of God and obey it!"**

Luke mentions no change of scene, but Jesus is clearly no longer in seclusion with the disciples as in the preceding episode. Instead, they are in the midst of "crowds" that keep growing during the next section of teachings (11:14, 29; 12:1). The opening summary report of Jesus' exorcism of a demon, to the amazement of the crowds, introduces a controversy over the source of Jesus' power. At issue is not whether he has power over demons: The previously mute person's restored speech is ample testimony to that. But some of the onlookers try to challenge Jesus' credibility by claiming that the demons obey him because he is working for their boss, "Beelzebul, the ruler of the demons." Others ask for a sign from heaven. That "sign" would presumably not be another exorcism or demonstration of the *fact* of Jesus' power, but rather something that would settle the issue of the *source* of Jesus' power. The first of the challenges is addressed in 11:17–23, and the second in 11:29–32.

The response to the first challenge is two-pronged. First, if Jesus is working against the demons under the authority of Satan, that would mean that Satan's own power is divided and surely on the verge of collapse (11:17–18)—a genuine cause for rejoicing if it were true. The second line of argument refers Jesus' audience to the work of other exorcists, whom they do not challenge, to resolve the question of where Jesus' authority comes from (11:19). The conclusion of this part of the argument, which represents the view that prevailed in the source shared by Luke and Matthew (11:20; Matt. 12:28), is that God's own power is at work in Jesus, and therefore God's reign has come. That also would be a cause for rejoicing.

Luke in no way ridicules the challenge, but rather recognizes the power of the evil forces of which they have reason to be afraid (11:21–22). Their comfort lies in the fact that the power at work in Jesus is stronger still, and fully able to neutralize the threat represented in the other powers. But the two ways—that of Jesus and that of the powers of evil—are fundamentally incompatible. Those who are under the power of evil are opposed to Jesus. The saying in 11:23 reflects a change from the similar saying in 9:50, where, just before the start of the journey to Jerusalem, Jesus' followers were urged to welcome outsiders ("whoever is not against you is for you"). Now the issue is not human beings who come to the same place by different routes, but rather, the issue is the contradictory agenda of evil and good.

The earlier report of the exorcism provides the thematic link to the account of the behavior of exorcised spirits in 11:24–26. A spirit that has been driven out of a person finds itself suddenly homeless and seeks another place to inhabit. "Waterless regions" provide no resting place, since these spirits were thought to have their origins in, and thus to long to return to, watery depths (8:26–39). In the absence of a proper home, the spirits return to the person they used to inhabit. The order of that newly healed person—in the metaphor, cleansed of the evil powers, but still like an empty house into which the new "furniture" of good has not yet been moved—is an enticing place to camp, and the emptiness is filled by the old spirit and all its friends. The fundamental incompatibility of the powers of evil and of Jesus is further elaborated on: What is present in Jesus is not simply the absence of evil, but a positive power for good, symbolized in the reign of God. Only that presence can finally safeguard human beings, and by implication the whole created order, from becoming the unholy habitations of the forces of evil.

What at first appears as a woman's pious interjection to break the mounting tension of the previous teachings (11:27–28) turns out to further the point that Luke is making in this section of the Gospel. Her declaration that Jesus' mother is blessed simply for having given birth to him may indeed be intended to express her recognition of, and her rejoicing in, the truth of what Jesus has been saying. Jesus' response does not refute her or deny her blessing, but rather it recalls the true basis for blessing and for kinship with Jesus (8:19–21), God's word—by implication, the word of God's reign—heard and embodied in action.

## THE SIGN FOR THIS GENERATION
### Luke 11:29–32

11:29 **When the crowds were increasing, he began to say, "This generation is an evil generation; it asks for a sign, but no sign will be given to it except the sign of Jonah. 30 For just as Jonah became a sign to the people of Nineveh, so the Son of Man will be to this generation. 31 The queen of the South will rise at the judgment with the people of this generation and condemn them, because she came from the ends of the earth to listen to the wisdom of Solomon, and see, something greater than Solomon is here! 32 The people of Nineveh will rise up at the judgment with this generation and**

**condemn it, because they repented at the proclamation of Jonah, and see, something greater than Jonah is here!"**

A word about the increasing size of the crowd signals the shift to the second aspect of the challenge to Jesus, the demand for a sign (11:16). Early in the Gospel, Simeon identified Jesus himself as "a sign that will be opposed" (2:34). The people later on request some sign to indicate when the temple would be destroyed as Jesus predicted (21:7), and during the judicial proceedings against Jesus, Herod is said to have hoped to see Jesus perform some sign (23:8). Simeon's voice prevails, however, for no sign is ever provided on demand. The only sign given is Jesus himself.

The sayings concerning the sign that are found in 11:29–32 find echoes in Matthew 12:38–42. In both passages "this generation" is called evil for seeking a sign, and in both they are told that Jonah will be their sign. In Matthew that sign is elaborated on in terms of Jonah's three days and nights in the belly of the sea monster, but then the sayings go on to recall Jonah's power to bring about the repentance of Nineveh. Luke retains the focus on Jonah as a sign to Nineveh, without referring to the three-day period, but referring instead to Jonah's preaching of repentance: "Just as Jonah became a sign to Nineveh, so the Son of Man [here clearly meaning Jesus himself] will be [a sign] to this generation" (11:30).

The parallels are established between Jesus and Jonah, and between Nineveh and "this generation." But neither of those parallels remains static. The first shifts to affirm that Jesus is even greater than Jonah (11:32c). The second shifts in the opposite direction: At the final judgment, the people of Nineveh—who repented in response to Jonah, will condemn this generation, which (by implication) does not repent even though one greater than Jonah has brought God's word.

A similar pattern of unequal parallelism is developed around the "queen of the South" (or the queen of Sheba, 1 Kings 10:1–13; 2 Chron. 9:1–12) and "this generation." The queen of the South traveled from a great distance to witness the wisdom of Solomon. At the judgment she will judge "this generation" who have failed to recognize something greater than Solomon right in their very midst, the very Wisdom or *Sophia* of God present in Jesus (11:31; see also 7:35; 21:15).

As Simeon said, Jesus himself is their sign, as both divine Wisdom and divine Word—greater than the wisdom of Solomon and the word of Jonah alike—but he is a sign that is opposed. Why he is not recognized or received Luke does not explain. The connection of the request for a sign and the debate about the source of Jesus' authority implies that people fail to recognize him as the sign they seek because they are not "with" him (11:23). They are still aligned with the forces of evil, which make them more ready to live with the destructive powers that harm human lives than they are to hear and obey the word of God.

## LIGHT IN THE BODY
## Luke 11:33–36

> 11:33 "No one after lighting a lamp puts it in a cellar, but on the lampstand so that those who enter may see the light. [34] Your eye is the lamp of your body. If your eye is healthy, your whole body is full of light; but if it is not healthy, your body is full of darkness. [35] Therefore consider whether the light in you is not darkness. [36] If then your whole body is full of light, with no part of it in darkness, it will be as full of light as when a lamp gives you light with its rays."

The link between these teachings and the preceding ones is elusive at best. The first affirmation is a variation of the proverb cited in 8:16. It seems to be a sort of proverbial footnote added to the powerful affirmation of Jesus' superiority to Solomon and Jonah, and thus of the need to pay attention to him (9:35). Surely God's intent is that such a "light" be made visible!

The remaining sayings about lamps and light (11:34–36) appear to have been joined here simply on the basis of those catchwords. (They are found in Matthew too, but in the totally different context of the Sermon on the Mount, Matt. 6:22–23.) These sayings do not apply to Jesus in particular, instead, they express general truths about human beings. The reference is not to the eye as an organ of sight, but to the eye which, along with the heart, was understood to be the seat of human thought and emotion—in short, of one's entire personality. According to this metaphor, if one's "eye," which is the core of a person's intellect, feeling, judgment, will, and capacity for relationship, is healthy, that health permeates one's entire being the way the light of a lamp fills every corner of a room. On the other hand, if the lamp gives no light, the room—or, in this case, the whole person—suffers from its absence.

# 8. Dire Warnings
*Luke 11:37–13:9*

## WARNINGS TO THE
## RELIGIOUS LEADERS
## Luke 11:37–12:1

11:37 While he was speaking, a Pharisee invited him to dine with him; so he went in and took his place at the table. 38 The Pharisee was amazed to see that he did not first wash before dinner. 39 Then the Lord said to him, "Now you Pharisees clean the outside of the cup and of the dish, but inside you are full of greed and wickedness. 40 You fools! Did not the one who made the outside make the inside also? 41 So give for alms those things that are within; and see, everything will be clean for you.

42 "But woe to you Pharisees! For you tithe mint and rue and herbs of all kinds, and neglect justice and the love of God; it is these you ought to have practiced, without neglecting the others. 43 Woe to you Pharisees! For you love to have the seat of honor in the synagogues and to be greeted with respect in the marketplaces. 44 Woe to you! For you are like unmarked graves, and people walk over them without realizing it."

45 One of the lawyers answered him, "Teacher, when you say these things, you insult us too." 46 And he said, "Woe also to you lawyers! For you load people with burdens hard to bear, and you yourselves do not lift a finger to ease them. 47 Woe to you! For you build the tombs of the prophets whom your ancestors killed. 48 So you are witnesses and approve of the deeds of your ancestors; for they killed them, and you build their tombs. 49 Therefore also the Wisdom of God said, 'I will send them prophets and apostles, some of whom they will kill and persecute,' 50 so that this generation may be charged with the blood of all the prophets shed since the foundation of the world, 51 from the blood of Abel to the blood of Zechariah, who perished between the altar and the sanctuary. Yes, I tell you, it will be charged against this generation. 52 Woe to you lawyers! For you have taken away the key of knowledge; you did not enter yourselves, and you hindered those who were entering."

⁵³ **When he went outside, the scribes and the Pharisees began to be very hostile toward him and to cross-examine him about many things, ⁵⁴ lying in wait for him, to catch him in something he might say.**
12:1 **Meanwhile, when the crowd gathered by the thousands, so that they trampled on one another, he began to speak first to his disciples, "Beware of the yeast of the Pharisees, that is, their hypocrisy."**

The tension of the previous section of the narrative continues to escalate, along with the size of the crowds (11:14, 29; 12:1), in a series of warnings about dangers that threaten to lead Jesus' followers astray. The first of the warnings is expressed in a list of woes spoken against the very religious leaders who ought to be giving the people reliable guidance for their lives. The episode is set at table in the home of a Pharisee, where Jesus offends his host by not following the purity rules about hand-washing before eating. Every child has dreamed of finding a place where Jesus condemns hand washing, but that is not the point of this passage. Neither is this a place where Jesus condemns the Pharisee's concern with purity. Instead, purity is reinterpreted in categories of justice.

What is implied to be the host's preoccupation with the purity of the outside of the body whereas the inside is "full of greed and wickedness" is as foolish as washing only the outside of a dish while leaving the inside dirty (11:39–40). Thus the whole human being is a unity, and it is the health of the inside that finally determines the well-being of the whole. The crucial transition to Luke's principal point in this section of the Gospel is made in his connection of purity and giving for alms "those things that are within . . . you" (11:41). The word translated "within" can also be translated "among," and it appears that Luke uses the word both ways. In the discussion of purity, the former meaning seems more appropriate, but the following "woe" implies material and social resources that link one person to another as well.

The warning unfolds in the form of three woes against the Pharisees, followed by three against the lawyers. The first woe against the Pharisees contrasts concern about precision in tithing garden herbs (which would go beyond what Torah required) with the neglect of "justice and the love of God" (11:42). Love of God and appropriate treatment of the neighbor are held together here, as they are in 10:25–28 (in the combination of Deut. 6:5 and Lev. 19:18) and in Micah 6:8. Alms-giving is thus interpreted as not referring to the bestowing of trifles from one's surplus or from the optional "herbs and spices" of life. Instead, it has to do with attention to the material substance of life that conveys or impedes justice.

The second and third woes (11:43–44) elaborate on the first by irony and insult. The Pharisees are charged with thriving on the very prestige and honor inherent in their highly stratified society (see also 20:46), which a commitment to justice should lead them to undercut. In the process, these people so preoccupied with purity become invisible or hidden contaminants: "unmarked graves." As such, they spread the impurity of injustice, while passing themselves off as models of the religious life.

Those charged with the interpretation of the law, who may also have been connected to the Pharisees, come under equally harsh fire in a parallel series of three woes. The first woe has an economic bite, for the struggle simply to meet basic needs would prevent the poor people of both the city and the countryside from being able to pay attention to the detailed interpretations of the law developed with increasing precision by the legal experts (11:46). The second woe against the lawyers is the most fully elaborated (11:47–51). Jesus charges them with condoning the killing of the earlier prophets in two ways. First, they build tombs for them, honoring them in death, apparently, instead of heeding their words. Second, they join in the chain of killing by killing "prophets and apostles" sent to them by the Wisdom of God. This generation thus becomes guilty of the deaths of all of the prophets of all generations.

The phrase "from the blood of Abel to the blood of Zechariah" is puzzling for several reasons. In the Roman alphabet, the convenient parallel representing inclusiveness—"from A to Z"—comes to mind, but that does not work for the Greek alphabet in which Luke wrote. Given that Abel figures in the early narratives of Genesis and the book of the prophet Zechariah is the next to the last book in what Christians know as the "Old Testament," that also suggests itself as a way of including all of the martyred ancestors. It is not clear, however, whether the prophetic books would have been listed in the same order in the Bible Luke knew. Furthermore, there is no tradition that the prophet Zechariah suffered a violent death, nor is there any such tradition related to the Zechariah who was the father of John the Baptist. A third man named Zechariah—this one a priest, and the son of Jehoiada (2 Chron. 24:20–22)—was reported to have been stoned during the reign of King Joash, but neither that Zechariah nor Abel was known as a prophet. The meaning of the phrase thus remains a mystery.

The third woe against the lawyers again picks up on the reference to

Wisdom in the previous one. In the second woe, the Wisdom of God was the one who sent prophets and apostles for whose deaths this generation is being held responsible, but in the third, the lawyers are charged with removing access to Wisdom's "house" (Prov. 9:1), especially in the form of the salvation of God.

The three woes against the lawyers thus encompass all of Scripture—Torah, prophets, and wisdom. These sources of life and of connection to God, which the lawyers ought to make accessible to the people, they keep from the people instead. Like the Pharisees, who ought to help people learn the ways of purity but instead are themselves sources of contamination, so the lawyers also are charged with doing the opposite of their proper calling. That deliberate inversion of the truth is called "hypocrisy" (12:1). Since Luke does not go into an elaborate explanation about what he means in this section of the Gospel, we must conclude that Luke's audience too must have been aware of cases of similar confusion of truth and lies.

## WARNINGS ABOUT DENYING GOD
## Luke 12:2–12

12:2 **Nothing is covered up that will not be uncovered, and nothing secret that will not become known.** [3] **Therefore whatever you have said in the dark will be heard in the light, and what you have whispered behind closed doors will be proclaimed from the housetops.**

[4] **"I tell you, my friends, do not fear those who kill the body, and after that can do nothing more.** [5] **But I will warn you whom to fear: fear him who, after he has killed, has authority to cast into hell. Yes, I tell you, fear him!** [6] **Are not five sparrows sold for two pennies? Yet not one of them is forgotten in God's sight.** [7] **But even the hairs of your head are all counted. Do not be afraid; you are of more value than many sparrows.**

[8] **"And I tell you, everyone who acknowledges me before others, the Son of Man also will acknowledge before the angels of God;** [9] **but whoever denies me before others will be denied before the angels of God.** [10] **And everyone who speaks a word against the Son of Man will be forgiven; but whoever blasphemes against the Holy Spirit will not be forgiven.** [11] **When they bring you before the synagogues, the rulers, and the authorities, do not worry about how you are to defend yourselves or what you are to say;** [12] **for the Holy Spirit will teach you at that very hour what you ought to say."**

The tremendous crowd—perhaps an incipient mob—identified at the end of the previous story is also the audience for the next set of warnings.

The mood of these verses is of a time of suffering and testing. They begin with a proverb or wisdom saying similar to that found in 8:17, pointing to a time of revelation. What is to be revealed is not something about God, but rather, the things people have been trying to keep secret (12:2–3). Perhaps Luke's reference here is to people's Christian confession itself, which, when it becomes known, can lead to their being called to account before religious and civil authorities (12:4, 11). The revelation thus becomes an occasion for testimony that is a time of reckoning before God.

The sayings approach that moment of reckoning from several directions. The first emphasizes the finite power of the human authorities, which have authority only over one's biological survival, in contrast with God's judgment, which has eternal consequences (12:4–5). Those consequences are conveyed by the reference to Gehenna (NRSV, "hell"), literally a valley running along the western and southern boundaries of Jerusalem in which there were continuously burning garbage dumps—an image evocative of Sheol (Deut. 32:22). The implication is that God alone has the ability to consign one there, to eternal punishment. That frightening image is contrasted, however, with God's loving intent and persistent care even for sparrows and the hairs of one's head. In an argument from the lesser to the greater, Luke affirms that the God who cares for things of little value will be even more attentive to the people who hear these warnings (12:6–7).

The moment of judgment is then approached from the perspective of the crucial factor in determining the outcome (12:8–10). In a saying that recalls 9:26, people's public testimony to Jesus on earth (presumably now no longer able to be kept hidden) is mirrored in the testimony, borne by Jesus as "Son of Man," before God in the celestial courtroom (see Ezekiel 33–34). In other words, one's recognition or denial of Jesus has eternal consequences. That strong declaration is modified, however, in 12:10. Even those who testify against the "Son of Man" will be forgiven. Such speaking "against the Son of Man" would logically extend to include even the ultimate testimony against Jesus that will lead to his death. As serious as that is, the assurance that it can be forgiven is crucial for Luke, who is determined to hold open the way of salvation to "all flesh" (3:6), Jews and Gentiles alike.

"Blasphemy against the Holy Spirit" is another matter, according to Luke. For that there is no forgiveness. What exactly is meant by that phrase, and why is it unforgivable? To "blaspheme" is to abuse the name of God or to attack something that belongs to God (see the discussion of

5:21). To blaspheme against the Holy Spirit would mean to deny that the Spirit is an expression of God. It would amount to negating or turning one's back on the very source from which all forgiveness comes. Such "blasphemy" is not the last straw that collapses God's patience. Rather, it is a person's rejection of God's grace, a refusal to be forgiven. Blasphemy against the Holy Spirit cannot be forgiven because by it one has cut one's self off from the source of forgiveness.

The section concludes by returning to the likelihood that one will be called to account before religious and secular authorities (12:11–12). At such times, both the assurance of God (12:6–7) and the advocacy of the Holy Spirit (12:12) will be one's only, and sufficient, protection.


## WARNINGS ABOUT FALSE SECURITY
## Luke 12:13–34

### The Parable of the Rich Fool (Luke 12:13–21)

12:13 Someone in the crowd said to him, "Teacher, tell my brother to divide the family inheritance with me." [14] But he said to him, "Friend, who set me to be a judge or arbitrator over you?" [15] And he said to them, "Take care! Be on your guard against all kinds of greed; for one's life does not consist in the abundance of possessions." [16] Then he told them a parable: "The land of a rich man produced abundantly. [17] And he thought to himself, 'What should I do, for I have no place to store my crops?' [18] Then he said, 'I will do this: I will pull down my barns and build larger ones, and there I will store all my grain and my goods. [19] And I will say to my soul, 'Soul, you have ample goods laid up for many years; relax, eat, drink, be merry.' [20] But God said to him, 'You fool! This very night your life is being demanded of you. And the things you have prepared, whose will they be?' [21] So it is with those who store up treasures for themselves but are not rich toward God."

The context of a society built around the patterns of security and social position related to one's economic status meant that questions related to the distribution of estates occupied a great deal of attention. According to Jewish custom, one heir (one brother, for example) could demand that an estate be divided among all of them. In the setting of the parable, Jesus is asked to mediate in that process. The reply—a warning against greed and centering one's life on the accumulation of wealth (12:15)—provides the framework in which to interpret the parable that follows (12:16–21).

The parable features a man who is successful in his business, and who operates within an economy where wealth and security are measured in the goods one has accumulated. We get to know the man's attitude as he talks to himself, first making his plans, then relishing the bright future before him. There is a catch, though, for death intervenes the very night everything is finally in order. God also speaks directly, calling the man a "fool" for trusting in his own storehouses and not being "rich toward God." That puzzling phrase is elaborated on in the set of teachings that follow. Far from referring to a life of generalized "spiritual" discipline, worship, or prayer, it reflects a different posture toward wealth and possessions.

## Confidence and Anxiety (Luke 12:22–34)

12:22 **He said to his disciples, "Therefore I tell you, do not worry about your life, what you will eat, or about your body, what you will wear. 23 For life is more than food, and the body more than clothing. 24 Consider the ravens: they neither sow nor reap, they have neither storehouse nor barn, and yet God feeds them. Of how much more value are you than the birds! 25 And can any of you by worrying add a single hour to your span of life? 26 If then you are not able to do so small a thing as that, why do you worry about the rest? 27 Consider the lilies, how they grow: they neither toil nor spin; yet I tell you, even Solomon in all his glory was not clothed like one of these. 28 But if God so clothes the grass of the field, which is alive today and tomorrow is thrown into the oven, how much more will he clothe you—you of little faith! 29 And do not keep striving for what you are to eat and what you are to drink, and do not keep worrying. 30 For it is the nations of the world that strive after all these things, and your Father knows that you need them. 31 Instead, strive for his kingdom, and these things will be given to you as well.**

32 **"Do not be afraid, little flock, for it is your Father's good pleasure to give you the kingdom. 33 Sell your possessions, and give alms. Make purses for yourselves that do not wear out, an unfailing treasure in heaven, where no thief comes near and no moth destroys. 34 For where your treasure is, there your heart will be also."**

The surrounding crowd fades away as subsequent teachings focus on the disciples. The initial teachings contrast the frenzied construction projects of the rich man in the parable with the life of birds and flowers, to whom God provides everything necessary for their life and well-being. How much more, then, God will provide everything necessary for human life (12:22–28; see also 12:6–7). The concerns here, however, like the retirement plan of the rich man, are concerns about future security. Such worries plague the well-to-do, while the very poor are concerned with immediate survival needs. These teachings, like the saying about giving alms, make it clear that the audience in view consists of people who are the "haves" of their society, whose sense of well-being must shift and come not from the amassing of more and more goods but from the reallocation of social and material goods that is the expression of justice.

The affirmation with which the teachings began—"life is more than food, and the body more than clothing"—is echoed in 12:29–30, where these concerns of the surrounding society are contrasted with the ethos of the reign of God (12:31–34). That reign is not marked by poverty and deprivation of material goods that are due to the competitive accumulation of possessions, but by their abundance that flows out of God's own sufficiency and generosity. "Sell your possessions and give alms" (12:33) is the hallmark of this different economy, where alms-giving is not just a doling out of extras, but it is a fundamental reallocation of material and social goods according to the canons of justice (12:41–44). Such heavenly treasure is indeed what makes one "rich toward God" (12:21) in the flowing together of love of neighbor and of God (10:25–28; 11:42) that characterizes God's reign.

## WARNINGS ABOUT THE URGENCY OF THE TIMES
## Luke 12:35–48

12:35 "Be dressed for action and have your lamps lit; 36 be like those who are waiting for their master to return from the wedding banquet, so that they may open the door for him as soon as he comes and knocks. 37 Blessed are those slaves whom the master finds alert when he comes; truly I tell you, he will fasten his belt and have them sit down to eat, and he will come and serve them. 38 If he comes during the middle of the night, or near dawn, and finds them so, blessed are those slaves.

39 "But know this: if the owner of the house had known at what hour the thief was coming, he would not have let his house be broken into. 40 You also must be ready, for the Son of Man is coming at an unexpected hour."

41 Peter said, "Lord, are you telling this parable for us or for everyone?" 42 And the Lord said, "Who then is the faithful and prudent manager whom his master will put in charge of his slaves, to give them their allowance of food at the proper time? 43 Blessed is that slave whom his master will find at work when he arrives. 44 Truly I tell you, he will put that one in charge of all his possessions. 45 But if that slave says to himself, 'My master is delayed in coming,' and if he begins to beat the other slaves, men and women, and to eat and drink and get drunk, 46 the master of that slave will come on a day when he does not expect him and at an hour that he does not know, and will cut him in pieces, and put him with the unfaithful. 47 That slave who

**knew what his master wanted, but did not prepare himself or do what was wanted, will receive a severe beating.** [48] **But the one who did not know and did what deserved a beating will receive a light beating. From everyone to whom much has been given, much will be required; and from the one to whom much has been entrusted, even more will be demanded."**

In a series of teachings that emphasize the need for preparedness and alertness, the comforting mood of the previous section, which established a firm basis for a person's security in lieu of the competition to accumulate possessions that marks the prevailing wisdom of society, gives way to a renewed sense of urgency. The first section urges that Jesus' hearers (the disciples, 12:22) model themselves on servants who remain alert through the night, ready to do their work whenever it is required of them (12:35–38). The twice-repeated language of benediction ("Blessed are those slaves"), the references to the lamps and the wedding banquet (which echo the parable of the ten bridesmaids in Matt. 25:1–13), and the reversal of roles of servant and master (12:37; see also 22:27–30) all make it clear that more is at stake than simply a commandment to be ready for whatever tasks the day brings. The image is like a transparent overlay on a reference to the church's expectation of the return of the resurrected one. That theme is not found often in Luke, but clearly he continues to call his church to attentive waiting for that day, however delayed it may be in coming.

The image then shifts abruptly from servants ready to work, to a householder alert to defend the house from a would-be thief (12:39–40). Again the reference is to the coming one (this time identified as the Son of Man). If the emphasis in the previous verses was on the likelihood of a delay, here the emphasis is on the unexpectedness of the arrival.

Peter's question about the audience of the remarks (12:41) is a device that Luke uses in order to clarify the particular role of the disciples and their successors, who are the leaders of Luke's church. The image returns to that of the servants, with the added focus on the managers who are in charge of securing the well-being of the rest (12:42–44). The servants chosen as managers are those in the first image (12:35–38), who are found alert when the householder returns. If they continue to fulfill their duties, they are given increased responsibilities, but if they mistreat those entrusted to their care, words can hardly describe the punishment that awaits them (12:45–46).

Although the warnings about the urgency of the times apply to everyone, they are directed in a particular way to the leaders of the community. A higher standard of behavior is expected from them than from the others (12:47–48). Whether Luke's church has simply lost its sense of the urgency of waiting for Jesus' return after so many years, or whether that very delay has led to abusive behavior on the part of the leaders, the warning carried by these words attributed to Jesus says pointedly: "To whom much has been entrusted, even more will be demanded."

## WARNINGS ABOUT CONFLICT
## Luke 12:49–59

12:49 **"I came to bring fire to the earth, and how I wish it were already kindled!** [50] **I have a baptism with which to be baptized, and what stress I am under until it is completed!** [51] **Do you think that I have come to bring peace to the earth? No, I tell you, but rather division!** [52] **From now on five in one household will be divided, three against two and two against three;** [53] **they will be divided:**

**father against son**
  **and son against father,**
**mother against daughter**
  **and daughter against mother,**
**mother-in-law against her daughter-in-law**
  **and daughter-in-law against mother-in-law."**

[54] **He also said to the crowds, "When you see a cloud rising in the west, you immediately say, 'It is going to rain'; and so it happens.** [55] **And when you see the south wind blowing, you say, 'There will be scorching heat'; and it happens.** [56] **You hypocrites! You know how to interpret the appearance of earth and sky, but why do you not know how to interpret the present time?**

[57] **"And why do you not judge for yourselves what is right?** [58] **Thus, when you go with your accuser before a magistrate, on the way make an effort to settle the case, or you may be dragged before the judge, and the judge hand you over to the officer, and the officer throw you in prison.** [59] **I tell you, you will never get out until you have paid the very last penny."**

The previous warnings about the sense of urgency and demand that surrounds Jesus, and that carries over with even greater clarity into the period of the church, are joined by warnings about the divisions that often result from Jesus' ministry, despite the "peace" that surrounded Jesus' birth (2:14) and that will characterize his entry into Jerusalem (19:38). This set of warnings is divided into two sayings about the critical quality of the present time (12:49–50, 54–55) and two references to the social divisions that Jesus' ministry provokes (12:51–53).

The vivid imagery of the initial saying (12:49–50) recalls the earlier preaching of John the Baptist (3:16), which pointed to Jesus as coming to baptize with the Holy Spirit and fire. Here the baptism lies ahead for Jesus himself, and that second baptism can only refer to his approaching death. As did his baptism by John, death too represents a turning—a *metanoia*—from which there is no turning back. And the fire—burning heat that judges and refines—is one Jesus longs to kindle. Both images convey urgency as well as threat.

Of all social units, the family was the most tightly knit of Jesus' and Luke's societies. A person's family gave one a history and a place in the social order—an identity. The more highly placed one's family was, the more important it was to preserve its integrity. Obligations to other family members were most strictly observed of all the obligations that accompanied the social and economic relationships by which the society was structured. In language that recalls Micah 7:6, Jesus' words speak of the dissolution of the family in the face of various members' responses to his program (12:51–53). The numbers—divisions of five into groups of two and three—stand for the breaking up of a previous wholeness into the dynamics of a new community (Matt. 18:20).

The urgency of the time is again conveyed in 12:54–56 by an image drawn from meteorology. In Israel, clouds coming from the direction of the Mediterranean Sea to the west mean approaching showers. Conversely, a south wind blowing from the Negeb desert brings sudden, scorching heat. Everyone knows how to read such signs—of the sun and rain that fall on evil and good, on just and unjust alike (Matt. 5:45)—and the signs of the time are even clearer. Those hearing Jesus' words are "hypocrites," because their inability to perceive something so self-evident has to be pretended.

Their alleged inability to discern the times is matched by their inability, even after all that has been said on the subject, to make a judgment on the side of "justice." The translation of the NRSV, "judge for yourself what is *right*" (emphasis added), obscures the underlying issue by its ambiguity. In English, "right" can mean "correct" or "true" as well as "morally appropriate." The Greek makes it clear that the ethical dimension is what is referred to. A more precise translation would be, "Judge for yourself what is *just*."

The social and economic context for the saying is the rampant debt that was destroying families and communities throughout Palestine. If disputes about debts reached the Roman legal system, one of two verdicts would greet the debtor. Either the debtor would be forced into indentured service to work off the debt, or the debtor would be thrown into prison until family members managed to scrape together the needed money to pay off the debt (usually by selling off any remaining lands). It was a system that allowed the rich to get richer, and that spelled the ruin of the poor. (It is little wonder that when the Zealots entered Jerusalem at the start of the war in 66 C.E., the first thing they did was to burn the debt records!) In order to avoid playing into such blatant injustice, the only solution would be to settle cases before they went to court. Whatever the actual patterns of debt and credit, justice required that the system be brought to an end. The debts and credits of "business as usual" must be canceled in this present time, with the realization that God's reign is at hand (see 4:18).

## WARNINGS TO REPENT
## Luke 13:1–9

13:1 **At that very time there were some present who told him about the Galileans whose blood Pilate had mingled with their sacrifices. ² He asked them, "Do you think that because these Galileans suffered in this way they were worse sinners than all other Galileans? ³ No, I tell you; but unless you repent, you will all perish as they did. ⁴ Or those eighteen who were killed when the tower of Siloam fell on them—do you think that they were worse offenders than all the others living in Jerusalem? ⁵ No, I tell you; but unless you repent, you will all perish just as they did."**
**⁶ Then he told this parable: "A man had a fig tree planted in his vineyard; and he came looking for fruit on it and found none. ⁷ So he said to the gardener, 'See here! For three years I have come looking for fruit on this fig tree, and still I find none. Cut it down! Why should it be wasting the soil?' ⁸ He replied, 'Sir, let it alone for one more year, until I dig around it and put manure on it. ⁹ If it bears fruit next year, well and good; but if not, you can cut it down.'"**

The catalog of warnings concludes with a pair of examples and a parable warning the hearers to repent—to turn their lives in a different direction—or face dire consequences. The first example is introduced by Jesus' audience. It features an incident in Galilee, in which Pilate killed a number of people and mingled their blood with that of their sacrifices (13:1). Josephus and others mention several episodes in which representatives of Rome took harsh action against Jews. None of those episodes sounds exactly like the incident referred to here, however, so it is impossible to connect this to any specific historical event. Of all of the Gospel writers, only

Luke mentions this incident, and it is possible that his account reflects an event of limited local importance, which Luke may have uncovered in the course of his study. The specific underlying event, however (if in fact there was one), is not germane to the point Luke is making.

Having been informed of the action of Pilate, Jesus responds by addressing not just this incident but the larger and very human question, Why do bad things happen to people? Jesus denies that their suffering occurred because they were worse sinners than other people who were not killed. Instead, the question, Why? is set aside in favor of a warning to the hearers: "But unless you repent, you will all perish as they did" (13:3). Of what they are to repent, we are told, nor is there any explanation of why death should follow.

The second example is presented as part of Jesus' response, and it is parallel to the first: Those killed in Jerusalem when the tower of Siloam collapsed were no worse than other residents of the city, "but unless you repent, you will all perish just as they did" (13:5).

The nature of the two specific examples is as important as the words of denial and warning, as a way to move people away from linking suffering and disobedience toward recognizing the need to repent. The first example tells of an act of officially sanctioned terrorism and exemplary violence used by political authorities to enforce control over a captive population. Luke's readers would probably readily recognize that no connection can be drawn between being "sinners"—doing something that merits punishment—and suffering at the hands of people obsessed with maintaining power by any means necessary. The second example is an "accident": Why did the victims just happen to get caught by the falling tower? Life experience, however, leads one to look with a certain skepticism at such "accidents" too. Are they perhaps the product of construction shortcuts in methods or material, disregarding the consequences for workers or members of the public? Both of the examples point not to a specific cause-and-effect connection between guilt and death for the particular victims, but rather to a moment for "repentance" or turning by the persons responsible for causing them, if such events are not to continue. Suffering results, not from any "sin" of the sufferer, but from injustice left unchallenged and unrepented.

The parable of the fig tree (13:6–9) underlines the importance of "repentance" in shaping the future. The parable is found only in Luke, and though it also features a fig tree, it does not appear to be related to the episode of Jesus' cursing of the fig tree found in Matthew 21:18–22 and Mark 11:12–14, 20–26. The parable in Luke turns on the logic of agriculture in the Palestinian context of absentee landowners. The owner has had a tree planted with the intent of profiting from its produce. When no fruit has appeared, he orders it chopped down. The gardener pleads for more time and instead proposes to give the tree extra attention. Then if it still does not produce, he will remove it.

In this parable, we do not have the usual allegorical equation of the householder with God and the servant with the human being who is more or less faithful to God's will. Instead, it is the gardener who is the "reliable" character presenting the author's agenda. The owner's judgment is based only on past performance, but the gardener opens the story toward the future. Far from offering cheap grace, or forgiveness with no reckoning, he advocates that every chance—even extra attention—be given before a final decision is made. What is held out is a time of reprieve and then of reckoning in this painful meantime of human reluctance to recognize God's project or reign and its bearer, and to bear the fruit of that promised harvest.

# 9. Holiness Redefined
*Luke 13:10–15:32*

At the heart of the travel narrative Luke presents a series of stories and teachings that explore the basis for one's association with Jesus and for one's participation in the ministry related to God's reign. What makes a person fit to be set apart for such holy purposes, and on what basis is one called to such a holy task?

## SABBATH HEALING:
## THE BENT-OVER WOMAN
## Luke 13:10–17

13:10 Now he was teaching in one of the synagogues on the sabbath. [11] And just then there appeared a woman with a spirit that had crippled her for eighteen years. She was bent over and was quite unable to stand up straight. [12] When Jesus saw her, he called her over and said, "Woman, you are set free from your ailment." [13] When he laid his hands on her, immediately she stood up straight and began praising God. [14] But the leader of the synagogue, indignant because Jesus had cured on the sabbath, kept saying to the crowd, "There are six days on which work ought to be done; come on those days and be cured, and not on the sabbath day." [15] But the Lord answered him and said, "You hypocrites! Does not each of you on the sabbath untie his ox or his donkey from the manger, and lead it away to give it water? [16] And ought not this woman, a daughter of Abraham whom Satan bound for eighteen long years, be set free from this bondage on the sabbath day?" [17] When he said this, all his opponents were put to shame; and the entire crowd was rejoicing at all the wonderful things that he was doing.

This section begins with the final reference in the Gospel to Jesus' teaching in a synagogue, in the second of three accounts of Jesus' healing on a sabbath that led to a dispute with religious authorities (see also

6:6–11; 14:1–6). The three sabbath-healing controversy stories may reflect a continuing dispute between the synagogue and the church for which Luke was writing, concerning the proper keeping of the sabbath. In each of the stories, the core question is not *whether* to keep the sabbath, but rather *how* to keep it, and, specifically, how keeping the day "holy" to God (Exod. 20:8) relates to healing in circumstances not overtly life-threatening, which, therefore could wait until sundown for treatment.

The woman is described as having, literally, "a spirit of weakness" that kept her bent double for eighteen years—about half of her adult life, given the short life expectancy of women in the first century. Apparently we should understand that she had come to the synagogue to worship, for nothing is said about her taking the initiative to seek out Jesus to request healing. As is the case also for the other two sabbath-healing controversies and for many of the healing stories of the Gospel of John (but unlike most of the other healing stories in the Synoptic Gospels), Jesus is said to take the initiative in the woman's cure. The steps of the healing story are clear and straightforward: Jesus summons her, pronounces her free from her "weakness," and lays his hands on her. Immediately the symptoms disappear, and she praises God (13:12–13).

Her weakness itself is regarded as the power that holds her captive to restricted movement, to the inability to meet another person face-to-face, and to a world defined by the piece of ground around her own toes or looked at always on a slant. The words that effect the healing deal with what has enslaved her. The power of her weakness is treated in the same way as the power of demons in the various exorcisms (4:31–37; 8:26–39). Just as the man healed at Gerasa was instructed to do, the woman praises God as the true source of her healing. Nothing is said about her own faith or about any recognition or confession of Jesus.

The mood shifts abruptly after the healing is accomplished, when the leader of the synagogue raises the issue of the sabbath law (13:14). His implication is that the crowd (not just the woman) has come deliberately to seek healing—to which they are entitled, but which is appropriate to the six ordinary work days and not to the sabbath. Jesus' response, citing the accepted practice of untying farm animals so they could get water to drink on the sabbath, is an argument from the lesser to the greater: If it is appropriate to "untie" farm animals on the sabbath, it is so much more appropriate to "untie" (the same word is used) a daughter of Abraham on the sabbath after her eighteen years of imprisonment.

The phrase "daughter of Abraham" is found only here in all of the

Gospels. The masculine parallel "sons of Abraham," in contrast, is a common way to identify the people of God. John the Baptist has already warned against presuming on that identity (3:8), and Zacchaeus—a tax collector whose profession would have marginalized him from his people—receives the blessing of being restored to being a "son of Abraham" (19:1–10). Here, this woman who has been captive to Satan (identified in 13:16 as the power behind the spirit of weakness that has held her) is brought from the margins to the heart of her people. The crowd's celebration (13:17) is ample testimony to the appropriateness of such an act on the sabbath as a way to make the day holy.

## PARABLES OF THE MUSTARD SEED
## AND THE LEAVEN
## Luke 13:18–21

13:18 He said therefore, "What is the kingdom of God like? And to what should I compare it? ¹⁹ It is like a mustard seed that someone took and sowed in the garden; it grew and became a tree, and the birds of the air made nests in its branches."
²⁰ And again he said, "To what should I compare the kingdom of God? ²¹ It is like yeast that a woman took and mixed in with three measures of flour until all of it was leavened."

With no indication of any literary break, and with a close logical link to the preceding narrative ("therefore"), the inclusive thrust of the narrative is specifically connected to the reign of God by means of two parables attributed to Jesus. A version of the first parable is found in Mark 4:30–32, and both are found together in Matthew 13:31–33. Details common to Matthew and Luke but different from Mark's version (the claim that the mustard becomes a "tree" instead of a "shrub," and that the birds nest in its "branches" instead of in its "shade," for example) suggest that a parable about a mustard plant was found in both Mark and the other source shared by Luke and Matthew, where it was probably already paired with the parable of the leaven.

At face value, Luke's parable of the mustard seed has several odd details. First, in Palestine, mustard is a weed growing abundantly on the hillsides. No one would sow it in a garden; rather, a farmer would wage a constant battle to keep it out of cultivated areas. The suggestion that the seed would be sown in a garden probably reflects Luke's own experience, where the herb was recognized as useful for food and seasoning, and where it may have been cultivated fairly commonly in the kitchen gardens of houses in urban areas.

In any case, at its very largest, the mature mustard plant is a shrub and not a tree. Birds could easily nest in the shade underneath the shrub, but the branches would be both too dense and too fragile to support nests. Although it is possible that Matthew's version of the parable, which appears to blend the versions in Mark and Q, may have been intended to echo the allegory of the tree that shelters the nations in Nebuchadnezzar's dream (Dan. 4:9–18), Luke's version lacks the clues that would support an allegorical reading. For Luke, mustard is simply a plant that grows to a size substantial enough to provide shelter.

In a similar way, in the second parable, common substances—yeast and flour—and the common daily activity of making bread are compared to the reign of God (13:20–21). In this parable, the yeast does not play its usual role as a cause of contamination and a metaphor for evil (see 12:1), though probably those qualities are not too far in the background. It is simply the invisible cause ("hidden" in the flour) of the effect of the leavened bread. Only the quantity of flour stands out as at all unusual in the second parable. The yield from three measures of leavened flour would far exceed the amount of bread that a family could consume in a day or two, and in the absence of preservatives, that is as long as bread could be kept. It is clear that the product will be shared far beyond the baker's family. The motif of hospitality is hinted at in the loaves of bread as in the sheltering branches of the "tree."

Two themes, then, appear to connect the parables to each other and to the preceding narrative: commonness and hospitality. The juxtaposition of the common and the holy in the parables is striking. The ordinary daily work of a woman preparing bread and the ordinary daily work of a man sowing a garden are set side by side as glimpses of God's reign. The same juxtaposition marks the preceding narrative as well. There the chronic condition (attributed to a "spirit of weakness") of an ordinary woman becomes the occasion for a new definition of sabbath keeping—of the nature of a day kept holy. And at the same time, this woman who has been viewing and barely participating in life from the margins—literally looking at it from the side—is affirmed as a full member of the community, even a "daughter of Abraham." Her inclusion as a formerly outcast individual is mirrored and expanded in the pictures of the hospitable branches and abundant loaves of the parables.

## A BASIS FOR EXCLUSION
## Luke 13:22–30

13:22 **Jesus went through one town and village after another, teaching as he made his way to Jerusalem.** 23 **Someone asked him, "Lord, will only a few be saved?" He said to them,** 24 **"Strive to enter through the narrow door; for**

**many, I tell you, will try to enter and will not be able.** [25] **When once the owner of the house has got up and shut the door, and you begin to stand outside and to knock at the door, saying, 'Lord, open to us,' then in reply he will say to you, 'I do not know where you come from.'** [26] **Then you will begin to say, 'We ate and drank with you, and you taught in our streets.'** [27] **But he will say, 'I do not know where you come from; go away from me, all you evildoers!'** [28] **There will be weeping and gnashing of teeth when you see Abraham and Isaac and Jacob and all the prophets in the kingdom of God, and you yourselves thrown out.** [29] **Then people will come from east and west, from north and south, and will eat in the kingdom of God.** [30] **Indeed, some are last who will be first, and some are first who will be last."**

As if in counterpoint to the narrative and the parables of welcome and inclusion, the next phase of the journey (marked by the second note about Jesus' progress toward Jerusalem, 13:22; see also 9:51 and 17:11) will explore criteria for exclusion and judgment. That theme is set explicitly in the collection of sayings in 13:22–30, which Matthew scatters in six different locations (Matt. 7:13–14, 22–23; 8:11–12; 19:30; 20:16; 25:10b–12), with only the last having a parallel in Mark (Mark 10:31). It is impossible to know for certain whether the sayings were already linked in Luke's source, or whether Luke assembled them. However, they are found together in Luke's Gospel, and in that context they cast a variety of lights on the question of exclusion from the salvation present in Jesus.

The section begins with a question that is also the reader's question: How easy is it for us to gain access to the blessings carried in these promises? The answer attributed to Jesus paints a scenario whose parts are connected more by image and allusion than by strict logic. The first saying (13:24) depicts a door that will entice many, but admit only a few. The difficulty of access because of the narrowness of the door (presumably the stringency of the requirements) shifts to the image of a door that is closed at a certain moment and that the householder will not subsequently reopen (13:25). The earlier affirmation of the need and time for repentance (13:1–9) here acquires a sense of temporal urgency: There will be a moment after which it will be too late.

The focus of the collection of sayings then shifts from the picture of the door—always narrow, and at some point finally shut—to the questioner's concern about being saved, and to Jesus' role in the response to that concern. Simply claiming that one has had prior contact with Jesus (having heard his teachings or even shared food together) will not suffice to allow one to claim access to the promises. The real issue is whether one is known by the "Lord" (in this case, the word refers both to the householder of the metaphor and to Jesus, 13:25–27). Such memories of contact with Jesus will make exclusion even more bitter, because those who have met Jesus will have glimpsed the promised salvation (13:28). Those who have once known Jesus also now see the rich variety of people who share in the eternal banquet of God's reign (13:29). The collection of sayings ends with a proverb about a reversal of order (of "firsts" and "lasts,"—13:30), which, by extension, addresses the unpleasant surprise encountered when those who assume they will be on the inside find themselves settling for a glimpse of the party through a crack in the door.

Luke's collection of sayings reminds his audience that none of the criteria according to which they might presume that they hold a place of privileged access to the blessings of salvation will be of any avail. The warning of Simeon (2:34–35) that the child is destined for the fall and rising of many, and that he will reveal the schemes, worries, and thoughts of human hearts, continues to prove true in the church as well as in Israel. The human religious quest for guarantees and the competition for positions of privilege and priority lead instead to exclusion and remorse.

## JESUS IN TENSION:
## GALILEE AND JERUSALEM
## Luke 13:31–35

13:31 **At that very hour some Pharisees came and said to him, "Get away from here, for Herod wants to kill you."** 32 **He said to them, "Go and tell that fox for me, 'Listen, I am casting out demons and performing cures today and tomorrow, and on the third day I finish my work.** 33 **Yet today, tomorrow, and the next day I must be on my way, because it is impossible for a prophet to be killed outside of Jerusalem.'** 34 **Jerusalem, Jerusalem, the city that kills the prophets and stones those who are sent to it! How often have I desired to gather your children together as a hen gathers her brood under her wings, and you were not willing!** 35 **See, your house is left to you. And I tell you, you will not see me until the time comes when you say, 'Blessed is the one who comes in the name of the Lord.'"**

The subject shifts when some Pharisees warn Jesus that Herod is plotting his death (13:31). They have come as Jesus' friends, identifying with him against a common opponent, Herod. Herod, whose specific responsibilities are located in Galilee where he is Tetrarch (9:7–9; 23:7), nevertheless represents the political power of Rome that is lodged in Jerusalem, which is reaffirmed as Jesus' destination. Jesus' response connects that warning of danger in Jerusalem to a warning and a lament in which the name "Jerusalem" provides the link.

The warning and Jesus' response unfold in a series of contrasting parallels. The Pharisees warn Jesus to "[go] away," and he in turn tells them to "go" to Herod (13:31, 32). Herod wants to "kill" Jesus (13:31), and Jesus reminds them of Jerusalem's reputation for killing prophets (13:33–34; see 4:16–30). A three-day pattern is presented in 13:32 to set the shape of Jesus' ministry of healing and exorcism being completed in all its fullness, and in 13:33 for the journey to Jerusalem that will end in his death. The power of God to effect God's will is portrayed in language of necessity and impossibility governing Jesus' journey and his fate, respectively (13:33; see also 9:22; 17:25; 18:31–33; 24:44–46).

The starkest contrast of all is between Jesus' will or "desire" concerning Jerusalem and that of the city itself (13:34). That contrast is expressed in the form of a lament that has the added dire consequences of linking Jesus' fate to the fate of the city. Jesus expresses his desire in the tender picture of a mother bird who wants to shelter her young, but that desire is met by a conflicting one—the people's stark refusal to accept that shelter.

The consequence of their rejection is that their "house is left" (or "abandoned," 13:35). The saying is puzzling, but probably refers to the desolation of Jerusalem and the razing of the temple during the war between the Jews and Rome (66–70 C.E.). If that is the case, Luke has linked that disaster to the city's refusal to receive Jesus and, in fact, to its hostility to him, which provides the climax of Luke's account of Jesus' arrest and trials (23:13–25). For Luke, that connection is a great cause for lament, because he has affirmed from the very beginning of the Gospel that God's will has always been that Israel and all the nations would enjoy blessings and salvation (for example, 1:68–79; 3:6). When God's gracious will is thwarted by human refusal to accept it, Jesus' proclamation turns into lament.

In keeping with that overarching affirmation by Luke, the final sentence of the section also draws the reader forward to Jesus' coming time in Jerusalem by the preview of the song that accompanies Jesus' entrance into the city (19:38; Ps. 118:26). That conclusion asserts that even the sly Herod ("that fox") will not be able to thwart Jesus until his work has been accomplished, yet, at the same time, it holds out Luke's own hope that the city (as a symbol for the Jews) will finally "see" Jesus and recognize that he is "the one who comes in the name of the Lord." The house *is* abandoned, not to divine delight, but to divine lament and tender yearning that there still might be another outcome. In the power of the divine will to effect what is longed for, Luke ends this section of the journey narrative on a note of promise.

## BANQUET ETIQUETTE
## Luke 14:1–24

A banquet held on the sabbath at the home of a leader of the Pharisees provides the symbolically weighted setting for the next collection of stories and teachings along the way to Jerusalem. The setting includes a festive event and a holy time, but in a company that would have led Luke's audience to anticipate opposition to Jesus and confrontation by the religious authorities. The episode is set off from the surrounding narrative by the introductory phrase with which the section begins—"On one occasion" (14:1)—and by the change in audience between this episode and the teachings that follow (14:25).

### Another Sabbath Healing Story (Luke 14:1–6)

14:1 **On one occasion when Jesus was going to the house of a leader of the Pharisees to eat a meal on the sabbath, they were watching him closely. ² Just then, in front of him, there was a man who had dropsy. ³ And Jesus asked the lawyers and Pharisees, "Is it lawful to cure people on the sabbath, or not?" ⁴ But they were silent. So Jesus took him and healed him, and sent him away. ⁵ Then he said to them, "If one of you has a child or an ox that has fallen into a well, will you not immediately pull it out on a sabbath day?" ⁶ And they could not reply to this.**

The sabbath setting and the presence of the religious leaders are important in the unfolding of the story of Jesus' healing of the man with edema (14:1–6). Stories of two other sabbath healings that turned into controversies have already been told (6:6–11; 13:10–17). This one seems to reflect details from both of the other stories. As he does in both of the other stories, Jesus himself initiates the healing. Here, as in 6:6–11, he initiates the discussion as well. He does so in a way that raises the general question of what it means to keep the sabbath, rather than immediately focusing on the limits or special conditions for sabbath keeping according to the law.

The question, "Is it lawful to cure people on the sabbath, or not?" calls for a yes-and-no answer: Yes, in matters of life and death, but generally no, because healing would have been considered work, and therefore prohibited. This question, as does the question in 6:9, "Is it lawful to do good or to do harm on the sabbath, to save life or to destroy it?" would cause an audience of expert interpreters to choose words carefully. As does the story of the woman who was healed on the sabbath, in 13:10–17, though, this passage also introduces a rationale from within the law itself: A living being in danger on the sabbath must be rescued (14:5). The silence of Jesus' audience (14:6) suggests that the parallel between the man's condition and other life-threatening (or at least life-inhibiting) circumstances was clear.

In one sense, one could say that Luke has not advanced his account at all by including this story, for he is reiterating points already made. If his church was still involved in controversies with the synagogue about proper sabbath observance, the silence of the Jewish religious leaders in this story might be designed to suggest that Luke thinks his arguments have carried the day. The reason for the inclusion of this healing story becomes even more difficult to discern in light of the fact that the sabbath setting does not appear to be an issue in any of the teachings that follow, but would be equally appropriate on any day. We will leave that question unanswered until we have had a chance to explore the accompanying teachings.

The remainder of the episode falls into three parts: Verses 7–11 deal with the conduct of guests at a banquet; verses 12–14 address people who would host a banquet; and verses 15–24 convey a parable about a banquet. The festive occasion itself has shaped the dinner-table conversation. The host, identified as a leader of the Pharisees, is implied to be a person of comfortable means, if not necessarily from the richest class of the society. Nothing is said about the identity of the other guests, but the implication is that they were people who would be concerned about their prestige or standing relative to other guests, and people who might be in a position to give parties themselves to reciprocate for such an invitation. We are not told whether the man who was healed was among the invited guests, or whether he might have entered the house in order to benefit from the distribution of leftover food to poor people from the neighborhood (see 7:36–50). The man who is healed may be a living example of "the poor, the crippled, the lame, and the blind" (14:13, 21) who figure both in the teachings and in the parable.

## Table Manners and Guest Lists (Luke 14:7–14)

14:7 **When he noticed how the guests chose the places of honor, he told them a parable.** 8 **"When you are invited by someone to a wedding banquet,** do not sit down at the place of honor, in case someone more distinguished than you has been invited by your host; 9 and the host who invited both of you may come and say to you, 'Give this person your place,' and then in disgrace you would start to take the lowest place. 10 But when you are invited, go and sit down at the lowest place, so that when your host comes, he may say to you, 'Friend, move up higher'; then you will be honored in the presence of all who sit at the table with you. 11 For all who exalt themselves will be humbled, and those who humble themselves will be exalted."

12 He said also to the one who had invited him, "When you give a luncheon or a dinner, do not invite your friends or your brothers or your relatives or rich neighbors, in case they may invite you in return, and you would be repaid. 13 But when you give a banquet, invite the poor, the crippled, the lame, and the blind. 14 And you will be blessed, because they cannot repay you, for you will be repaid at the resurrection of the righteous."

The teachings in 14:7–14 are unique to Luke (except for 14:11, other versions of which are found in Matthew 18:4; 23:12; and Luke 18:14). Like the story in 14:1–6, they all point to an unexpected turn or interruption in a very proper occasion, though these teachings focus on social customs, whereas the earlier story has to do with a point of law. The teachings can be divided into two groups on the basis of their content and their address to guests (14:7) and to hosts (14:12).

The teachings addressed to guests (14:7–11) sound like a page taken from a first-century book of etiquette. As is the case for most rules of etiquette, these teachings depend on common sense and ways to minimize discomfort and awkwardness. In a highly stratified society, where places at table carried great social weight, to misjudge one's status relative to the other guests was a serious matter. To overestimate one's position and take a better seat than "deserved" would lead to great embarrassment when the host asked one to give that place up for another. On the other hand, to exhibit modesty by choosing a less prestigious seat than one's status indicated could reflect even greater honor on the humble guest, who would be asked to move up. The fact that the teachings are included, however, hints that the hearers might not think through that possibility, and might be inclined toward social climbing and jealousy. The saying in 14:11 changes the impact of these teachings, however, because in that saying the reversal of first and last becomes a matter of principle, not a matter of prudence. In the larger context of Luke 14, verse 11 seems to be an artificial attempt to bring the previous teachings into line with the reversal of common sense and "normal" values mandated in 14:12–14 and in the parable that follows.

The teachings directed at people who might host a banquet (14:12–14) contradict the usual reasons a host in the society assumed by the Gospel writer might have for drawing up a guest list. According to these teachings, people who might be in a position to reciprocate are to be omitted, in favor of people who could not invite the host in return—people from outside the host's social circle. Furthermore, the invited guests are even to be the sort of people whose presence would make more typical guests uncomfortable. These teachings thus echo those found earlier in the sermon on the plain (6:27–36), where reciprocal relationships between friends and enemies alike are transformed by new standards of generosity.

We should note that in these teachings in chapter 14, Luke takes for granted the assumptions that all persons with physical disabilities are poor, and that hospitality is a matter of mutual obligations between social equals. On the contrary, even in Jesus' or Luke's day, there were probably lame or blind people who were economically well off due to their families' wealth. More important, Luke does not make what to modern hearers is an obvious point, that society has an obligation to make it possible for persons with disabilities to participate as valued and productive members of the society. There is no more reason to assume, let alone to justify, their poverty than to justify the poverty of any other man, woman, or child.

Furthermore, these teachings ignore the extraordinary generosity and hospitality of many people who are poor, which far surpass the carefully calculated reciprocal invitations assumed as the norm. Travelers from Europe and North America often return from visits to Africa, Asia, or Latin America with stories of "banquets" shared with them by poor villagers who pooled the last bits of food in their homes in order to welcome those who had come to visit them. By analogy, it is not at all unlikely that poor people of Luke's day also lived more open and generous lives than did those who were busy calculating benefits and obligations of their actions.

As radical as is Luke's portrayal of a new framework for human life and society, then, the specific stories and teachings by which that vision is conveyed are limited by the author's own social context. Examples like these teachings serve as a reminder that the vision of the gospel is always deeper and broader than any sustained human expression of it, even that of the Gospels themselves.

The reversal of values away from business-as-usual that is always a part of the expression of the gospel is underlined in 14:14b, where one's table community is said to have eternal consequences. Those consequences are elaborated on in a beatitude pointing to the "messianic banquet" (14:15), the great feast symbolizing the joys and the splendor of God's ultimate triumph. The words of blessing both introduce the parable and link it (and, by implication, the preceding teachings) to the reign of God. While the beatitude might seem at first glance to be a pious platitude uttered to defuse a tense social moment, the connection drawn is crucial to the unfolding of Luke's argument. Once again, as in the story and the parables of 13:10–21, divine truths unfold in the stuff of everyday life, and there they show a surprising new side: Those who "will eat bread in the kingdom of God" turn out not to be the ones we thought were on the guest list.

## The Parable of the Great Feast (Luke 14:15–24)

**14:15  One of the dinner guests, on hearing this, said to him, "Blessed is the one who will eat bread in the kingdom of God!"** [16] **Then Jesus said to him, "Someone gave a great dinner and invited many.** [17] **At the time for the dinner he sent his slave to say to those who had been invited, 'Come; for everything is ready now.'** [18] **But they all alike began to make excuses. The first said to him, 'I have bought a piece of land, and I must go out and see it; please accept my regrets.'** [19] **Another said, 'I have bought five yoke of oxen, and I am going to try them out; please accept my regrets.'** [20] **Another said, 'I have just been married, and therefore I cannot come.'** [21] **So the slave returned and reported this to his master. Then the owner of the house became angry and said to his slave, 'Go out at once into the streets and lanes of the town and bring in the poor, the crippled, the blind, and the lame.'** [22] **And the slave said, 'Sir, what you ordered has been done, and there is still room.'** [23] **Then the master said to the slave, 'Go out into the roads and lanes, and compel people to come in, so that my house may be filled.** [24] **For I tell you, none of those who were invited will taste my dinner.'"**

The parable (14:16–24) develops in much greater detail the picture of a banquet at which the guest list and the rules of etiquette have been changed. A parable similar to this one is found in Matthew 22:1–10, and another version is found in the noncanonical Gospel of Thomas. Although each version has acquired particular accents that result in different stories, they point to an original parable that included the following elements: a feast or banquet, prior invitations repeated, excuses from the original guests, and new invitations to different guests.

The specific excuses of the first guests and the identity of the new guests are the points at which Luke develops his particular concern about the poor. Custom dictated that an original invitation to an event scheduled for a future date would be repeated when the party was ready to begin. Guests could arrive at a dinner party any time up to the end of the first course and expect to be welcomed. The first two excuses (14:18–19) seem to anticipate just such a delay, though perhaps a bit longer than custom allowed: The guests would complete their business, then they would go to the party. Buying land unseen or five yoke of oxen (a number of animals which suggests that the buyer had fairly extensive landholdings) without examining them would seem to be rather sloppy business practices. The determination to complete business on one's own schedule also shows a certain disregard for the host. The third excuse (14:20) seems to anticipate absence from the banquet rather than a delay. As such, it either demonstrates even greater disregard for the host whose invitation had previously been accepted, or it reflects total absentmindedness.

The beatitude in 14:15 has already alerted Luke's audience (as well as the characters within the story) that this is no ordinary party, however, and the rules of etiquette are different. Guests who count on excuses of prior commitments and business as usual find themselves the targets of the host's anger (14:21), and they find their seats taken by a new cast of celebrants.

In Luke's version of the parable, the wealthy host relies on a servant or "slave" to deliver the invitations. We should note that despite the example of social reversals in the parable in particular and in this section of the Gospel in general, the slave's status is never questioned. The text assumes what our moral sense abhors, namely the institution of slavery.

As the story unfolds, the servant makes two trips in order to find enough new guests to fill the house. The second of the new invitations, where the guests are not described, resembles the versions of the parable found in Matthew and in the Gospel of Thomas. Luke's special emphasis is found in the first list, whose qualifications echo those of the guests to be invited to one's parties according to the teaching in 14:13. Traditional interpretations of the parable have read that first list as referring to outcasts in Israel to whom Jesus' proclamation was directed, while the second group (coming from outside the town) are Gentiles now being welcomed into the church. That sort of ethnic reading, however, masks the issues of social and economic class that are much closer to the heart of this section of Luke, and that might give some clues to how the parable fits into the section on banquet etiquette.

The contrast between the first guests and both groups of recipients of the second invitations is a contrast between people of means and people on the margins. The original guests who are buying land and the animals with which to work it would come from the class of large landowners who are benefiting from the hardships being suffered by owners of small farms. The latter would be forced to sell even their precious land and other capital goods in order to obtain the cash needed for their immediate survival. They, in turn, would be but a short step from the social marginalization of the urban and rural poor who constitute the first and second groups of new guests, respectively. Or, to look at the cast of characters from another angle, the first invitees all participate in the commerce and customs of the society, and the plot of the parable hangs on their assumption that those rules can always be counted on. They learn that for this particular banquet, such socially guaranteed privileges no longer count. On the other hand, the new guests—whether peasants or "people of the land," or the urban marginalized people who were poor, crippled, blind, and lame—are people in no position to make such assumptions in the social order presupposed by the parable. For them, the invitation to this banquet is an unexpected gift.

We have already seen such a guest list of outsiders and persons without privilege several times in Luke's Gospel. In 4:18, quoting Isaiah 61:1–2, people who are poor, captives, blind, and oppressed are identified as the recipients of the good news and release to be proclaimed by the one anointed by the Spirit. Similarly, in 7:22, healing and good news that has come to the people who are blind, lame, lepers, deaf, dead, and poor is the evidence that responds to John's question to Jesus from prison, "Are you the one who is to come, or are we to wait for another?" Finally, the blessings summarized in 6:20–22 are for those who are poor, hungry, weeping, hated, excluded, or defamed. In each case, those to whom Jesus' ministry (and in particular the reign of God of which he is the herald and proclaimer) is directed are the people whom both secular and religious society has relegated to the margins. For them, the celebration tastes especially sweet.

What at first appears to be the conclusion to the parable (14:24) turns out to be much more. In fact, it provides an important key to this section of Luke's Gospel. According to the parable, the host has been addressing the slave, giving orders for the second group of new invitations. Despite the tight link indicated by the conjunction "for," the situation has changed, for the "you" being addressed is a plural pronoun (a distinction that is clear in Greek). In other words, no longer is the host of the parable speaking to the servant, but rather, apparently, all the guests at the Pharisee's dinner party are addressed: "For I tell you [all], none of those who were invited will taste my dinner."

With this conclusion, Luke reminds his audience once again that the whole episode has been about the reign of God. The sabbath setting of the chapter does prove to be central, for the whole chapter is about the meaning and celebration of what is truly holy and appropriate to God's agenda of salvation—"good news to the poor" (4:18) and hence to "all the people" (2:10). In the initial story (14:1–6), the healing has made it clear that in that reign, holy times are times for life, health, and wholeness that stretch the boundaries of religious law. Presumptions of privilege, whether on the basis of one's religious identity (seen in traditionally proper sabbath observance) or one's social status (seen in schemes to assure privilege or to protect one's economic status by business as usual), crumble in the face of the invitation to drop everything that contributes to one's system of security, and to join the party. For those who come, it is a splendid feast indeed.

## THE COST OF DISCIPLESHIP
### Luke 14:25–35

> 14:25 Now large crowds were traveling with him; and he turned and said to them, 26 "Whoever comes to me and does not hate father and mother, wife and children, brothers and sisters, yes, and even life itself, cannot be my disciple. 27 Whoever does not carry the cross and follow me cannot be my disciple. 28 For which of you, intending to build a tower, does not first sit down and estimate the cost, to see whether he has enough to complete it? 29 Otherwise, when he has laid a foundation and is not able to finish, all who see it will begin to ridicule him, 30 saying, 'This fellow began to build and was not able to finish.' 31 Or what king, going out to wage war against another king, will not sit down first and consider whether he is able with ten thousand to oppose the one who comes against him with twenty thousand? 32 If he cannot, then, while the other is still far away, he sends a delegation and asks for the terms of peace. 33 So therefore, none of you can become my disciple if you do not give up all your possessions.
>
> 34 "Salt is good; but if salt has lost its taste, how can its saltiness be restored? 35 It is fit neither for the soil nor for the manure pile; they throw it away. Let anyone with ears to hear listen!"

The seam between the scene at the banquet and the teachings that follow appears to have been carelessly joined. With no indication of a change of location from the banquet in the home of the Pharisee, Jesus is said to turn to the large crowds that accompanied him (14:25). Luke expects us to move with him to the more public setting, because his purpose is not to achieve dramatic polish, but theological parallelism. Just as the privileged guests at the banquet have had to deal with the overturning of the rules for social discourse that would have sustained their relative privilege and security, so now all of Jesus' followers are confronted with a collection of teachings about the cost of following Jesus.

That theme is all that connects the teachings. They include three sayings about criteria that prevent people from being Jesus' disciples (14:26, 27, 33), amplified by short parables (14:28–30, 31–32, 34–35a). The first requirement (14:26)—"hating" father and mother, wife and children, brothers and sisters, and even one's own life—does not prescribe the emotion we know as "hatred," or in the case of one's own life, self-hatred or contempt. Rather, it means even being willing to live without these loved ones, not being so attached to them that their well-being, or even one's own survival, is one's first priority. The saying is powerful precisely because one's own life and family relationships *are* a baseline of one's personal security and identity, regardless of one's social position.

The lack of a reference to husbands on the list of family members makes it clear that men are the principal audience envisioned by the Gospel writer. They would be the people in a position of authority in some portion of their family and the ones most clearly in a position to benefit from the prestige or honor of the household. The literature of the early church makes it clear that women as well as men were prominent in the church, as they had been among Jesus' followers from the very beginning. For an author to address principally the dominant or most powerful members of a group, and to allow others to hear themselves included as best they can, is a practice that is deeply entrenched in the literature of many cultures.

While Luke's harsh wording certainly gets our attention, Matthew's parallel reading, "Whoever loves father or mother more than me is not worthy of me; and whoever loves son or daughter more than me is not worthy of me" (Matt. 10:37) may convey more clearly the point being made. Indeed, that reading echoes the sayings about the priority of discipleship over family obligations Luke gives in 9:59–62.

The second saying (14:27) also has a parallel in Matthew (Matt. 10:38), and a similar saying occurs also in Matthew 16:24b, Mark 8:34b, and Luke 9:23b. The version of the saying that has a parallel in Mark assumes that each follower will have to take up his or her own cross, while the other version refers to "the" cross—presumably Jesus' cross. The focus in the latter is more narrowly on following Jesus on the dangerous journey to Jerusalem (of which this passage is roughly the midpoint in Luke's Gospel).

It would be easy to read both of the sayings in 14:26–27 as equating discipleship with neglect of one's own family in the pursuit of some higher goal, out of self-hatred or contempt, or even in the quest for martyrdom. They have sometimes been misread in that way. The two parables that follow the sayings, however, make it clear that Luke's point is different. The first parable (14:28–30) is drawn from the life of peasants who would need to build watchtowers in their fields in order to be sure no animal or human predators threatened them. To begin to build such a tower and have to abandon the project when it was half completed because one had run out of funds would make the builder a laughingstock.

Similarly, the second parable (14:31–32), set in the context of international politics, assumes common sense on the part of a king contemplating waging war on an enemy. No king would knowingly lead an army into a slaughter or into a situation where he could be forced into an unconditional surrender, but rather, the king whose troops are outnumbered will pursue a diplomatic solution. We should beware of an unfortunate implication of this parable, which is clearly not part of Luke's agenda. The situation envisioned in the parable seems to suggest that the pursuit of a peaceful solution to political and military conflicts is a strategy growing out of weakness. The effect is to portray war as the more desirable and honorable course for political leaders who want to be seen as powerful players on the world stage. To draw such a conclusion pushes the parable beyond its role in this part of Luke's Gospel, where the issue of prudent action is clearly the principal theme.

The point of the two parables is precisely that at the very least one will try to avoid disaster. One will recognize the cost before beginning a venture, and one will choose one's course prudently and realistically. So it is also, Luke implies, with discipleship. One needs to go into the venture with forethought, aware of where it might lead, and ready to pay the price if necessary. Discipleship does not mean simply to run after Jesus—or, in Luke's setting, to become part of the church—in a rush of enthusiasm that evaporates as quickly as it appears when the going gets rough.

The third saying (14:33) again underlines that cost and need for forethought: "None of you can become my disciple if you do not give up all your possessions." The "possessions" include everything at one's disposal, everything that gives shape and substance to one's life, and everything in which one might find one's security. Nothing is said here about selling material goods and giving the proceeds to the poor. Instead, the possessions themselves must be relinquished. The main idea is not what their value can do for others, but what the fact of having them—which becomes more like being possessed by them—makes impossible for the owner.

The concluding warning about salt that loses its taste, and as a result is good for nothing (14:34–35a), seems to take the previous warnings a step farther. Not only is the potential cost of discipleship great, but the bills may come in over a long time. A disciple who begins with energy and enthusiasm risks running short of both before the journey is completed. The judgment on such "flash-in-the-pan" followers is harsh: They are not merely worthless, but actually dangerous, just as even flavorless salt will contaminate the chemistry of soil or fertilizer (literally, "manure") that is exposed to it.

The teachings are hard, whether they are delivered over tea and cookies at a banquet or to crowds in the open air. Just as not everyone who learns of it will get the point about the bounty of God's reign (8:8b), so also it would appear that not everyone will understand the costly discontinuity between life and business as usual and the life of discipleship (14:35b): "Let anyone with ears to hear listen!"

## PARABLES OF "LOSTS" AND "FOUNDS"
## Luke 15:1–32

### The Sheep (Luke 15:3–7)

15:1 **Now all the tax collectors and sinners were coming near to listen to him. ² And the Pharisees and the scribes were grumbling and saying, "This fellow welcomes sinners and eats with them."**

**³ So he told them this parable: ⁴ "Which one of you, having a hundred sheep and losing one of them, does not leave the ninety-nine in the wilderness and go after the one that is lost until he finds it? ⁵ When he has found it, he lays it on his shoulders and rejoices. ⁶ And when he comes home, he calls together his friends and neighbors, saying to them, 'Rejoice with me, for I have found my sheep that was lost.' ⁷ Just so, I tell you, there will be more joy in heaven over one sinner who repents than over ninety-nine righteous persons who need no repentance.**

The setting remains the same as in the previous teachings, but a transition to a new section of teachings is indicated by Luke's elaborate description of the crowd. Now the multitude is said specifically to include tax collectors and sinners, much to the consternation of the scribes and Pharisees who are also present. The three parables about the lost and found sheep, coin, and sons respond to the challenge of the latter groups, "This fellow welcomes sinners and eats with them" (15:2). The first parable is found also in Matthew 18:12–14, and the other two are found only in Luke.

The differences between Matthew's and Luke's versions of the parable of the sheep are subtle. Both rely on the audience's agreement that the shepherd's action is appropriate. In Matthew's version the sheep has strayed from the flock—an occurrence that fits Matthew's inclusion of the parable in a collection of warnings not to allow any of the "little ones" in the community to stray away. In Matthew, whether the stray will be found again is left unknown: "And if he finds it, . . . he rejoices" (Matt. 18:13), whereas in Luke, the finding is only a matter of time ("until he finds it," 15:4). In Luke's parable, the sheep is not one that has "strayed," but one that is "lost"—an assessment Jesus' challengers might also make of the sinners and tax collectors.

The losing and finding of the sheep constitute simply the introductory question of the parable. The answer is self-evident: A valuable sheep that is lost merits one's full attention until it is found. What is not said, but is taken for granted, is that during the search for the one sheep, the others are left to their own devices "in the wilderness." Apparently those in the audience readily accept the risk as worth taking to recover the valuable animal.

In contrast to that brief summary, Luke elaborates in considerable detail on the joy that follows the finding: the shepherd's tender carrying of the sheep, his rejoicing already out in the wilderness by himself, his return home, and his summoning of the community to share in his celebration (15:5–6). The richly textured description of the mood of celebration invites the audience to join in.

That mood is tempered, however, by the application with which Luke concludes the parable (15:7). In the heavenly economy, a repentant sinner evokes similar joy to that which greets the finding of the one lost sheep. While Jesus' challengers might be convinced to accept that much of the argument, at least given adequate evidence of repentance, the suggestion that the return of that one sinner evokes more joy than their own habitual "righteousness" would certainly grate on their nerves. The implication is that it is worth risking their "safety" (in this case, their "righteousness") in order to recover even one who is "lost".

## The Coin (Luke 15:8–10)

15:8 **"Or what woman having ten silver coins, if she loses one of them, does not light a lamp, sweep the house, and search carefully until she finds it? ⁹ When she has found it, she calls together her friends and neighbors, saying, 'Rejoice with me, for I have found the coin that I had lost.' ¹⁰ Just so, I tell you, there is joy in the presence of the angels of God over one sinner who repents."**

The second parable features a woman who searches diligently for a lost silver coin—perhaps a part of her dowry. Again the situation is posed as a question whose answer is self-evident to any woman of modest means (and perhaps even to the husband of such a woman). This time the thoroughness of her search is noted (15:8), and again the details multiply in the description of her joy at finding the coin, which becomes the basis for a celebration in the whole community (15:9). Since the search for the lost coin does not place the other coins in jeopardy and set up the question of the relative appreciation of the one and the many, the concluding application of the second parable stops with an affirmation of the heavenly rejoicing that greets the repentance of one sinner (15:10).

The concluding applications in both of these parables underline the difference between the value system of Jesus' challengers and that of "heaven," which Jesus represents. While Jesus' challengers have objected to the presence of sinners and tax collectors who are not said to have repented and mended their ways, even those challengers would probably find reason to rejoice in the repentance of a sinner. But the fit between parables and setting is still not exact, for nothing is said about those who have gathered around Jesus having shown any signs of repentance that the scribes and Pharisees would recognize. For the parables to address the setting at all, the challengers would need to recognize the simple fact that the tax collectors and others had gathered around Jesus as evidence of the "turning" (*metanoia*) of which the summaries speak.

Another aspect of the gap between Jesus and his challengers can be seen in that while all in the audience would recognize both the lost sheep and the lost coin as objects of value, that is not the way Jesus' challengers would view the groups of people to whose presence they object. The sheep and coin are of value, and that is the reason they are searched for so diligently. Sinners, on the other hand, would be valued only after they had repented. For these parables to respond to the objections of Jesus' challengers, the scribes and Pharisees would have needed to have begun to look at the sinners and tax collectors in a different way.

## The Sons (Luke 15:11–32)

15:11 **Then Jesus said, "There was a man who had two sons.** 12 **The younger of them said to his father, 'Father, give me the share of the property that will belong to me.' So he divided his property between them.** 13 **A few days later the younger son gathered all he had and traveled to a distant country, and there he squandered his property in dissolute living.** 14 **When he had spent everything, a severe famine took place throughout that country, and he** began to be in need. [15] So he went and hired himself out to one of the citizens of that country, who sent him to his fields to feed the pigs. [16] He would gladly have filled himself with the pods that the pigs were eating; and no one gave him anything. [17] But when he came to himself he said, 'How many of my father's hired hands have bread enough and to spare, but here I am dying of hunger! [18] I will get up and go to my father, and I will say to him, "Father, I have sinned against heaven and before you; [19] I am no longer worthy to be called your son; treat me like one of your hired hands.' " [20] So he set off and went to his father. But while he was still far off, his father saw him and was filled with compassion; he ran and put his arms around him and kissed him. [21] Then the son said to him, 'Father, I have sinned against heaven and before you; I am no longer worthy to be called your son.' [22] But the father said to his slaves, 'Quickly, bring out a robe—the best one—and put it on him; put a ring on his finger and sandals on his feet. [23] And get the fatted calf and kill it, and let us eat and celebrate; [24] for this son of mine was dead and is alive again; he was lost and is found!' And they began to celebrate.

[25] "Now his elder son was in the field; and when he came and approached the house, he heard music and dancing. [26] He called one of the slaves and asked what was going on. [27] He replied, 'Your brother has come, and your father has killed the fatted calf, because he has got him back safe and sound.' [28] Then he became angry and refused to go in. His father came out and began to plead with him. [29] But he answered his father, 'Listen! For all these years I have been working like a slave for you, and I have never disobeyed your command; yet you have never given me even a young goat so that I might celebrate with my friends. [30] But when this son of yours came back, who has devoured your property with prostitutes, you killed the fatted calf for him!' [31] Then the father said to him, 'Son, you are always with me, and all that is mine is yours. [32] But we had to celebrate and rejoice, because this brother of yours was dead and has come to life; he was lost and has been found.' "

The third parable (15:11–32) suggests a more immediate connection to the setting in Luke: The younger son fits the role of "sinner" very well. Tradition has provided the title "parable of the prodigal son" to emphasize that character whose behavior and fate capture our attention. In fact, however, there are two sons whose stories unfold, and a father whose love and generosity encompass both. Perhaps a better name would be "the parable of two beloved sons" or "the parable of the compassionate father." All three of these characters come into focus at different points in the narrative.

The complexity of this parable is remarkable, especially in comparison with the two preceding ones. Instead of the simple movement from lost to found, resulting in a celebration, this parable is developed through two scenes, one featuring each of the two brothers. Each scene unfolds with an economy of detail that nevertheless presents a richly colored and textured picture. That richness is conveyed by glimpses of the family's social circumstances and of the customs and laws that encompassed them, through the dialogue between the characters or in one character's heart, through their ways of moving away from and toward each other, and through the symbolic quality of their actions.

The introductory statement alerts the reader to the double plot line: "There was a man who had two sons." According to the laws of the Roman Empire, the two sons would have been able to live off the family estate during their father's lifetime, but the property would remain in his hands until his death. After his death, the older son would inherit two-thirds of the property, and the remaining third would be divided among the remaining heirs. The younger son's request to receive his property during the father's lifetime was thus very irregular and deeply disrespectful. It amounted to his treating his father as if he were dead.

The father's compliance with the request is noted simply: "So he divided his property between them" (15:12c). By contrast, the younger son's downfall is described in slow motion, forcing the reader to take in every detail of the journey. The country to which he travels is "distant," the property is "squandered," his lifestyle is "dissolute," a famine strikes, and this son from a well-to-do household (as the subsequent mention of servants, the lavish feast, and the symbols of a robe, sandals, and signet ring make clear) suddenly finds himself among the poor. More than simply poor, he is so desperate that he becomes a farm worker on someone else's estate. The depth of his desperation is seen in that he not only cares for pigs, but envies them their food (15:13–16). The scribes and Pharisees in Jesus' audience would hear that as a particularly dismal fate, because for them pigs were "unclean" animals. Although we are not told the ethnic identity of the family in the parable, from the audience's perspective the point would be clear.

The journey to the distant country is resolved in an even more difficult journey: The young man "came to himself" (15:17). The journey home begins with an internal dialogue in which he resolves to throw himself on his father's mercy (in the hope of being allowed to live the better life of a servant on his family's estate), and he rehearses in detail his speech of repentance (15:18–20a). The audience is prepared by his words of earnest repentance to hear that he is welcomed back and allowed to work on the estate once again, and they would be ready to join in the rejoicing. But the son never actually finishes his carefully rehearsed speech.

The father's compassion outruns the son's penitence, and the speech of repentance is cut off in mid-sentence. Instead of accepting the son as one of his servants, the father tells the servants to wait on the son, preparing a feast and bringing a robe, sandals, and signet ring, which were the symbols of his restoration as son and heir (15:20–23). Like the two preceding parables, this scene ends with the celebration that accompanies the finding of something precious that was lost (15:24). Whatever the audience has come to think of the younger son, and however that character seems to assess his own worth in the context of the parable, the father's complete acceptance of him as a son does not waver.

If the parable ended here, the father's compassion would be an efficient corrective to the grumbling of the scribes and the Pharisees in Luke's setting of the parable. The father recognizes the value of this repentant sinner, and the grumblers should do the same for the tax collectors and sinners who gather around Jesus. But the story cannot end yet, because the man had *two* sons.

The second son returns from nearby fields to the house that is bursting with the celebration. A servant's words rehearse the story of what has happened. In contrast to the younger son's penitent but hopeful return, the older son's response is anger and a refusal to join the party. Just as the father went out to meet the younger son (15:20), so he does for the older son (15:28). This time, he is met with a lengthy recital of the older son's faithful service and of the evidence of the father's ingratitude for his relentless goodness (15:29–30).

By the usual criteria of justice and fairness, the older son has a point. His brother took his share of their father's estate and wasted it. Meanwhile the older son worked hard—albeit with a certain self-interest, since now it would all be his someday—caring for the estate and presumably increasing its value. His brother's return would cost more than the calf that was the main dish at the feast, for with the younger son not only home again but restored to his full status in the family, the estate would be divided again. The lavish celebration adds insult to the financial injury caused by the younger brother's homecoming. The scribes and Pharisees in Luke's setting of the parable would not be the only ones to understand such a reaction on the part of the older son. So would almost everyone else in the crowd.

But the father's response invokes a different value system—one that can rejoice in the presence of both sons (15:31–32). The love and constancy of the obedient older son is a treasured fact of the father's life. It is no surprise, but part of the context of life that allows compassion to flourish. What evokes the celebration is the wondrous news that "this brother of yours was dead and has come to life; he was lost and has been found."

The parable does not tell us how the older brother responds to this statement, which echoes the invitations to celebration in the previous two parables. The uncomfortable feeling lingers that perhaps there is still one lost son. That is the question posed to Jesus' challengers in Luke's setting. While all three of these parables portray God's rejoicing when those who are "lost" are "found," the last story may provide a glimpse of divine sadness at human resentment of divine compassion.

A word of caution is in order, however, lest especially the last parable be thought to provide a clear and unambiguous reflection of divine compassion and generosity. As a parable, the story is built on details of the social conditions and assumptions of its world of origin, and it is told to evoke the audience's response to specific issues and questions.

However, both the characters and actions that are mentioned and those that are ignored convey messages and impressions that may cloud the central voice of the parable. For example, as complex as the interactions of the characters in this parable are, we should note that only the father and the two sons occupy the stage as active characters. Servants are the only other human beings mentioned, and they are treated (as domestic workers often are) not as characters, but as instruments for conveying information (15:26–27) and preparing the party for the householder's family and their peers (15:22–24). Female members of the family are never mentioned: It is the "parable of the absent mother" as much as of the compassionate father. Women had little role in the complexities of inheritance and estate management as long as there were men to fulfill those roles. Furthermore, the whole story focuses on an estate of a fairly wealthy family, far removed from the concern for simple survival that, then as now, framed the daily life of the poor. In this parable, the father's compassion and generosity do not result in a celebration for the servants, but only added work.

Although the first two parables of this chapter seem not to address the grumbling of Jesus' challengers in the setting in the Gospel, they do speak to the experience of poor women and men who would rejoice to find a lost possession. The very simplicity and self-evidence of these two parables allow them to function as parables of joy and good news to the poor. It is different, however, with the third parable. The bite of the third is felt primarily by people of privilege, especially those who see themselves as relentlessly good and faithful, and so as deserving the blessings they enjoy. In fact, we probably side with the younger brother only because we know the outcome of the parable ahead of time. In our heart of hearts we know that the older brother has a point, and we grumble too at love that makes a home for both sons.

# 10.  Further Warnings and Teachings for Daily Life
*Luke 16:1–17:37*

## DIVINE LAW AND HUMAN GREED
### Luke 16:1–31

### The Parable of the Shrewd Manager (Luke 16:1–13)

16:1 Then Jesus said to the disciples, "There was a rich man who had a manager, and charges were brought to him that this man was squandering his property. ² So he summoned him and said to him, 'What is this that I hear about you? Give me an accounting of your management, because you cannot be my manager any longer.' ³ Then the manager said to himself, 'What will I do, now that my master is taking the position away from me? I am not strong enough to dig, and I am ashamed to beg. ⁴ I have decided what to do so that, when I am dismissed as manager, people may welcome me into their homes.' ⁵ So, summoning his master's debtors one by one, he asked the first, 'How much do you owe my master?' ⁶ He answered, 'A hundred jugs of olive oil.' He said to him, 'Take your bill, sit down quickly, and make it fifty.' ⁷ Then he asked another, 'And how much do you owe?' He replied, 'A hundred containers of wheat.' He said to him, 'Take your bill and make it eighty.' ⁸ And his master commended the dishonest manager because he had acted shrewdly; for the children of this age are more shrewd in dealing with their own generation than are the children of light. ⁹ And I tell you, make friends for yourselves by means of dishonest wealth so that when it is gone, they may welcome you into the eternal homes.

¹⁰ "Whoever is faithful in a very little is faithful also in much; and whoever is dishonest in a very little is dishonest also in much. ¹¹ If then you have not been faithful with the dishonest wealth, who will entrust to you the true riches? ¹² And if you have not been faithful with what belongs to another, who will give you what is your own? ¹³ No slave can serve two masters; for a slave will either hate the one and love the other, or be devoted to the one and despise the other. You cannot serve God and wealth."

211

The crowds, including the tax collectors and sinners, fade into the background, as Luke presents a series of teachings directed first to the disciples (16:1), then to the Pharisees (16:14), then again to the disciples (17:1). Not until 17:11 does Luke indicate that the journey is going forward, or tell a story that provides on-stage action (17:11–19). The first teachings directed to the disciples and those to the Pharisees both include parables that begin, "There was a rich man. . . ." Together, these parables provide some of Luke's most biting comments on wealth and poverty.

Luke offers no explanation for his abrupt turning from the Pharisees and scribes (15:2) to the disciples (16:1). He simply begins the parable. But where it stops, nobody knows! Clearly, a number of loosely related sayings have been appended to the core story. Most scholars recognize 16:10–13 as a collection of "morals" that have been connected to the parable either in the tradition of the church or by Luke himself. Opinions are divided on whether any or all of 16:8b–9 should also be seen as additions, or whether they are part of the parable itself. The very existence of these interpretive hints testifies to the puzzling nature of this parable, in which the manager seems to be praised for his financial finagling. Attention to the economic background presumed in the parable, and to some of the specific language by which it is told, begins to define its message about wealth.

At the outset, the parable poses the classical question, What's in a name? It is often referred to as the parable of the "dishonest" or "unjust" manager. Both of those labels influence one to see the manager in a negative light. The first is totally unjustified: The parable contains no language related to "honesty." The adjective "unjust" is closer to the text but still misleading, for in the Greek text of the Gospel, the manager is literally called "the manager *of injustice*" (16:8)—a phrase that will turn out to be related to Luke's view of wealth and its proper use. The manager is also described as having acted "shrewdly" or "intelligently," in what may well be the original ending to the parable (16:8a): It is the story of the "shrewd manager."

The parable assumes the practice of absentee landownership that prevailed in first-century Palestine, as well as in other places. The rich man is such an absentee landowner, who has put a manager in charge of overseeing the productivity of his holdings and collecting the various rents and other dues from those who farmed it. Such rents were often calculated and collected "in kind," in the form of produce from the anticipated harvest. The "bills" would also include a commission paid to the manager, which, in turn, constituted his salary for his managerial services (in addition, perhaps, to his own farming rights or other compensation from the land-owner). When crops failed or need arose, the tenants might find themselves at year's end unable to make the payments. Proceedings could then begin against them to force them to pay by selling their property or by becoming indentured servants to work off the debt.

The story opens with the statement that the manager is not doing his job: The property is being wasted or "squandered" instead of turning a profit. Nothing is said about any dishonest or illegal behavior on the manager's part, and it is unlikely that such action is implied, for any loss incurred in that way would have to be repaid. Nothing is said about any repayment, however, or any actual charges against him. The manager is simply dismissed for failing as a manager, with no provision for severance pay and little prospect of future employment with such a record (16:1–3).

The manager's solution is to act "quickly" (that is, before word of his dismissal, and thus of his lack of authority to act on the owner's behalf, reached the community) to reduce the amounts people owed to the owner. In that way the manager shifts from being a representative of the wealthy owner, to align himself instead with people who in gratitude, and out of a sense of their indebtedness to him, would provide him hospitality in the future (16:4–7). The owner will have to go along with the new arrangements, for to cancel them once the debtors know of them would leave the owner with angry tenants, who would be in a position to do even more damage to the estate. In one sense, one could call the manager "shrewd" for having protected himself from impending ruin. The owner's compliment thus acknowledges that the manager has him over the proverbial barrel, and has saved himself in the process. But more is involved in Luke's reading of the parable, as the sayings in 16:8b–9 make clear.

What, exactly, has the manager done that qualifies as intelligent or "shrewd"? Commentators often speculate about whether the manager has been charging excessively high commissions, and simply reduces them to something more justifiable. Or, they suggest, the owner has been charging usurious interest (in clear violation of Torah; see, for example, Lev. 25:36–37; Deut. 23:19–20), and the manager's act makes him obedient to Torah in spite of himself. Clearly, something "wrong" has been made right, but the problem may be deeper than such overt violations.

The key is in the manager's identification by the owner as a "manager of injustice" (16:8a), and in the subsequent identification of wealth, not as "dishonest," but as "wealth of injustice" (16:9). The underlying assumption is of an economy of scarcity, where the quantity of wealth available is fixed. Some have more only if others have less. Any excessive accumulation in the hands of one (such as the "rich man") is, by definition, evidence of injustice that must be redressed by that redistribution of wealth called "giving alms" (see the discussions of 11:41–42 and 12:13–21). By reducing the amount owed by the (obviously poorer) debtors to the rich man, the manager is doing justice—a way of doing his job as a "manager of injustice" that no longer aims at perpetuating and even adding to old inequities, but instead reflects the new "economy" of which Jesus is the herald.

The concluding comments in 16:8b–9 then make sense. Motivated by self-interest as a true "[child] of this age" (assuring himself a place in others' "households," 16:4), the manager has manipulated the wealth entrusted to him in a way that "children of light" (those so oriented toward "heavenly" things that they are reluctant to get their hands dirty with impure money) do not dare to do. As a good manager, then, he has used the very fruits of injustice in the forging of that new community of accountability based on justice that already participates in God's project or reign (the eternal "tents" or "dwelling places," 16:9; contrary to what the NRSV implies, the word is not the same as that in 16:4).

For the disciples, this parable provides a "management model" for their own role as leaders (12:41–48). Instead of urging upon them a lifestyle or even an ideal of poverty, or advice to keep themselves pure from contamination by wealth, it challenges them to manage wealth in the direction of justice. In the process, they will be creating new communities and relationships that will allow their mission to go forward and that will support the enjoyment of abundant life by all people.

The first group of the concluding sayings attached to the parable (16:10–12) links this story about wealth and accountability to other teachings in Luke's Gospel (for 16:10, see 12:43–48; for 16:11, see 12:21, 33; for 16:12, see 19:11–27). The final saying comes from the source shared by Luke and Matthew (where it is included in the Sermon on the Mount, Matt. 6:24). It is harsh, for it does not permit the argument that one can use wealth to "serve" God. Instead, it states that one cannot be "enslaved to" two "masters" at once. "Love" and "hate," and "be devoted to" and "despise" refer not to emotions (in which sense, one might "hate" anyone who makes one a slave), but rather to divided loyalties. Although a person may *use* wealth on behalf of God's justice, as the parable portrays, one cannot be committed to justice and to the pursuit of wealth at the same time (16:13b).

## Divine Law in Force (Luke 16:14–18)

16:14 **The Pharisees, who were lovers of money, heard all this, and they ridiculed him.** 15 **So he said to them, "You are those who justify yourselves in the sight of others; but God knows your hearts; for what is prized by human beings is an abomination in the sight of God.**

16 **"The law and the prophets were in effect until John came; since then the good news of the kingdom of God is proclaimed, and everyone tries to enter it by force.** 17 **But it is easier for heaven and earth to pass away, than for one stroke of a letter in the law to be dropped.**

18 **"Anyone who divorces his wife and marries another commits adultery, and whoever marries a woman divorced from her husband commits adultery."**

The Pharisees, who had moved to the background during the previous parable, resume center-stage. Their alleged love of money makes them victims of narrative stereotyping by Luke, both in 16:14–15 and earlier in 11:37–44 and 14:1–14. That narrative device should not be seen as representing historical truth about all Pharisees, or even as the general perception of them. In fact, the historian Flavius Josephus, whose writings are nearly contemporary with the Gospels, portrays the Pharisees as siding with the poor, whereas it is the Sadducees who exploit the poor.

The opening reference to the greed of the Pharisees and the following parable (16:19–31) bracket a series of sayings that are often dismissed as a random collection. In fact, however, the sayings in 16:14–18 are tied together in a double indictment of the Pharisees. The first aspect of that indictment is expressed in 16:16–17. These religious leaders, of all people, ought to recognize the eternal validity of Torah as the expression of God's law, which can only be strengthened the more God's sovereignty is in evidence. The irony, however, is that they have not heeded John's call to repentance (7:29–30), and they have resisted the subsequent urgent invitation to enter God's reign. (The clause translated, "everyone tries to enter it by force" can also be translated "everyone is urged into it with zeal," or "everyone is pressed by an urgent invitation to enter it.") On the contrary, Luke implies, their willingness to adapt the law for expediency's sake is evidenced in their reading of the laws about divorce (16:18; see also Matt. 5:31–32; 19:9).

The second indictment of the Pharisees becomes clear in 18:11–12, the prayer of another Pharisee who proclaims that he is not a thief, rogue, or adulterer. These roles also function as stereotypes—exaggerated signs of the same lawlessness mirrored in the charges of greed and pride, and the implied tolerance of what is defined as adultery. The prayerful self-image and the actual behavior of these religious leaders, at least as Luke portrays them, do not coincide.

The prohibition of marriage when either party has been divorced seems to have a particular role in Luke's larger agenda in this section of the Gospel, as an example of the willingness of at least some of the Pharisees to tinker with Torah even while pretending extreme piety. Despite that context, however, the words of the text are harsh. The text, which at least does not completely prohibit divorce, condemns persons whose marriage is loveless or even abusive to the alternatives of remaining in that marriage, spending the rest of their lives unmarried, or being guilty of adultery. There is no way to soften or explain away that reading. One can say that issues of marriage and divorce are clearly not the principal subject of this section of the Gospel, and one can also say that Luke's purpose in these words directed to adversaries was not to inform the pastoral care of persons within the church. Nevertheless, for people who would take the Bible seriously as a guide for their life, the sting of these teachings remains. So also does the responsibility for deciding what to do about such teachings in the context of communities called into being in response to the good news of God's reign (4:43).

## Human Faces of
## Wealth and Poverty (Luke 16:19–31)

16:19 **"There was a rich man who was dressed in purple and fine linen and who feasted sumptuously every day.** [20] **And at his gate lay a poor man named Lazarus, covered with sores,** [21] **who longed to satisfy his hunger with what fell from the rich man's table; even the dogs would come and lick his sores.** [22] **The poor man died and was carried away by the angels to be with Abraham. The rich man also died and was buried.** [23] **In Hades, where he was being tormented, he looked up and saw Abraham far away with Lazarus by his side.** [24] **He called out, 'Father Abraham, have mercy on me, and send Lazarus to dip the tip of his finger in water and cool my tongue; for I am in agony in these flames.'** [25] **But Abraham said, 'Child, remember that during your lifetime you received your good things, and Lazarus in like manner evil things; but now he is comforted here, and you are in agony.** [26] **Besides all this, between you and us a great chasm has been fixed, so that those who might want to pass from here to you cannot do so, and no one can cross from there to us.'** [27] **He said, 'Then, father, I beg you to send him to my father's house—** [28] **for I have five brothers—that he may warn them, so that they will not also come into this place of torment.'** [29] **Abraham replied, 'They have Moses and the prophets; they should listen to them.'** [30] **He said,**

**'No, father Abraham; but if someone goes to them from the dead, they will repent.'** [31] **He said to him, 'If they do not listen to Moses and the prophets, neither will they be convinced even if someone rises from the dead.'"**

The preceding indictments against the Pharisees and affirmations of the abiding power of God's law lead directly into the parable about the human faces of wealth and poverty: The Pharisees, like the disciples (16:1), are given a parable that begins with a rich man (16:19). At the root of the parable is a folk tale that appears to have originated in North Africa, and to have found its way to Palestine (or at least to Luke's church) from Egypt. The story proceeds with stereotypical contrasts and unexpected twists.

The rich man's regal clothing and abundant food identify him, and by implication indict him: He has wealth to share but does not do so (16:19; 12:13–21; Lev. 19:9–10; Isa. 58:6–7). In parallel fashion, gruesome details characterize the life of the poor man, but he is also named (16:20–21). How or why the name "Lazarus" was chosen is not explained, unless the reference to someone returning from the dead led the church to associate him with Lazarus of Bethany in the Gospel of John, whom Jesus is said to have resuscitated (John 11). In any event, Lazarus and the rich man have no contact, for they are separated by the chasm of their economic differences and are linked only by Lazarus's longing gaze.

Both characters die, and in death it is Lazarus whose circumstances are conveyed with the merest sketch (16:22a), whereas the rich man's fate is spun out in grim detail (16:22b–31). Everything has changed, yet nothing has changed. He and Lazarus are still separated by an abyss—this one made uncrossable by divine order (16:26)—but now the longing comes from the rich man. Still in character, he tries to order people to satisfy his needs (16:24), but the time has arrived for reckoning and reversal (1:46–55; 6:20–26). Abraham himself is present, providing a blessing to the reversal of privilege and to the end of presumption, just as Mary sang (1:55) and John the Baptist promised (3:8).

The first part of the story gives way to a second scene (16:27–31). Still in character, the rich man turns his attention to his five brothers: The biological family, and not a wider or more inclusive community, continues to function as his principal (even his only) point of reference, security, and concern. If it is too late for the rich man himself to escape his fate, maybe his brothers can be warned in time. That plea too is to no avail: Moses and the prophets have already said all that is necessary (24:25–27, 44–47; Acts 2:16–36). If they have not taught his brothers the ways of justice, neither will someone returning from the dead convince them. A double meaning to this part of Luke's parable appears here. The one to return from the dead is both Lazarus in the story and the risen Christ in the church, neither of whom will convince those whose tenacious greed defies divine law and stands in the way of justice.

## WARNINGS TO THE DISCIPLES
## Luke 17:1–10

17:1 **Jesus said to his disciples, "Occasions for stumbling are bound to come, but woe to anyone by whom they come! ² It would be better for you if a millstone were hung around your neck and you were thrown into the sea than for you to cause one of these little ones to stumble. ³ Be on your guard! If another disciple sins, you must rebuke the offender, and if there is repentance, you must forgive. ⁴ And if the same person sins against you seven times a day, and turns back to you seven times and says, 'I repent,' you must forgive."**

⁵ **The apostles said to the Lord, "Increase our faith!" ⁶ The Lord replied, "If you had faith the size of a mustard seed, you could say to this mulberry tree, 'Be uprooted and planted in the sea,' and it would obey you.**

⁷ **"Who among you would say to your slave who has just come in from plowing or tending sheep in the field, 'Come here at once and take your place at the table'? ⁸ Would you not rather say to him, 'Prepare supper for me, put on your apron and serve me while I eat and drink; later you may eat and drink'? ⁹ Do you thank the slave for doing what was commanded? ¹⁰ So you also, when you have done all that you were ordered to do, say, 'We are worthless slaves; we have done only what we ought to have done!'"**

The collection of teachings concludes with the focus shifting back to the disciples. They are given administrative guidelines for their work as leaders in the community that will carry on Jesus' mission—a pastoral handbook for the community that will become the church. They are warned, first, against bringing harm to others in the community, whatever the pressures and circumstances. On no account are the disciples to cause another to "stumble"—a Greek word which is related to the English verb "be scandalized" (17:1–2). Equally demanding is that they both correct and then forgive others in the community who do wrong and who repent of their acts (17:3–4).

In an interesting shift in wording, "the apostles"—those disciples specifically set apart for leadership roles in the missionary enterprise

(9:1–2, 10)—respond with a plea for greater faith, so that they will be adequate for the task given them (17:5). Jesus' response in 17:6 is not a "condition contrary to fact" (if you had such faith, you could do something, but since you do not have the faith, you cannot), but rather a "condition according to fact," which assumes that they do have such faith: "If you had faith [only] the size of a mustard seed, you could say to this mulberry tree, 'Be uprooted and planted in the sea,' and it would obey you." If the faith they have is that powerful, surely it is sufficient to sustain them in their responsibilities.

There is another side to the assurance, however, for though they need no additional faith to carry out their task, they also can expect no extra credit or compensation, regardless of how hard they work. The introductory question of the following example (17:7) assumes that no one would be so foolish as to reward or even thank a "slave" for doing the work that is commanded (17:7–9). The apostles are in the same situation. No matter how much they do, it is only what is expected of them (17:10).

Luke's point in presenting this teaching is clearly the all-encompassing nature of the ministry in which the disciples are engaged. The metaphor used to make that point, however, creates problems. Even though, in this example, "slavery" is a metaphor for the life of persons under authority, the fact is that the very premise of slavery—which is usually the lot of people who are poor or otherwise marginalized—remains unquestioned. According to that premise, one person can "own" another and have a claim on every waking and sleeping minute, as well as on every bit of his or her energy. The enslaved person becomes the object of the other's choices, decisions, and actions, and not the subject of the verbs of his or her own life. One must consider carefully whether such a social metaphor is appropriate for the lifestyle that bears a gospel of "good news to the poor."

## HEALING AND THANKSGIVING
## Luke 17:11–19

17:11 **On the way to Jerusalem Jesus was going through the region between Samaria and Galilee.** [12] **As he entered a village, ten lepers approached him. Keeping their distance,** [13] **they called out, saying, "Jesus, Master, have mercy on us!"** [14] **When he saw them, he said to them, "Go and show yourselves to the priests." And as they went, they were made clean.** [15] **Then one of them, when he saw that he was healed, turned back, praising God with a loud voice.** [16] **He prostrated himself at Jesus' feet and thanked him. And he was a Samaritan.** [17] **Then Jesus asked, "Were not ten made clean? But the**

**other nine, where are they?** [18] **Was none of them found to return and give praise to God except this foreigner?"** [19] **Then he said to him, "Get up and go on your way; your faith has made you well."**

Luke breaks into the string of teachings that he has been presenting without narrative settings and reminds readers of the purpose and destination of this journey. He then tells a story that begins as an account of the healing of ten persons afflicted with a skin disease called "leprosy" (see the discussion of 5:12–16). In conformity to the commandments of Torah, they are keeping themselves apart from other people (Lev. 13:45–46; Num. 5:2–3), but instead of crying, "Unclean, unclean!" as the Levitical law requires, they cry out to Jesus for mercy (17:12–13). No special words or actions communicate the act of healing, but instead, they are instructed to carry out the provisions in Torah for having themselves declared clean again, and free to return to their communities (Lev. 14:2–32). The healing story itself concludes with the good news that on the way to fulfill that requirement, they are indeed made clean (17:14).

The story suddenly changes direction: One of the ten, a Samaritan, returns to Jesus, thanking him and praising God (17:15–16). Praise and thanksgiving are appropriate responses to healing, but Jesus himself had sent all ten to the priests for their cleanness to be certified according to the law (see also 5:14). Jesus' questions (17:17–18) thus seem out of place, because the other nine simply have followed his instructions.

The key to understanding those questions, and thus also Luke's reason for telling the story, lies in the concluding blessing: "Get up and go on your way; your faith has made you well"—literally, "saved" you (17:19; see also 7:50; 8:48; 18:42). A fairly simple healing story is transformed into the story of the salvation of a foreigner, which echoes the story of Elisha's healing of Naaman (2 Kings 5:1–14). At issue is not whether the Samaritan in Luke's story had access to appropriate members of the priestly establishment to certify his healing, or whether he returned to Jesus because he would not be welcomed by Jewish priests. Instead, the point is that the Samaritan recognized that God could be praised—and that God's holy and saving power could be addressed—in Jesus' presence as well as in God's recognized "homes" in the temples of Jerusalem or (for Samaritans) Mount Gerizim.

This interlude of healing and thanksgiving provides a bridge from the preceding teachings about the tough demands of justice and the difficult burdens of leadership in the new community (16:1–17:10), to the following warnings about the end-time that awaited them (17:22–37). The energy of praise and of relationships built on thanksgiving sustains the community during the difficult meantime.

## WARNINGS ABOUT THE COMING OF GOD'S REIGN
### Luke 17:20–37

17:20  Once Jesus was asked by the Pharisees when the kingdom of God was coming, and he answered, "The kingdom of God is not coming with things that can be observed; 21 nor will they say, 'Look, here it is!' or 'There it is!' For, in fact, the kingdom of God is among you."

22 Then he said to the disciples, "The days are coming when you will long to see one of the days of the Son of Man, and you will not see it. 23 They will say to you, 'Look there!' or 'Look here!' Do not go, do not set off in pursuit. 24 For as the lightning flashes and lights up the sky from one side to the other, so will the Son of Man be in his day. 25 But first he must endure much suffering and be rejected by this generation. 26 Just as it was in the days of Noah, so too it will be in the days of the Son of Man. 27 They were eating and drinking, and marrying and being given in marriage, until the day Noah entered the ark, and the flood came and destroyed all of them. 28 Likewise, just as it was in the days of Lot: they were eating and drinking, buying and selling, planting and building, 29 but on the day that Lot left Sodom, it rained fire and sulfur from heaven and destroyed all of them 30 —it will be like that on the day that the Son of Man is revealed. 31 On that day, anyone on the housetop who has belongings in the house must not come down to take them away; and likewise anyone in the field must not turn back. 32 Remember Lot's wife. 33 Those who try to make their life secure will lose it, but those who lose their life will keep it. 34 I tell you, on that night there will be two in one bed; one will be taken and the other left. 35 There will be two women grinding meal together; one will be taken and the other left." 37 Then they asked him, "Where, Lord?" He said to them, "Where the corpse is, there the vultures will gather."

The warnings about the coming of God's reign come in two parts. The first is directed to the Pharisees, who again raise the issue of the timing and signs of God's reign (17:20; see also 9:27; 10:9, 11; 11:20, 29–32; 12:54–56). To them, the answer is simple: The reign of God is "among you" (17:21).

Luke's emphasis is on the timing—the present reality of God's reign. Modern readers, on the other hand, tend to raise more questions about where than about when God's reign is to be found. Although the preposition itself can be translated "among" or "within," the fact that the pronoun ("you") is plural makes "among" seem the more likely reading. To look at the question on a larger scale, in Luke's Gospel the reign of God has never been discussed as only an "inner" reality, although God's sovereignty clearly does shape human hearts. Rather, that sovereignty encompasses all of life—institutions and relationships that unite and divide people, as well as human hearts and spirits. It provides a new matrix for life: It lies within, among, and surrounding humankind. Anything less risks becoming an idol, and not the transcendent reality of God's reign.

The warnings to the disciples (17:22–37) focus not on the reign of God but on the Son of Man. The disciples are pictured as looking forward to the "days of the Son of Man," possibly because they see themselves destined to be vindicated, and even rewarded, for their righteousness (see Dan. 7:9–18). In their eagerness for that day, they search high and low for signs of it. Their enthusiasm is dampened in two ways. First, and most immediately applicable to this context near the end of Luke's travel narrative, the disciples are warned that before the day for which they long, Jesus—the Son of Man whom they know already—must suffer at the hands of "this generation." Second, the days of the Son of Man are linked not to triumph and glory, but to sudden, massive, and apparently arbitrary destruction, from which there is no way to protect oneself.

References to the days of Noah and Lot anchor the warnings to the disciples. In both cases, daily life and business as usual were interrupted by widespread destruction—flood and fire respectively—that consumed everything in its path (17:27–29). Similarly, in the days of the Son of Man there will be no escaping and no way of calculating who will or will not fall victim (17:31, 34–35. Some Greek manuscript copies of the Gospel include another example as verse 36, "Two will be in the field; one will be taken and the other left." The manuscript evidence in favor of including it is weak, however, and those that do include the verse seem to have borrowed it from Matt. 24:40). The saying about securing and losing life that earlier identified the demands of discipleship (9:24) now characterizes the coming cataclysm (17:33): The only option is to ride out the storm. The days of the Son of Man as days of glory and triumph? Not likely! Vultures in the sky mean corpses below (17:37; see Job 39:26–30). And that is the only sign the disciples are given.

# 11. Following Jesus
## Luke 18:1–19:28

## PARABLES OF GOD'S JUSTICE
## Luke 18:1–14

### The Parable of the
### Widow and the Judge (Luke 18:1–8)

18:1 Then Jesus told them a parable about their need to pray always and not to lose heart. ² He said, "In a certain city there was a judge who neither feared God nor had respect for people. ³ In that city there was a widow who kept coming to him and saying, 'Grant me justice against my opponent.' ⁴ For a while he refused; but later he said to himself, 'Though I have no fear of God and no respect for anyone, ⁵ yet because this widow keeps bothering me, I will grant her justice, so that she may not wear me out by continually coming.'" ⁶ And the Lord said, "Listen to what the unjust judge says. ⁷ And will not God grant justice to his chosen ones who cry to him day and night? Will he delay long in helping them? ⁸ I tell you, he will quickly grant justice to them. And yet, when the Son of Man comes, will he find faith on earth?"

The focus on the coming of the Son of Man in the preceding passage sets the stage for a parable "about their need to pray always and not to lose heart" (18:1). Luke has provided both this parable and the following one with introductory statements of purpose (18:1, 9) and concluding applications (18:6–8, 14). These interpretations by the author have the effect of giving away the punch line of a joke or the answer to a riddle. They mute the surprising and confronting qualities that parables usually have, as do paintings or photographs whose artistry gives new shape and meaning to a familiar scene or subject. Having these answers ahead of time makes these parables more like illustrations of concepts that merely add a bit of color or spice than like stories that reshape one's world.

Despite Luke's instruction about the point of the story, the parable of the widow and the judge shifts the focus from the announced model of prayerful persistence, to the granting of justice. The story begins with stark contrasts. The identification of the woman as a widow already marks her as one of the most vulnerable members of the society. A common theme in the Hebrew Bible is the need for people—particularly those in authority—to fulfill God's own purposes by caring for widows and orphans (see, for example, Exod. 22:22; Deut. 10:17–18; 24:17–22; Ps. 146:7b–9; Isa. 1:16–23; 10:1–4; Jer. 7:5–7; Ezek. 22:7; Zech. 7:8–10; Mal. 3:5). The parable does not say anything about this widow's actual circumstances or about the nature of the case at issue; such concerns are not important to the story. What is important is that the judge—whom both the narrator and the judge's own words identify as bound neither by loyalty to God nor by human concern—refuses even to do his job by ruling on her case (18:2–4a).

What moral obligation fails to compel, the effect of the woman's persistence accomplishes: She shames him into action. The verb translated in the NRSV as "wear out" means literally "give a black eye" to someone. Her constant claims for justice are a mark visible to everyone in the community of his failure as a judge, and consequently evidence of his loss of honor and prestige. Despite his claims that he does not "respect" people, he turns out to be vulnerable to embarrassment and to a threat to his privileged place in the society.

The argument of the concluding application (18:6–8), which is attributed to "the Lord," builds on the contrast between the judge, who is sensitive only to his own well-being, and God, who is identified with justice. If even the judge can eventually be badgered into granting justice, God will surely respond much more speedily to God's own people: The delay until the days of the Son of Man envisioned in the previous passage (17:22–37) will surely not be long. The final question (18:8b) appears to be almost an aside to the disciples, or, more precisely, an aside from Luke to his church. God's time and human time do not always coincide, and the passing of time with no glimmer of the longed-for days may be threatening the persistence of the church's prayers. The widow's untiring pursuit of justice is translated into the "faith" that should mark the church's welcome of the awaited Son of Man.

## The Parable of the Pharisee and the Tax Agent (Luke 18:9–14)

18:9 **He also told this parable to some who trusted in themselves that they were righteous and regarded others with contempt:** [10] **"Two men went up to the temple to pray, one a Pharisee and the other a tax collector.** [11] **The Pharisee, standing by himself, was praying thus, 'God, I thank you that I am not like other people: thieves, rogues, adulterers, or even like this tax collector.** [12] **I fast twice a week; I give a tenth of all my income.'** [13] **But the tax**

•

collector, standing far off, would not even look up to heaven, but was beating his breast and saying, 'God, be merciful to me, a sinner!' [14] I tell you, this man went down to his home justified rather than the other; for all who exalt themselves will be humbled, but all who humble themselves will be exalted."

A second parable that is ostensibly about prayer but is really about justice follows immediately. The focus provided by the introduction (18:9) is the relationship between the prayer and the person praying. Again, the characters are caricatures. The prayer of the Pharisee—model of piety and religious rectitude, but one of a group of people already unmasked by Luke as liable to hypocrisy and pretense (11:37–44; 16:14–18)—reminds God of the Pharisee's own righteousness that exceeds even what Torah requires (18:11–12; see Ps. 17:3–5). His prayer shines a spotlight on the second character, a tax collector. That professional identity makes this character also a model—model of greed, questionable honesty, ritual uncleanness—of everything an upright Pharisee would avoid (see 5:27–32; 15:1–2; 19:1–10). The tax collector's prayer (modeled on Psalm 51) suggests that he acknowledges with anguish that assessment of himself, and simply entrusts himself to God's mercy.

The two parables appear on the surface to represent a pair of simple instructions for effective prayer for different categories of people. Those whose cause is legitimate have only to persist in praying for it (18:1–8). Sinners have only to throw themselves on God's mercy and not try to make excuses or seem better than they are (18:9–14). On a deeper level, though, both prayers bring the attention of Luke's readers back to the issue of justice. The widow is granted justice in her case, and the tax collector returns to his home "justified" (18:5, 14a; in Greek, as in English, the two words share a common root). Both verdicts are portrayed as coinciding with God's will, and both fly in the face of the judgments of the judge and the Pharisee, who are locked into the systems of social and economic competition and the hierarchy of honor and prestige that favor the dominant classes in their society. In both parables, prayer is about the reversal of the rules of those systems, as the concluding proverb confirms (18:14b; see also 14:11; Matt. 18:4; 23:12).

## JESUS AND THE CHILDREN
## Luke 18:15–17

18:15 People were bringing even infants to him that he might touch them; and when the disciples saw it, they sternly ordered them not to do it. [16] But

Jesus called for them and said, "Let the little children come to me, and do not stop them; for it is to such as these that the kingdom of God belongs. $^{17}$ Truly I tell you, whoever does not receive the kingdom of God as a little child will never enter it."

At this point Luke's narrative rejoins the order of events in Mark, from which Luke has diverged since the beginning of the account of Jesus' journey to Jerusalem (9:51). From here on, all three Synoptic Gospels move relentlessly toward Jesus' final approach to the holy city where his death will take place. Suddenly one has the sense that the stakes are higher, as teachings and incidents move to a closer focus on the crisis that is impending for both Jesus and the disciples.

The reversal of position of humble and exalted that is announced in the proverb concluding the preceding parable (18:14b) is dramatized by Jesus' welcome of little children (18:15–17). In the ancient world, where many children did not even survive infancy, rituals welcoming a child into the larger community often took place only when he or she reached the threshold of adulthood, and after the worst of the threats to survival were past. Only then did the child become a person to be reckoned with. Even in the modern world, as priceless as infants are to their parents and to others who love them and vest their hopes in them, they have no place in public hierarchies. To the world outside their families, children are the paradigms of powerlessness, which sometimes leads to their being made victims of outright abuse, but more often leaves them simply ignored or pushed out of the way.

In terms of common values, then, the disciples' attempt to protect Jesus and his important mission from interruptions by children is understandable. In terms of the values of the reign of God, however, the disciples have missed the point. Children, who possess nothing and bring no merit or claim to privilege (like the widow and the tax collector of the preceding parables), are in a position to "receive" God's reign in the only way it can be received, as a free gift (see also 9:48).

## DISCIPLESHIP AND SECURITY
## Luke 18:18–30

18:18 A certain ruler asked him, "Good Teacher, what must I do to inherit eternal life?" $^{19}$ Jesus said to him, "Why do you call me good? No one is good but God alone. $^{20}$ You know the commandments: 'You shall not commit adultery; You shall not murder; You shall not steal; You shall not bear false witness; Honor your father and mother.'" [21] He replied, "I have kept all these since my youth." [22] When Jesus heard this, he said to him, "There is still one thing lacking. Sell all that you own and distribute the money to the poor, and you will have treasure in heaven; then come, follow me." [23] But when he heard this, he became sad; for he was very rich. [24] Jesus looked at him and said, "How hard it is for those who have wealth to enter the kingdom of God! [25] Indeed, it is easier for a camel to go through the eye of a needle than for someone who is rich to enter the kingdom of God."

[26] Those who heard it said, "Then who can be saved?" [27] He replied, "What is impossible for mortals is possible for God."

[28] Then Peter said, "Look, we have left our homes and followed you." [29] And he said to them, "Truly I tell you, there is no one who has left house or wife or brothers or parents or children, for the sake of the kingdom of God, [30] who will not get back very much more in this age, and in the age to come eternal life."

Following the story about Jesus and the children (18:15–17) comes another story that is its polar opposite. Instead of infants who are without power, prestige, or deeds that merit reward, and who are brought to Jesus by others, a man identified as one of the powerful (and who later is called rich) approaches Jesus on his own. He comes with the question that in some form grounds all religious life: Where is the ultimate meaning and validation of my life to be found?

The ruler's way of posing the question further contrasts him with the infants who receive the reign of God in an appropriate way. He begins by addressing Jesus as "Good Teacher"—a bit of flattery that seems harmless enough, and that even seems appropriate to Jesus according to our Christian confession. That designation, however, is greeted with a rebuke (18:18–19), the real meaning of which is not clear until later in the story. The ruler also asks his question in a way that shows he does not understand what is involved, for one "does" things in order to earn payment, while an inheritance is really a gift. Jesus' reply to the ruler fits his question, however, for it lists ethical commandments found in the Decalogue (Exod. 20:12–16; Deut. 5:16–20). The ruler's response digs him deeper into the hole he is creating for himself (18:21): If he really wants to do all that is necessary, he must keep *all* of the commandments.

The "one thing lacking" confronts the one commandment that has eluded the ruler all along: "You shall have no other gods before me" (Exod. 20:3; Deut. 5:7). The ruler's willingness to flatter Jesus with an attribute to be reserved for God (18:18–19) turns out to be a symptom of his willingness to let other things take the place of God in his life. The "one thing" that Jesus demands is that the ruler divest himself of all of the wealth that has established his position in society—possessions, home, land—everything that he has come to count on and that is at the center of his life where only God belongs. To do that "one thing" would restore God to God's rightful place, and it would leave the ruler in the position of receiving God's gift of eternal life "as a little child."

Unlike Matthew and Mark (Matt. 19:22; Mark 10:22), Luke does not tell us whether the ruler complied, but only that he became sad. One has the sense that he probably did not, for "treasure in heaven" often seems a risky venture for those whose treasure has been accumulated elsewhere (12:21, 33). Jesus' lament (18:24) reflects not a condemnation of wealth as somehow inherently evil but rather a recognition, so widespread as to have become proverbial (18:25), that wealth is particularly susceptible to becoming an idol that displaces God.

The proverb plays on the image of the ridiculous impossibility of a huge and bulky camel getting through a needle's eye. To interpret it as referring to a gate so small that camels had to be unloaded and led through on their knees before being loaded with their cargo again simply misses the point. Only God could get a camel through a needle, and only God's grace—not something human beings can "do"—can overcome human idolatry (18:26–27).

By reminding Jesus that he and the other disciples have done what was asked of the ruler (18:28), Peter comes dangerously close to joining the ruler in missing the point. Pride in what they have done could easily become a new claim to merit that displaces God's grace. Jesus' response makes of their discipleship not a meritorious accomplishment but already part of the blessing they enjoy: The new family into which they are received (18:29–31). That they have left their old homes and families "for the sake of the kingdom of God" links their new life to the earlier blessing of the children (18:15–17), and the promise of "eternal life" in the age to come closes the parentheses around this story that were opened by the ruler's question (18:18). The way to eternal life is in the life of discipleship.

## A PREDICTION NOT UNDERSTOOD
### Luke 18:31–34

> 18:31 Then he took the twelve aside and said to them, "See, we are going up to Jerusalem, and everything that is written about the Son of Man by the prophets will be accomplished. 32 For he will be handed over to the Gen-

tiles; and he will be mocked and insulted and spat upon. ³³ After they have flogged him, they will kill him, and on the third day he will rise again." ³⁴ But they understood nothing about all these things; in fact, what he said was hidden from them, and they did not grasp what was said.

Luke provides occasional reminders to the audience of the Gospel about the destination and purpose of the journey, but these things are first identified by Jesus' own words in the prediction of his passion in 18:31–34. Almost within sight of Jericho, as they are about to begin their climb up the mountain to Jerusalem, the disciples are told a third time (see also 9:22, 43b–45) about what awaits the Son of Man there. All three predictions emphasize that the events will happen according to divine plan or necessity: Jesus' death is no coincidence, no failure, and no fluke. The first of the predictions speaks of the role that Jewish religious authorities play, and the second mentions only "human hands." In this prediction, the role of Gentile authorities is forecast, and with that inclusion, the passion account is now complete.

As dire as the prediction is, the note of deepest sadness in the passage is in the word of the disciples' failure to "grasp what was said." Despite having been with Jesus from the beginning of his ministry and having heard many things in plain speech and not parabolic puzzles (8:9–10), there are things they still do not understand—such as where their journey must end (18:34). Whether Jesus actually predicted his fate in such fine detail as the formal predictions suggest, or whether he spoke simply out of the wisdom that the path they were on would evoke the punishing wrath of powerful people, is unknown. In any case, the Synoptic Gospels are unanimous in saying that the disciples fail to understand the verbal rehearsals of what lies ahead. The Gospels are also unanimous in showing how the horror of the actual experience swallows them up, driving most of them to betrayal, denial, and flight (Luke 22 and 23). Only in the memories of Jesus' last hours and of his entire ministry that are shared in the midst of the new community that will become the church does the meaning of words and events alike become clear.

## HEALING AND DISCIPLESHIP
## Luke 18:35–43

18:35 As he approached Jericho, a blind man was sitting by the roadside begging. ³⁶ When he heard a crowd going by, he asked what was happening. ³⁷ They told him, "Jesus of Nazareth is passing by." ³⁸ Then he shouted,

"Jesus, Son of David, have mercy on me!" 39 Those who were in front sternly ordered him to be quiet; but he shouted even more loudly, "Son of David, have mercy on me!" 40 Jesus stood still and ordered the man to be brought to him; and when he came near, he asked him, 41 "What do you want me to do for you?" He said, "Lord, let me see again." 42 Jesus said to him, "Receive your sight; your faith has saved you." 43 Immediately he regained his sight and followed him, glorifying God; and all the people, when they saw it, praised God.

The final episodes of the travel narrative are set around Jericho. The actual location of the town is uncertain, but the implication is that it is the town at the base of the mountain on top of which sits the city of Jerusalem. Jericho is the last place for the travelers to regroup and ready themselves to retrace the route of Israel's kings at the annual enthronement festival. At the festival, the king would leave Jerusalem and descend the mountain, and wearing the clothing of ordinary people, the king would make his way back to the place of power chanting the Songs of Ascent (Psalms 120–134). With these reaffirmations of the royal obligations of faithfulness to God's will, and this reminder of where the true power in Israel is lodged, the king would reassume the throne. As Jesus' own words have just declared (18:31–33), he and his followers are moving toward a different end, but the music of their journey up to Jerusalem will be the same: "I lift up my eyes to the hills—from where will my help come? My help comes from the LORD, who made heaven and earth. . . . The LORD will keep you from all evil; [God] will keep your life. The LORD will keep your going out and your coming in from this time on and forevermore" (Psalm 121:1–2, 7–8).

A blind person begging by the side of the road near the entrance to Jericho becomes the occasion for the fourth and final healing story in the narrative of the journey to Jerusalem (18:35–43; see also 13:10–17; 14:1–6; 17:11–19). Physical blindness, however, masks insight about Jesus' identity. At this place where the earlier royal "sons of David" began their annual pilgrimages to power, this man becomes the only character in the Gospel to recognize and call on Jesus as "Son of David." And call on him he does, despite efforts by some in the crowd to get him to stop. Like the friend who asks for bread at midnight (11:5–8), and like the widow claiming justice (18:1–8), this man does not let his claim be silenced (18:38–39).

The account of Jesus' interaction with the man sets this story apart from other healing stories at several points, making it not simply a healing story, but a model of how people become disciples of Jesus. Instead of Jesus approaching the man, Jesus has the man brought to him. With that movement, the man has already left his old life as a beggar sitting by the side of the road—everything that defined his identity and place in society —just as the other disciples have done (18:28). The man has already cried out for mercy, but the story depicts Jesus asking him to make explicit what he wants (see also John 5:6). Does the mercy the blind man asks for mean simply charity—something to sustain him more comfortably in his present circumstances? Only with the man's request for healing does Jesus issue the command, but then he immediately attributes the man's healing or "salvation" to his own "faith" (18:42; again, the blessing is literally, "Your faith has saved you"; see also 7:50; 8:48; 17:19). The man's response to his new sight is to join the onlookers in praising God (see also 5:25–26; 17:15, 18), then to take the final step into discipleship by following Jesus. Even with Jerusalem nearly in sight, the ranks of the disciples are swelling—as indeed they will continue to do in the time of the church, when Jerusalem is a dim memory. And the process of becoming disciples always looks the same.

## ZACCHAEUS AND SALVATION
## Luke 19:1–10

19:1 **He entered Jericho and was passing through it.** 2 **A man was there named Zacchaeus; he was a chief tax collector and was rich.** 3 **He was trying to see who Jesus was, but on account of the crowd he could not, because he was short in stature.** 4 **So he ran ahead and climbed a sycamore tree to see him, because he was going to pass that way.** 5 **When Jesus came to the place, he looked up and said to him, "Zacchaeus, hurry and come down; for I must stay at your house today."** 6 **So he hurried down and was happy to welcome him.** 7 **All who saw it began to grumble and said, "He has gone to be the guest of one who is a sinner."** 8 **Zacchaeus stood there and said to the Lord, "Look, half of my possessions, Lord, I will give to the poor; and if I have defrauded anyone of anything, I will pay back four times as much."** 9 **Then Jesus said to him, "Today salvation has come to this house, because he too is a son of Abraham.** 10 **For the Son of Man came to seek out and to save the lost."**

Luke introduces yet another character as Jesus' journey continues out of Jericho. Zacchaeus is identified as a chief tax collector who is rich. We have met his kind before. His story echoes that of Levi, set early in Jesus' ministry in Galilee (5:27–32). In the story of Levi, however, Jesus' table community with Levi provokes a controversy principally with the religious leaders. Complaints about Jesus' association with Zacchaeus are more widespread than just from the religious establishment (19:7). As a chief tax collector, Zacchaeus attracts an instinctive contempt that comes from many quarters. Especially as a "rich" tax collector, he would have been assumed by many in the early church (as well as by other residents of a Palestinian city) to be lining his own pockets at others' expense.

People who have been following along in Luke's Gospel, though, know that tax collectors have fared pretty well. They are not only received by Jesus, but they even serve as positive models of prayer and piety (18:9–14). However, people who are rich—whether characters in parables (12:13–21; 16:19–31) or characters in the Gospel narrative itself (18:18–25)—have not fared as well. At the beginning of the story, then, Zacchaeus is an ambiguous character, and not easily categorized.

The story begins as a comedy. Zacchaeus is drawn, not by devotion to Jesus or any high-sounding confession of faith, but by simple curiosity to try to get a glimpse of him. Being short, he decides to climb a tree to get a better view. A sycamore tree should provide good cover and let him get away with his covert surveillance without jeopardizing his dignity. No such luck. Jesus not only spots Zacchaeus, but makes a spectacle of him by inviting himself to Zacchaeus's home. You have to chuckle, at least a little (unless you happen to be Mrs. Zacchaeus, left with the problem of rearranging household plans to provide dinner for the unexpected guest and his entourage).

Suddenly, at 19:8 the mood shifts, and a story that has invited playfulness becomes stark and serious. Two statements, the first by Zacchaeus and the second by Jesus, cut off the laughter. For no reason other than Jesus' presence in his home, Zacchaeus makes a solemn vow. He speaks of his intended future actions with such determination that the verbs are already in the present tense (literally, "I give," and "I pay back").

The distribution of half of his goods, although falling short of what was required of the rich man seeking eternal life (18:22), more than meets the standards of almsgiving that have been so important earlier in the Gospel (12:13–21; 16:19–31). Concerning the second part of his promise, Torah and custom provide that if anyone has defrauded another and offers to make amends, the one who has done wrong must make restitution of the original amount, plus an additional 20 percent (Lev. 6:5; Num. 5:7). If restitution is involuntary, the wrongdoer must repay two, four, or even five times the original amount (Exod. 22:1–3, 5–14; 2 Sam. 12:6). Not only is Zacchaeus's action portrayed as voluntary, but it is not even clear that he is guilty of fraud in the first place (19:8). Clearly his offer to divest himself of his wealth is extraordinary.

If the intent of his promise is hard to understand, so is the relationship between that promise and Jesus' response (19:9–10). With no explanation at all, Zacchaeus is suddenly declared to be a "son of Abraham." Because of his political and economic role as a chief tax collector, Zacchaeus has never been in a position to consider membership in the people of God something on which he can presume (note John the Baptist's warning in 3:8). In fact, some would say that his profession has made him the equivalent of a Gentile. Suddenly his membership in the chosen people is reinstated. His earnest promise is not mentioned as a reason, but one is left with the sense that they are connected. His embrace of the opportunity to give alms—to redistribute his excess wealth to "the poor"—does not earn his new identity, for that identity can be his only through the same divine grace by which Israel was chosen by God in the first place. But the lifestyle he has embraced makes his identity evident. That identity names Zacchaeus's new reality as surely as the parallel designation "daughter of Abraham" identified the woman freed from the weakness that kept her bent double (13:10–17). The whole event is summed up in the statement that salvation has come, not just to Zacchaeus in some private religious experience, but to his entire household.

Salvation is identified also as one of the tasks of the Son of Man (19:10). The Gospel has been full of stories of Jesus' presence on the margins of society, reaching out to those whom sin, illness, lifestyle, or the disintegration of their personalities has made into nonpersons. That role has not been coincidental; it is central to Jesus' identity and mission from God. The saying draws us back to the parables of Luke 15—the lost sheep, the lost coin, and the lost sons. Not simply clever or perplexing stories, they live at the heart of God's purpose of salvation.

## INVESTMENT AND PREPAREDNESS
## Luke 19:11–28

19:11 **As they were listening to this, he went on to tell a parable, because he was near Jerusalem, and because they supposed that the kingdom of God was to appear immediately.** [12] **So he said, "A nobleman went to a distant country to get royal power for himself and then return.** [13] **He summoned ten of his slaves, and gave them ten pounds, and said to them, 'Do business with these until I come back.'** [14] **But the citizens of his country hated him and sent a delegation after him, saying, 'We do not want this man to rule over us.'** [15] **When he returned, having received royal power, he ordered these slaves, to whom he had given the money, to be summoned so that he might**

find out what they had gained by trading. [16] **The first came forward and said, 'Lord, your pound has made ten more pounds.'** [17] **He said to him, 'Well done, good slave! Because you have been trustworthy in a very small thing, take charge of ten cities.'** [18] **Then the second came, saying, 'Lord, your pound has made five pounds.'** [19] **He said to him, 'And you, rule over five cities.'** [20] **Then the other came, saying, 'Lord, here is your pound. I wrapped it up in a piece of cloth,** [21] **for I was afraid of you, because you are a harsh man; you take what you did not deposit, and reap what you did not sow.'** [22] **He said to him, 'I will judge you by your own words, you wicked slave! You knew, did you, that I was a harsh man, taking what I did not deposit and reaping what I did not sow?** [23] **Why then did you not put my money into the bank? Then when I returned, I could have collected it with interest.'** [24] **He said to the bystanders, 'Take the pound from him and give it to the one who has ten pounds.'** [25] **(And they said to him, 'Lord, he has ten pounds!')** [26] **'I tell you, to all those who have, more will be given; but from those who have nothing, even what they have will be taken away.** [27] **But as for these enemies of mine who did not want me to be king over them—bring them here and slaughter them in my presence.'"**
[28] **After he had said this, he went on ahead, going up to Jerusalem.**

The narrative of Jesus' journey to Jerusalem ends on a note of caution. Ostensibly the word of warning is to the disciples, lest they confuse the coming events in Jerusalem with the arrival of the reign of God (19:11). The account of those events (Luke 22 and 23) shows that Jesus' followers seem little inclined to that confusion. Rather, the account shows that the real threat lies in their confusion, born of their despair that, with Jesus' arrest and execution, all seems lost. The warning is more appropriately directed to Luke's church—and to the church ever since—that *we* not confuse the events at the core of our faith with the realization of God's sovereign will. Central as Jesus' crucifixion and resurrection are to God's saving purposes, Luke maintains that more is yet to come. We cannot think that the story of the saving work of God ends in Jerusalem, but instead, it goes out even to the ends of the earth (Acts 1:8).

Luke's word of caution comes in the form of a parable consisting of two interwoven stories. Whatever may have been the meaning of either or both of the stories for Jesus' own audience or for the early church, in Luke's reading, both are allegories in which each detail in the story has two distinct references in the reality of the hearers. One tells the story of Jesus, and the other sets the agenda for the disciples and the church.

Jesus' story is the story of a noble who journeys to a distant country to be vested with royal power, despite the objections of other citizens of his

home country. Before leaving, he places servants in charge of his possessions. When he returns with the power of his new office, he settles accounts with the servants and orders the execution of his enemies
(19:12–15, 27). The allegorical equivalents are clear: After the crucifixion
and resurrection, Jesus leaves the disciples and ascends to sit at God's right
hand. In the meantime, until his return at the final judgment, Jesus has entrusted his followers to carry on his ministry and to make it "prosper" and
grow into the mission of the church. At an appropriate time, the risen
Christ will return to demand an account of what they have done with the
responsibility entrusted to them and to punish those who have been his
enemies.

The disciples' story is seen through the account of the servants—all of
them, as is seen in the "complete" number ten. Each receives the same
amount of the property, with the charge to "do business" with it until the
noble returns. At the time of reckoning, the reports of three of the servants are presented. (The other servants mentioned earlier simply fade
into the background, following the standard storyteller's pattern of three
cycles of action [see also, for example, 10:29–37].) The first two servants
have earned phenomenal returns on the resources entrusted to them (one
thousand and five hundred percent, respectively). Consequently, they are
rewarded with corresponding shares of the new king's territory. The third
servant gives back only the same amount entrusted in the beginning, because, for fear of losing the coin and angering the noble, he has simply
stashed it away. He has lost nothing, but that was not the assignment, and
so he receives the harsh judgment that led to his caution in the first place.
This third servant loses the carefully guarded coin to the one who has
made the best investment (19:13, 15–25). The judgment is explained by a
saying that echoes earlier warnings about accountability (19:26; see also
8:18; 12:48; Matt. 13:12; 25:29; Mark 4:24–25).

The warning to the disciples and to the church emphasizes the need for
them to be "profitable" managers of what has been entrusted to them in
the interim between Jesus' imminent departure and his eventual return in
judgment. They are not simply to preserve what they have received from
Jesus, but rather they are to work with it and develop it. In other words,
the gospel and ministry of Jesus must not simply be kept as he left them,
but rather they must be transferred into the mission of the whole church.

With that warning, Jesus completes the journey begun in 9:51. The
soon-to-be king (19:12) completes the pilgrimage to Jerusalem (see the
discussion of 18:35). If we listen, we can hear the Psalms that accompany
his way:

Come, bless the LORD, all you servants of the LORD,
who stand by night in the house of the LORD!
Lift up your hands to the holy place, and bless the LORD.
May the LORD, maker of heaven and earth,
bless you from Zion.

(Psalm 134)

# 4. Endings and Beginnings: The Time in Jerusalem

*Luke 19:29–24:53*

# 12. Ministry in Jerusalem
## Luke 19:29–21:38

## JESUS ENTERS THE CITY
### Luke 19:29–38

19:29 **When he had come near Bethphage and Bethany, at the place called the Mount of Olives, he sent two of the disciples,** 30 **saying, "Go into the village ahead of you, and as you enter it you will find tied there a colt that has never been ridden. Untie it and bring it here.** 31 **If anyone asks you, 'Why are you untying it?' just say this, 'The Lord needs it.'"** 32 **So those who were sent departed and found it as he had told them.** 33 **As they were untying the colt, its owners asked them, "Why are you untying the colt?"** 34 **They said, "The Lord needs it."** 35 **Then they brought it to Jesus; and after throwing their cloaks on the colt, they set Jesus on it.** 36 **As he rode along, people kept spreading their cloaks on the road.** 37 **As he was now approaching the path down from the Mount of Olives, the whole multitude of the disciples began to praise God joyfully with a loud voice for all the deeds of power that they had seen,** 38 **saying,**

> **"Blessed is the king**
> **who comes in the name of the Lord!**
> **Peace in heaven,**
> **and glory in the highest heaven!"**

All four Gospels tell of Jesus' entry into the city of Jerusalem from the region around Bethany and the Mount of Olives (Matt. 21:1–9; Mark 11:1–10; Luke 19:28–38; John 12:12–19; see Zech. 14:4–5). The accounts are quite similar in all the Gospels (as is the case for many of the events of Jesus' final days), and it is difficult to pay attention to the particular accents of Luke's account. For example, the account is so much a part of the church's Palm Sunday liturgy that it is easy to overlook the fact that Luke does not even mention such branches—and for a very good reason.

One gets the impression that arrangements have already been made by

Jesus to enter the city in a particular way. Two disciples are sent ahead, as has been the case, apparently, during most of the journey to Jerusalem (10:1), and as Jesus does again to prepare for the supper with his disciples on the night of his arrest (22:8). The instructions are explicit, complete with identifying questions and replies (19:30–31). The same words convey both the instructions and the report of how they are carried out (19:32–35a).

The animal they are to seek is a young donkey. As an animal that has not been ridden, the donkey is symbolically suitable for a sacred use. A donkey, however, is not an animal one thinks of for ceremonies. Rather, it is a draft animal—humble, common, and singularly unimposing. One would never ride a donkey to war—at least not if one were serious about it, and that is precisely the point: The little donkey carries a king who comes in peace (Zech. 9:9).

In keeping with the peaceful scene, in Luke's version of the story no crowds waving palm branches and shouting hosannas greet Jesus as they might greet a general returning victorious from battle, or someone who has come to wage war on their behalf. Instead, people cushion Jesus' ride with their own clothing (19:35b–36), divesting themselves of symbols of their status instead of putting on the trappings of war. The disciples—the large group that has been traveling with him—direct their praises to God, not in anticipation of a victory still ahead, but for the "deeds of power" (healings and exorcisms, for example) that they have already witnessed (19:37). Their first chorus of praise (19:38a; see Ps. 118:26) fulfills the time foretold in Jesus' lament over Jerusalem (13:35): Now the city will indeed see him, but with its will and his more sharply opposed than ever. The second chorus (19:38b) echoes 2:14: The angels' song that greeted Jesus' birth becomes the disciples' song at the end of his life, but peace now is known only in heaven, no longer on earth.

## A JUDGMENT ON THE TIMES
## Luke 19:39–48

### Warnings about the City (Luke 19:39–44)

19:39 **Some of the Pharisees in the crowd said to him, "Teacher, order your disciples to stop."** [40] **He answered, "I tell you, if these were silent, the stones would shout out."**

[41] **As he came near and saw the city, he wept over it,** [42] **saying, "If you, even you, had only recognized on this day the things that make for peace!**

But now they are hidden from your eyes. [43] Indeed, the days will come upon you, when your enemies will set up ramparts around you and surround you, and hem you in on every side. [44] They will crush you to the ground, you and your children within you, and they will not leave within you one stone upon another; because you did not recognize the time of your visitation from God."

The Pharisees do not appreciate the disciples' songs and try to silence them (19:39). The motive behind their effort is not stated. Are they opposed to Jesus? Do they fear trouble from the Roman authorities if Jesus' popularity becomes too evident? Luke reported in 13:31 that Pharisees warned Jesus about Herod's intent to kill him, and perhaps they should be seen as speaking a similar word here. Jesus' reply, however, rejects their warning: If the disciples are silenced, the stones themselves will take up the song of the salvation God intends (3:8; see also Josh. 4:20–24).

Jesus' lament over the city (19:42–44) is Luke's lament as he looks back through the intervening years of war and destruction, especially during the Jewish-Roman War (66–70 C.E.). The city whose name means "Seeing of Peace" does not know its own name, and does not recognize its "visitation from God." Luke connects the awful siege and destruction suffered by the city to the people's rejection of Jesus' way of peace in favor of open rebellion against their Roman occupiers (19:43–44). There is no glee or gloating on Luke's part. Instead, his lament, just as Jesus', conveys love and care as well as frustration and grief, and above all a vision of what might have been.

## Warnings about the Temple (Luke 19:45–48)

19:45 Then he entered the temple and began to drive out those who were selling things there; [46] and he said, "It is written,

'My house shall be a house of prayer';
     but you have made it a den of robbers."
[47] Every day he was teaching in the temple. The chief priests, the scribes, and the leaders of the people kept looking for a way to kill him; [48] but they did not find anything they could do, for all the people were spellbound by what they heard.

Jesus' time in Jerusalem is spent mostly in and around the temple. Like the city itself, the temple has a hold on Luke's heart. His Gospel began in the temple, with Zechariah, Simeon, and Anna, and it will end with Jesus' followers "continually in the temple blessing God" (24:53). But at the same time, Luke identifies the temple as contradicting God's purposes, and as the site of growing and powerful opposition to Jesus. First, instead of being the house of prayer it was intended to be (Isa. 56:7; Jer. 7:11), the temple has become a place where greed and exploitation are carried out by the very persons conducting the temple's business (19:45–46).

Luke does not identify the type of commerce, but one can surmise that it involved especially the sale of animals for the temple sacrifices and the exchange of imperial money into the currency used for temple offerings. Both of those would have been types of commerce on which the temple itself enjoyed a monopoly, and thus the merchants could charge exorbitant rates of exchange that left poor pilgrims with no recourse. Luke's language is ironic. He is talking about the deeds of those carrying out the official business of the temple. He refers to them, however, as "robbers." The word is the same one usually used to refer to the roving bands who stole from the wealthy as a form of protest against the officially sanctioned exploitation going on around the temple. Luke does not describe Jesus' action against these legally sanctioned "robbers," and there is no mention of the destruction of property described in the other Gospels (see Matt. 21:12–13; Mark 11:15–17; John 2:13–17). Instead, simply by driving out those responsible, Jesus protests the temple's desertion of its true vocation.

Ominous notes are sounded, however, in the mounting opposition to Jesus by the temple authorities (19:47). For the moment, the crowd's support provides Jesus temporary protection. The city would have been bursting with people who had come to Jerusalem for the approaching festival. To anger the people by taking action against someone with a popular following would be risky for those with a stake in maintaining the public order (19:48). One can sense the wheels begin to turn, however: If only that popular support can be eroded, the crowds themselves might be used against him.

## A DISPUTE WITH THE
## TEMPLE AUTHORITIES
## Luke 20:1–19

### The Source of Jesus' Authority (Luke 20:1–8)

20:1 One day, as he was teaching the people in the temple and telling the good news, the chief priests and the scribes came with the elders [2] and said to him, "Tell us, by what authority are you doing these things? Who is it who gave you this authority?" [3] He answered them, "I will also ask you a question, and you tell me: [4] Did the baptism of John come from heaven, or was it of human origin?" [5] They discussed it with one another, saying, "If we say, 'From heaven,' he will say, 'Why did you not believe him?' [6] But if we say, 'Of human origin,' all the people will stone us; for they are convinced that John was a prophet." [7] So they answered that they did not know where it came from. [8] Then Jesus said to them, "Neither will I tell you by what authority I am doing these things."

The setting in Jerusalem and in the temple precincts leads to a shift in Jesus' opponents (19:47; 20:19) and challengers (20:1, 20, 27). Instead of the Pharisees who kept tabs on his ministry in rural Galilee and on the way to Jerusalem, once he is inside the city, the temple functionaries take over: Sadducees, chief priests, and the scribes who serve them. Their first and most obvious challenge addresses the source of Jesus' authority (20:2).

Jesus' strategy mirrors earlier encounters with the Pharisees, when Jesus was said to trap them by responding to their questions with other questions, to which any answer would be incriminating. This time, Jesus' question turns them back to John the Baptist. Their dilemma is obvious in their discussion among themselves (20:4–6). Their solution—to plead ignorance—gets them out of the trap, but without an answer to their question (20:7–8). According to all three Synoptic Gospels (see also Matt. 21:23–27 and Mark 11:27–33), even with Jesus' death only a short time away, John the Baptist is still the point of entry to understanding Jesus and his ministry. Those who have not reckoned with John cannot know Jesus, and further discussion with the authorities is pointless.

## The Parable of the
## Wicked Tenants (Luke 20:9–19)

20:9 He began to tell the people this parable: "A man planted a vineyard, and leased it to tenants, and went to another country for a long time. [10] When the season came, he sent a slave to the tenants in order that they might give him his share of the produce of the vineyard; but the tenants beat him and sent him away empty-handed. [11] Next he sent another slave; that one also they beat and insulted and sent away empty-handed. [12] And he sent still a third; this one also they wounded and threw out. [13] Then the owner of the vineyard said, 'What shall I do? I will send my beloved son; perhaps they will respect him.' [14] But when the tenants saw him, they discussed it among themselves and said, 'This is the heir; let us kill him so that the inheritance may be ours.' [15] So they threw him out of the vineyard and killed him. What then will the owner of the vineyard do to them? [16] He will come and destroy those tenants and give the vineyard to others." When they heard

this, they said, "Heaven forbid!" [17] But he looked at them and said, "What then does this text mean:
   'The stone that the builders rejected
     has become the cornerstone'?
[18] Everyone who falls on that stone will be broken to pieces; and it will crush anyone on whom it falls." [19] When the scribes and chief priests realized that he had told this parable against them, they wanted to lay hands on him at that very hour, but they feared the people.

The religious leaders hover in the background as Jesus tells a parable ostensibly to the people (20:9), but actually to the leaders themselves (20:19). The parable is another one that assumes the prevailing system of absentee landownership and tenant farming (see also 16:1–13 and 19:11–28, for example). Rents and taxes often took most of the tenants' income and left them with not even enough to live on. Given the economic abuses of that system, it is likely that many of Jesus' hearers would have identified with the tenants who finally rose up in rebellion against the owner of the vineyard. The traditional storytellers pattern of three servants who come to collect on behalf of the owner, and who suffer escalating abuse from the tenants, is broken by the sending of the fourth emissary. This one is different—the heir, who presumably is the only obstacle between the tenants and freedom from exploitation. Should they be punished for seizing the chance to get some of the owner's wealth? "Heaven forbid!" (20:16b), the people reply.

The Jerusalem elites who benefited from that system of land management (and may in fact have included some of the owners), on the other hand, would likely have listened in horror to the story and nodded in agreement at the decision to destroy the tenants and give the land to others (20:16a). And that is precisely the response counted on in the parabolic twist on the parable itself in the Gospels (see also Matt. 21:33–46; Mark 12:1–12). There, the parable functions as a thinly veiled allegory.

In the allegory, the vineyard owner is not the wicked exploiter, but represents God. The tenants, then, are the people with whom God is in covenant, and the servants are the prophets sent by God to recall the people to their covenant responsibilities. Insofar as the parable may have been directed to Jesus' contemporaries, the owner's son would probably have been equated with John the Baptist, about whom they have just been talking (20:3–8). For the Gospel writers' audiences whose point of view was shaped by the experience of Jesus' death and resurrection, of course, the "son" is Jesus himself. In either case, the authorities are caught in Jesus' trap, for they have rejected both John and Jesus, thus directly or indirectly colluding in their deaths.

The quotation from Psalm 118:22–23 (20:17) springs the trap, for the authorities have just made public their rejection of John and Jesus. The image shifts a bit to drive home the point about the fatal mistake they have made (20:18; see 2:34; Isa. 8:14–15; Dan. 2:34–35, 44–45). The chief priests and scribes recognize themselves in those charged with violating the covenant with God and rejecting God's spokespersons sent to remind them of it. Their response is rage against Jesus, and once again their fear of the people is his only protection (20:19).

## A DOUBLE TRAP
## Luke 20:20–40

### The Question about
### Paying Taxes (Luke 20:20–26)

20:20 **So they watched him and sent spies who pretended to be honest, in order to trap him by what he said, so as to hand him over to the jurisdiction and authority of the governor.** [21] **So they asked him, "Teacher, we know that you are right in what you say and teach, and you show deference to no one, but teach the way of God in accordance with truth.** [22] **Is it lawful for us to pay taxes to the emperor, or not?"** [23] **But he perceived their craftiness and said to them,** [24] **"Show me a denarius. Whose head and whose title does it bear?" They said, "The emperor's."** [25] **He said to them, "Then give to the emperor the things that are the emperor's, and to God the things that are God's."** [26] **And they were not able in the presence of the people to trap him by what he said; and being amazed by his answer, they became silent.**

The temple authorities' hostility toward Jesus escalates into a plot to "hand him over" (the verb is the same used for Judas's act of betrayal, 22:22) to the civil authorities (20:20). The question by which their spies try to trap him is indeed central to the charge against Jesus that they eventually bring to Pilate (23:2).

The spies' initial flattery actually speaks the truth about Jesus (20:21), but they intend it merely to curry his favor before they ask the fatal question. The issue of paying taxes to Rome went to the heart of the suffering of the poor people of first-century Palestine. In addition to taking bread from their mouths, the tax system was a constant reminder that they were an occupied people who were essentially aliens in the very land that God had given to their ancestors. In that context, advocates of open rebellion against Rome, like Judas the Galilean (who lived just before and during the time of Jesus), were reported to have equated paying taxes to Rome with committing treason against God.

If Jesus responds to the question by saying that paying the Roman taxes is lawful for Jews, he faces charges of advocating treason against God, and, at the same time, he courts the wrath of people whose backs are being broken by that burden. That would be the end of his protection against the plots and wrath of the religious leaders (19:48; 20:19). On the other hand, if he forbids paying taxes to the emperor, he faces charges of treason against Rome (which is precisely the ploy the ruling council attempts when they turn him over to Pilate, 23:2).

Once again, it is Jesus who sets the trap (20:24–25). The denarius he gets the spies to produce bears the emperor's picture, and the inscription "Tiberius Caesar, Augustus, Son of Divine Augustus." "Divine Augustus"? The coin these official representatives of the religious authorities are carrying amounts to a confession of another God, and so they themselves are on the very shakiest religious ground! His response is a model of ambiguity and clarity at the same time. The coin bearing the emperor's image might as well be given to the emperor: Jesus has thus sidestepped the charge of treason against Rome. But before the wrath of poor and pious alike can be mobilized, Jesus turns the saying around. If the coin is recognized as the emperor's by his image on it, then everything bearing God's image belongs to God. That means human beings (Gen. 1:26)—even the emperor. By the very image it bears, the coin itself belongs to God.

The silence that greets Jesus' response (20:26) has unraveled into often strident debate in the church about the question of the appropriate relationship between Christians and the political authorities. The debate has been colored by the various experiences different groups of people have had of political authorities that are more or less respectful of human worth and dignity, and more or less tolerant of their practice of their religion. Jesus' response, however, directs that discussion away from strategic questions about feasibility and expediency, and back to the central issue of idolatry (see also 18:18–27)—to the meaning of giving to God the things that are God's.

## The Question about Resurrection (Luke 20:27–40)

20:27 **Some Sadducees, those who say there is no resurrection, came to him** [28] **and asked him a question, "Teacher, Moses wrote for us that if a man's brother dies, leaving a wife but no children, the man shall marry the widow and raise up children for his brother. 29 Now there were seven brothers; the first married, and died childless; 30 then the second 31 and the third married her, and so in the same way all seven died childless. 32 Finally the woman** also died. ³³ In the resurrection, therefore, whose wife will the woman be? For the seven had married her."

³⁴ Jesus said to them, "Those who belong to this age marry and are given in marriage; ³⁵ but those who are considered worthy of a place in that age and in the resurrection from the dead neither marry nor are given in marriage. ³⁶ Indeed they cannot die anymore, because they are like angels and are children of God, being children of the resurrection. ³⁷ And the fact that the dead are raised Moses himself showed, in the story about the bush, where he speaks of the Lord as the God of Abraham, the God of Isaac, and the God of Jacob. ³⁸ Now he is God not of the dead, but of the living; for to him all of them are alive." ³⁹ Then some of the scribes answered, "Teacher, you have spoken well." ⁴⁰ For they no longer dared to ask him another question.

The second of the trick questions by which temple authorities try to trap Jesus focuses on one of the principal points of contention between Pharisees and Sadducees, the resurrection of the dead. The questioner— a Sadducee, the party that says there is no such thing as resurrection— poses a problem of interpretation of the law that becomes a problem only for Pharisees, who believe in a resurrection of the dead at the end of time. The problem is created by the levirate law (Deut. 25:5–6), which required that if one brother died without leaving an heir, his brother must marry the widow. The first son born to that couple is then considered the heir of the woman's first husband.

The problem posed to Jesus assumes multiple cases of levirate marriage—seven, to be exact—thus leading to the question, "In the resurrection, therefore, whose wife will the woman be?" (20:28–33). Presumably, the riddle would force Jesus to declare his allegiance either with the Pharisees or with the Sadducees, and thus would probably divide the audience whose unified support has been Jesus' defense so far.

Jesus' response is twofold, each part addressing one of the premises underlying the riddle. First, he speaks to the nature of the resurrected life (20:34–36). Without engaging in speculation about the architecture of heaven or the anatomy of angels, he simply affirms that the resurrected life will not mirror life here: Resurrection is not simply the resuscitation of corpses to the same human dilemmas further complicated by wings and white robes. (Paul deals with the same delicate issue in response to questions raised by the Corinthians [1 Cor. 15:35–57], finally cutting off speculation with the acclamation, "But thanks be to God, who gives us the victory through our Lord Jesus Christ.")

The second part of Jesus' response addresses the core debate over whether there is a resurrection. Jesus comes down on the Pharisees' side in a Pharisee's manner, namely by arguing from the heart of Torah itself (20:37–38; see Exod. 3:6). His point is simple: If Moses could refer to God as the God of the patriarchs who had long since died, and if God is clearly the God of the living, then the patriarchs must be alive to God—in other words, living the resurrected life. Jesus' questioners—and we today—might be left still wondering how, where, and in what form, but no further explanation is given. Note also that the response in no way echoes the church's tendency to make resurrection for other people depend on Jesus' resurrection. Resurrection is simply part of who God is.

Jesus' response ends the riddles (20:39–40) but not the opposition. One who speaks so well that he is able to defuse the arguments of the powerful presents a clear and present danger to the public order, and appropriate steps must be taken.

## JESUS' QUESTION ABOUT THE SON OF DAVID
### Luke 20:41–44

20:41 **Then he said to them, "How can they say that the Messiah is David's son?** 42 **For David himself says in the book of Psalms,**
> **'The Lord said to my Lord,**
> **"Sit at my right hand,**
> 43 **until I make your enemies your footstool." '**
> 44 **David thus calls him Lord; so how can he be his son?"**

Jesus takes the initiative away from the religious leaders by a question (20:41–44) and a warning (20:45–21:4). Matthew and Mark identify Pharisees and scribes, respectively, as those to whom the question refers (Matt. 22:41; Mark 12:35). The first occurrence of the pronoun in Luke "them" appears to address the question to the Sadducees, who have just tried to trap Jesus (20:27), but it is not clear who "they" are who call Jesus "David's son."

Even less clear is why the title "David's son" is a problem. The title has been accepted in a positive sense, in the cry of the person (or persons, according to Matthew) begging beside the road near Jericho (18:35–43; Matt. 20:29–34; Mark 10:46–52). Luke has also referred to Jesus several times as a descendant of David (1:32; 2:4; 3:31). Some scholars have argued that "son of David" can also mean "David-like"—a mighty military and political leader, with all of the trappings of royalty—and thus that the main idea is that the Messiah will not be that sort of figure. The biblical "proof," however, suggests that the problem is of another sort.

The text assumes that David wrote the Psalms attributed to him, including Psalm 110. It further assumes that that psalm refers to the coming Messiah (see also Acts 2:34–36). Thus, in the opening line, David says: "The LORD (meaning God) said to my Lord (meaning the coming Messiah)." Jesus argues that David would not use a title of honor (Lord) to refer to a descendant, to whom David as the ancestor would be considered superior. Thus, the Messiah cannot be David's "son." The title is inappropriate because it does not reflect the appropriate hierarchy of honor between King David and God's Messiah.

It is interesting, however, that Luke never refutes the title on the basis of the manner of Jesus' conception and birth. Jesus' Davidic lineage is traced through Joseph (2:4; 3:23, 31), who—if Luke intended to portray Jesus as born of a union of Mary and the Holy Spirit—would not be Jesus' father at all. The door is open wide in this passage for an aside to Luke's own audience reminding them of Jesus' identity as Son of God, not son of David. But Luke never walks through that door. One must wonder again, therefore, whether the church has built on the foundation of Luke's Gospel beliefs that Luke himself did not share.

## WARNINGS ABOUT THE RELIGIOUS LEADERS
## Luke 20:45–21:4

### Piety and Injustice (Luke 20:45–47)

**20:45 In the hearing of all the people he said to the disciples, ⁴⁶ "Beware of the scribes, who like to walk around in long robes, and love to be greeted with respect in the marketplaces, and to have the best seats in the synagogues and places of honor at banquets. ⁴⁷ They devour widows' houses and for the sake of appearance say long prayers. They will receive the greater condemnation."**

Jesus retains the initiative in the discussion, addressing the disciples, but in the hearing of "all the people." That double audience makes his words all the more dangerous, for they risk inciting public contempt and opposition to the religious leaders. The first charge—this time against temple officers—echoes an earlier charge against the Pharisees (11:43); its double occurrence suggests its importance to Luke, perhaps also as an implied warning against such behavior among the leaders of Luke's own church.

The second charge is aimed at an obvious abuse (20:45–47). Instead of defending widows (see 18:1–8)—perhaps even those for whom they function as legal guardians—these religious authorities exploit them. They thus violate a basic principle of the very religion to which their piety makes claim (Deut. 10:18; 14:29; 24:17, 19–21; 26:12; Job 22:9; 24:3; 31:16; Ps. 68:5; 94:6; Isa. 1:23; 10:2; Jer. 49:11; Mal. 3:5). Because of that, their condemnation is certain.

### The Impoverished Widow (Luke 21:1–4)

21:1 **He looked up and saw rich people putting their gifts into the treasury; ² he also saw a poor widow put in two small copper coins. ³ He said, "Truly I tell you, this poor widow has put in more than all of them; ⁴ for all of them have contributed out of their abundance, but she out of her poverty has put in all she had to live on."**

A "teachable moment" presents itself, in which the previous point can be driven home with even greater force. Among those placing offerings in the temple treasury is a poor widow. For her to meet her religious obligations demands every cent she has, leaving her nothing to live on. She is the embodiment of the charge Jesus has just made against the scribes (20:47). One should not regard this story as praise for her piety, but rather as a scream against the distortion of religion that makes her a victim of abuse.

### SIGNS OF THE END
### Luke 21:5–38

The moral and religious decay that has greeted Jesus in Jerusalem leads into Luke's version of what is often called "the Synoptic apocalypse" (see also Matt. 24:4–36; Mark 13:5–37). That "revelation," which is what the word "apocalypse" means, brings together a series of warnings and signs of what will mark the interval before all time is resolved in the coming of God's final judgment. The specific warnings represent Luke's perspective on the time of Jesus, as he looks back through events that have already taken place—times of persecution, for example, and the destruction of Jerusalem and the temple. These are historical events interpreted according to their meaning beyond history. The warnings represented in these specific events are couched in more generic warnings of the human trauma that ensues when human pretense and injustice come face to face with God.

### The Destruction of the Temple (Luke 21:5–6)

21:5 **When some were speaking about the temple, how it was adorned with beautiful stones and gifts dedicated to God, he said, ⁶ "As for these things**

that you see, the days will come when not one stone will be left upon another; all will be thrown down."

The perversion of the temple, making it into a den of robbers (19:46)
and a place where abuse is masked by piety (21:1–4), has just been revealed. The temple, therefore, is the place to begin to observe the consequences of that perversion. What was predicted of the city itself—that not
one stone will be left on another (19:44)—now focuses on the temple. Not
even its splendor can protect it from the disaster that lies ahead.

## Political and Cosmic Signs (Luke 21:7–11)

21:7 **They asked him, "Teacher, when will this be, and what will be the sign
that this is about to take place?"** 8 **And he said, "Beware that you are not led
astray; for many will come in my name and say, 'I am he!' and, 'The time is
near!' Do not go after them.**

9 **"When you hear of wars and insurrections, do not be terrified; for these
things must take place first, but the end will not follow immediately."** 10 **Then
he said to them, "Nation will rise against nation, and kingdom against kingdom;** 11 **there will be great earthquakes, and in various places famines and
plagues; and there will be dreadful portents and great signs from heaven."**

Two questions greet the prediction of any disaster: When will it happen? and What will be the signs of its beginning? (21:7). Jesus' response
points to three signs. The first is the arrival of people making false claims
that they know the answers (21:8). The other two signs are warfare and
political chaos on the one hand (21:9–10), and natural disasters on the
other (21:11).

## Times of Persecution (Luke 21:12–19)

21:12 **"But before all this occurs, they will arrest you and persecute you;
they will hand you over to synagogues and prisons, and you will be brought
before kings and governors because of my name.** 13 **This will give you an opportunity to testify.** 14 **So make up your minds not to prepare your defense
in advance;** 15 **for I will give you words and a wisdom that none of your opponents will be able to withstand or contradict.** 16 **You will be betrayed even
by parents and brothers, by relatives and friends; and they will put some of
you to death.** 17 **You will be hated by all because of my name.** 18 **But not a
hair of your head will perish.** 19 **By your endurance you will gain your souls."**

The first of the signs (21:8) comes into focus in times of persecution
that will become occasions for Jesus' followers to bear witness to him and

to the truth of their faith (21:12–13). Members of the church will testify before both religious and political authorities (see Acts 4–5 and 24–26). Earlier words of assurance that they will not be abandoned in those times are repeated (21:14–15; 12:11–12), and so are earlier warnings about the betrayal and hatred that will be theirs (21:16–17; 12:52–53; 6:22). Even a false assurance (21:18)—for many would indeed suffer harm—echoes an earlier word of comfort (12:7). The final promise is not that they will be spared the suffering, but rather that their hope lies in "endurance" (21:19)—standing firm and refusing to give in to the evil around them.

## The Destruction of Jerusalem (Luke 21:20–24)

21:20 **"When you see Jerusalem surrounded by armies, then know that its desolation has come near.** [21] **Then those in Judea must flee to the mountains, and those inside the city must leave it, and those out in the country must not enter it;** [22] **for these are days of vengeance, as a fulfillment of all that is written.** [23] **Woe to those who are pregnant and to those who are nursing infants in those days! For there will be great distress on the earth and wrath against this people;** [24] **they will fall by the edge of the sword and be taken away as captives among all nations; and Jerusalem will be trampled on by the Gentiles, until the times of the Gentiles are fulfilled."**

The destruction of Jerusalem, ten to twenty years before Luke's Gospel was written, serves as the second sign (21:9–10). Many understood the horror of those days to be God's final condemnation of the people, and as already participating in the events of the final judgment. Luke's reading is different. The fall of the city (sketched in vivid images in 21:20–24a) is a sign only that those events of the end-time lie ahead. Furthermore, according to Luke, the triumph of the Gentiles over the Jews is not going to be permanent (21:24b): The Gentiles have joined *but not replaced* the Jews as God's holy people. Luke has affirmed since the beginning of the Gospel that salvation belongs to Israel as well as to the nations (for example, 1:54–55, 72–75; 2:29–32; 3:6), and he does not relinquish that affirmation in his vision of the last days.

## The Earth Returns to
the Edge of Chaos (Luke 21:25–27)

21:25 **"There will be signs in the sun, the moon, and the stars, and on the earth distress among nations confused by the roaring of the sea and the** waves. <sup>26</sup> **People will faint from fear and foreboding of what is coming upon the world, for the powers of the heavens will be shaken. <sup>27</sup> Then they will see 'the Son of Man coming in a cloud' with power and great glory."**

The third sign (21:11) completes the scene of panic and confusion (21:25–27). Not only human institutions like cities and governments, but even the earth, sea, and sky will reflect the coming times. The condition of these basic components of the created order will resemble again the moment before God's voice shaped them and called them good (Gen. 1:1–2). Once again, all is poised on the edge of space and time, between chaos and new beginnings.

## Final Assurances and Warnings (Luke 21:28–36)

21:28 **"Now when these things begin to take place, stand up and raise your heads, because your redemption is drawing near."**

<sup>29</sup> **Then he told them a parable: "Look at the fig tree and all the trees; <sup>30</sup> as soon as they sprout leaves you can see for yourselves and know that summer is already near. <sup>31</sup> So also, when you see these things taking place, you know that the kingdom of God is near. <sup>32</sup> Truly I tell you, this generation will not pass away until all things have taken place. <sup>33</sup> Heaven and earth will pass away, but my words will not pass away.**

<sup>34</sup> **"Be on guard so that your hearts are not weighed down with dissipation and drunkenness and the worries of this life, and that day catch you unexpectedly, <sup>35</sup> like a trap. For it will come upon all who live on the face of the whole earth. <sup>36</sup> Be alert at all times, praying that you may have the strength to escape all these things that will take place, and to stand before the Son of Man."**

For those to whom this revelation is given, the balance is tipped: What lies ahead of this moment on the brink is firmly in God's hand. In fact, this very moment signals that their "redemption" is near (21:28). The parable of the fig tree (21:29–31) pulls the cosmic images down to human scale. As surely and as reassuringly as the tree's leaves mark the beginning of summer, so these events are signs that God's reign is near. The "redemption" that is promised is not a private lifeboat to save a few privileged folk while everything else is destroyed. Rather, redemption is equated with the coming of God's reign, which spells transformation, healing, and wholeness for all of life.

How "near" the time will be is not exactly clear. The word "generation" can refer to the thirty or so years that one would normally assume for a human life cycle. It can also, however, refer to an entire era marked by a particular quality ("this age"), which could encompass all of human history. We do not know what Luke meant, either here or in the similar saying in 9:27. But the essence of the "revelation" has been to put an end to such calculation, emphasizing, instead, confidence in God's faithfulness to God's promises of salvation (21:33).

The apocalypse ends with a reminder of the need to stay alert (21:34–36; see also 12:35–46). Alertness involves an appropriate lifestyle, as well as the strength to get through all that will take place and to face the one in whose balances the judgment would be weighed.

## Jesus' Public Ministry
## Concludes (Luke 21:37–38)

21:37 **Every day he was teaching in the temple, and at night he would go out and spend the night on the Mount of Olives, as it was called.** [38] **And all the people would get up early in the morning to listen to him in the temple.**

Cataclysmic visions give way to the everyday rhythms of Jesus' ministry in Jerusalem: Days are given over to teaching in the temple, and nights are spent on the Mount of Olives. The summary marks the conclusion of Jesus' public ministry. This is the way it ends.

However, that same summary also draws us forward. Soon the Mount of Olives will bring not rest from the day's work, but arrest and betrayal (22:47–54a); early morning will not be a time for teaching, but for interrogation and judgment (22:66–71). But in the end, another early morning dawns (24:1), when life has the last word, and when the rhythms of life can go on (24:52–53).

# 13. The Final Day: Supper, Judicial Process, and Execution
## Luke 22:1–23:56

As richly detailed as the narrative of Jesus' final week in Jerusalem has been, the Gospel writers' lenses focus even more closely on the events of Jesus' final day. The basic pattern of the account—Jesus' final meal with his followers, arrest, hearings before Jewish and Roman authorities, verdict, and execution—is common to all four Gospels, but they differ at significant points. The differences in the four versions of the story, the weighty theological interpretation, and the symbolic embroidery with which almost every episode is adorned make it clear that none of the four is simply reporting the facts.

If they are not just conveying court records or news reports, then, questions about where the accounts came from and how fact and interpretation are interwoven become significant. Unfortunately, they do not yield certain answers. A number of scholars suggest that even Mark, the earliest of the Gospels to take written form, drew on one or more complete narratives of Jesus' "passion" or "suffering" in the final events of his life. It was a scandal that the one they called the Messiah or Christ was executed by Rome as a political criminal, instead of leading the people to freedom and victory and making God's triumph apparent. That scandal would have evoked efforts by his followers to explain and interpret his death, and somehow to make sense of their continued faith that this same one was resurrected and alive in their midst.

If Luke had Mark's Gospel as a basis for his new Gospel, it is probable that he also knew Mark's passion narrative (or at least a version of it very similar to the one now in that Gospel, allowing the probability that later editors might have altered a few details). The differences between Luke's passion account and Mark's have led to a debate among scholars about whether Luke had as one of his sources a different passion narrative, which he interwove with Mark's, or whether he simply incorporated isolated details he had found and then edited the result in order to emphasize his own theological interpretation of the passion and its aftermath. The evidence can be read both ways, and scholars are still divided about their conclusions.

The approach I have followed in this book is to focus on Luke's final form of the narrative, paying special attention to points he appears to emphasize. One way to identify such emphases is to take particular note of points at which Luke's narrative differs from Mark's, since it is at those points that he has most clearly chosen either to follow his other source (if he had one) or to adapt Mark's narrative himself.

## LOOKING FOR OPPORTUNITIES:
## DEATH PLOT AND BETRAYAL
## Luke 22:1–6

22:1 **Now the festival of Unleavened Bread, which is called the Passover, was near. ² The chief priests and the scribes were looking for a way to put Jesus to death, for they were afraid of the people.**

**³ Then Satan entered into Judas called Iscariot, who was one of the twelve; ⁴ he went away and conferred with the chief priests and officers of the temple police about how he might betray him to them. ⁵ They were greatly pleased and agreed to give him money. ⁶ So he consented and began to look for an opportunity to betray him to them when no crowd was present.**

The political dilemma that sets the context for the passion narrative is announced at the very beginning. The Passover festival was a time when crowds of people from the countryside entered Jerusalem in order to keep the feast in the holy city. In addition to attracting large numbers of people to the city, the Passover festival commemorating Israel's safe escape from slavery in Egypt to begin their journey toward the promised land reminded the people of God's commitment to their freedom. The theme of the festival and the occupation of Jerusalem by Rome stood in stark contrast. Feelings of anticipation that blended hope and dread covered the city during the week of the festival. These feelings would coalesce into tension-filled moments whenever there was a confrontation between gatherings of celebrants and the various forces of order (Roman soldiers and temple police alike).

Jesus' following may not have been massive, but apparently it was enough to attract attention and to represent a threat—potential flashpoints for protest and disruption of order. Whatever may have been their personal, political, and theological response to Jesus' message and ministry (to the extent that they would even have known of it), the temple authorities would have had very good reasons to oppose his movement. Given their responsibility for the well-being of the Jewish people in Jerusalem, they would not have wanted anything to bring about stronger Roman repression of the people. Popular charismatic leaders such as Jesus could evoke such a negative response from occupying forces already on edge because of the crowds and the mood of the festival. The temple authorities may have made a strategic decision that it would be wiser to remove Jesus from the scene than to risk a riot or an uprising that could only have been disastrous for the Jews.

All four of the Gospel writers, however, portray the temple authorities as having less pastoral or honorable motives. They agree in representing the leaders as plotting Jesus' disappearance in some way that would not attract the attention of his followers. The implication is that those leaders opposed Jesus, and that may have been the case, for the religious leaders would also have been reaping some benefits from their cooperation with the Roman authorities. Retaining the respect of the occupying forces might well have seemed like a strategically prudent move in order to hold on to their access to power and its accompanying economic benefits.

Thus, it is virtually impossible to know for certain how the official events surrounding Jesus' arrest unfolded, let alone what might have been the real motivations of the various participants in the process. Did the temple authorities initiate action against Jesus out of their own desires to be rid of him? Were they pushed to such action by a sense of their broader responsibilities for the well-being of the people? Could they even have been the unwilling agents of Rome, compelled to investigate Jesus (and possibly others) so that any blame would be lodged against Jewish leaders and would not become an added reason for the people to oppose Rome? Suffice it to say that the Gospel writers imply the first reason: The leaders wanted Jesus out of the way, and they were worried only about the people's reaction (22:1–2).

Luke goes on immediately to set the authorities' plan in motion: For a fee, Judas will help the authorities carry out the arrest at a time when no crowds will witness it (22:3–6). Both Matthew and Mark separate the statement of the authorities' plan to get rid of Jesus from the account of Judas's agreement to help them carry it out by telling the story of Jesus' being anointed "for burial" by an unnamed woman (Matt. 26:6–13; Mark 14:3–9). Luke does not include that account, having told of an anointing of Jesus by a woman earlier in the Galilean ministry (7:36–50). The effect of the omission is that in Luke there is nothing to alleviate the stark horror of the authorities' plan and its motives.

In Mark and Matthew, the anointing story includes the woman's "messianic" anointing of Jesus' head, affirming the ultimate triumph of God's purposes even in the midst of the horror. Furthermore, the affirmation that his body has been anointed, and thus properly prepared for burial, even before the execution is carried out sets that death in the context of a larger purpose. Although that purpose is not evident to Jesus' contemporaries, it is nonetheless known to and accepted by Jesus. In Luke's account, no such theological rationale or even human tenderness mitigates the moment. In fact, its horror is underlined by the careful reminder that this very Judas is "one of the twelve" chosen by Jesus as "apostles," selected from among all the disciples (6:13) for special preparation (6:20–8:56) and responsibility (9:1–6).

Furthermore, in Luke's account, Judas's collusion in the plot against Jesus represents the end of Jesus' public ministry, which was marked by the devil's temporary absence from the human scene. The "opportune time" for the devil to return (4:13) has arrived when the devil (here named "Satan") enters Judas. Just as the devil's final act prior to departing was to test Jesus during his time in the wilderness, Satan's return is marked by a new testing of Jesus in the holy city itself (see my comments on 22:43, 63–65; 23:7–11, 35–43).

## THE PASSOVER MEAL
## Luke 22:7–38

Action to carry out the death plot is suspended, however, while the narrator moves slowly through the late hours of the daytime and early evening before the arrest. Narrator's summaries give way to dialogue and to meticulous description of the liturgical movements and words of Jesus' final meal with the disciples. That Passover meal is like an opening bracket marking the beginning of the final portion of Luke's Gospel. The closing bracket is formed by the meals at Emmaus (24:13–35) and Jerusalem (24:36–49). Taken together, these meals give shape and meaning to what otherwise might be simply the report of another political execution by Rome, with the collusion of the Jewish authorities. Contained within the frame provided by the meals, the passion account finds its place not only at the pinnacle of the Gospel narrative but also at the heart of the life of Luke's church, where the Christ is known in the breaking of the bread.

## Preparation (Luke 22:7–13)

22:7 **Then came the day of Unleavened Bread, on which the Passover lamb had to be sacrificed.** [8] **So Jesus sent Peter and John, saying, "Go and prepare the Passover meal for us that we may eat it."** [9] **They asked him, "Where do you want us to make preparations for it?"** [10] **"Listen," he said to them, "when you have entered the city, a man carrying a jar of water will meet you; follow him into the house he enters** [11] **and say to the owner of the house, 'The teacher asks you, "Where is the guest room, where I may eat the Passover with my disciples?"'** [12] **He will show you a large room upstairs, already furnished. Make preparations for us there."** [13] **So they went and found everything as he had told them; and they prepared the Passover meal.**

Luke portrays Jesus and the disciples as spending the festival on the outskirts of Jerusalem, like most of the visitors without family in the city with whom they could lodge. They, therefore, must rent space in the "guest room" (see my comments on 2:7; the underlying Greek word is the same one translated there as "inn") of someone's home in order to have a suitable place to hold the Passover meal. Intrigue and mystery cloak the story. Luke gives the impression that Jesus has made prior arrangements for such space with someone living in Jerusalem, but that even the inner circle of the disciples have not been informed of the plans. Luke does not say who this confidant of Jesus may have been, or how Jesus happened to know him, or why Jesus had made the arrangements himself instead of entrusting the task to one of those traveling with him. Luke says only that Peter and John are given instructions, not about how to find the place of the banquet itself, but rather to look for a man who would identify himself by carrying a water jar. (Since drawing and carrying water was usually done by women, a man with a water jar would have been easy to spot. If the identifying action had any further significance, Luke provides no clue what it might be.) That man, in turn, would lead them to the upstairs room that had been readied for them: This time there would be room at the "inn" (2:7).

## The Supper (Luke 22:14–20)

22:14 **When the hour came, he took his place at the table, and the apostles with him.** [15] **He said to them, "I have eagerly desired to eat this Passover**

**with you before I suffer;** [16] **for I tell you, I will not eat it until it is fulfilled in the kingdom of God."** [17] **Then he took a cup, and after giving thanks he said, "Take this and divide it among yourselves;** [18] **for I tell you that from now on I will not drink of the fruit of the vine until the kingdom of God comes."** [19] **Then he took a loaf of bread, and when he had given thanks, he broke it and gave it to them, saying, "This is my body, which is given for you. Do this in remembrance of me."** [20] **And he did the same with the cup after supper, saying, "This cup that is poured out for you is the new covenant in my blood."**

The church's various accounts of Jesus' final meal with the disciples have been colored by the intense meaning and emotion that always surround last meals, last holidays, and last words shared with loved ones before their deaths. In addition to those powerful human factors, the liturgical practice from the earliest days of the church that carried forward the "words of institution" associated with that meal (1 Cor. 11:23–26) gave both shape and content to accounts of the event.

Luke's narrative of the meal and of the teachings that accompany it, however, seem to place less emphasis on the words of institution themselves and more on additional interpretations of the meal. In fact, the ancient manuscripts of Luke's Gospel present a number of different readings in 22:16–20. Various scribes charged with copying the text of the Gospel apparently tried to make sense of the many differences between Luke's version of the meal and those found in Matthew 26:26–29, Mark 14:22–25, and 1 Corinthians 11:23–26. For example, the wording of 22:19–20 is very similar to that of 1 Corinthians. The fact that some manuscripts of Luke do not contain portions of those verses suggests to a number of scholars that some scribes added the "missing" words in order to keep the sequence of bread and cup in the usual liturgical order (which is also reflected in 1 Corinthians and in the accounts of the last supper in Mark and Matthew). Such scholars identify the more "difficult" reading, a sequence of cup-then-bread (without the second cup mentioned in v. 20) as probably the original wording of Luke, which later copyists saw as an error needing correction. Both the external manuscript evidence and the internal coherence of Luke's account, however, seem finally to support the decisions by translators of the NRSV to include verse 20 in its entirety as part of the text.

The coherence of Luke's account can be seen if one considers the entire account as a narrative and not merely as a source for the liturgy of the supper. The dinner hour finds Jesus and the disciples at table, but the meal quickly loses its festive air. The account begins with what appears to be Jesus' double vow of fasting: He will neither eat the Passover meal nor even drink wine until the Passover is "fulfilled" in the reign of God, and until the reign of God comes (22:15–18). The wording of the text does not make it clear whether we are to understand that Jesus ate this meal with his friends and then vowed not to eat another until the condition of the vow was met, or whether the vow encompassed this meal too. However, the vow over the cup is clear: They are to divide the cup among themselves, and he does not drink from it. Because both vows are linked to the fulfillment of the reign of God, it seems logical to understand both as implying that Jesus himself did not partake of the meal.

The double vow of fasting is followed by words of institution in the traditional order of bread followed by cup (22:19–20). The meal is one of both remembrance and covenant for the Christian community, just as it is in 1 Corinthians. At this point, the purpose of Luke's double cycle of meal-then-cup followed by bread-then-cup becomes clear. This meal must be interpreted both in the context of Jesus' ministry and in the life of the church.

In the context of Jesus' ministry, this meal is yet another of the many meals that Jesus shared with the wider group of disciples and others touched by his ministry—the feeding of the five thousand (9:10–17); the meal when Jesus was anointed (7:36–50); the meal with Zacchaeus (19:1–10); the meal that was the setting for a healing, various teachings, and the parable of the great feast (14:1–24); and many others. Just as each of these meals was a sign of God's reign characterized by good news to the poor and release to captives, so also the meal that turned out to be their last meal together finds its meaning in people's longing for the fulfillment of that reign.

At the same time, this final meal of Jesus with the disciples looks forward to the life of the church that begins with the meals of Easter (24:13–49) and centers around the table community of the believers. As a meal that stands at the heart of the church's life, this Passover feast is reinterpreted in terms of covenant and remembrance focused through the approaching (and, for the church, remembered) death of Jesus.

In Luke's account of the supper, both cycles of interpretation—as a meal of Jesus and a meal of the church—are complete. There is no problem of an inverted liturgical order of cup and bread, and no dangling reference to a second cup that has to be resolved by an argument based on differences in ancient Greek manuscripts of the Gospel. Instead, Luke gives the entire meal a double interpretation appropriate to its situation on the boundary, where Jesus' own ministry is ending and the life of the church is already being called into being. The double focus continues in the remainder of the conversation at the table, where the disciples are shown as increasingly self-preoccupied, even as their time with Jesus is running out.

## The Unnamed Betrayer (Luke 22:21–23)

22:21 **But see, the one who betrays me is with me, and his hand is on the table.** 22 **For the Son of Man is going as it has been determined, but woe to that one by whom he is betrayed!"** 23 **Then they began to ask one another, which one of them it could be who would do this.**

Although Luke's readers know about Judas's conspiracy with the temple officials (22:3–6), the characters within the narrative (in particular, the other disciples) have not yet learned of the plot or the identity of the betrayer. In Matthew and Mark the plot is introduced before the meal is shared (Matt. 26:21–25; Mark 14:18–21), but Luke heightens the drama by having the betrayer already share in the covenant meal before his intentions are disclosed. Judas thus fulfills Psalm 41:9: "Even my bosom friend in whom I trusted, who ate of my bread, has lifted the heel against me." Just as Judas is always carefully identified as "one of the twelve," and not an outsider, so the betrayer here (though not named) is clearly shown to be someone inside the community. For Luke's church, the message is clear: The most dangerous enemies are insiders who can be tempted or persuaded to collaborate with authorities who are merely doing their job.

The mention of the Son of Man recalls the earlier passion predictions (9:22, 43b–45; 18:31–34), but the disciples make no such connection. Their attention is turned within their group, on *who* would do such a thing, not on *what* is being foretold.

## Standards for Leadership (Luke 22:24–30)

22:24 **A dispute also arose among them as to which one of them was to be regarded as the greatest.** 25 **But he said to them, "The kings of the Gentiles lord it over them; and those in authority over them are called benefactors.** 26 **But not so with you; rather the greatest among you must become like the youngest, and the leader like one who serves.** 27 **For who is greater, the one who is at the table or the one who serves? Is it not the one at the table? But I am among you as one who serves.**

28 **"You are those who have stood by me in my trials;** 29 **and I confer on you, just as my Father has conferred on me, a kingdom,** 30 **so that you may eat and drink at my table in my kingdom, and you will sit on thrones judging the twelve tribes of Israel."**

The sense of foreboding that has surrounded the scene gives way to a struggle over leadership in the community (22:24–27). The prevailing patronage system with its relationships of debt and mutual obligation once again is contrasted with the reversal of values that has marked Luke's Gospel from its very beginning. Just as the lowly are to be lifted up and the powerful brought down (1:47–55), the poor declared blessed and woe pronounced to the rich (6:20–26), and the guest list of the banquet turned completely around (14:12–14, 16–24), so also, within the community of disciples, criteria of power and honor are reversed (see also 9:46–48).

Jesus' own serving of the meal provides the standard for leadership in the community, about which the others are debating. By serving or distributing the food to the other guests, Jesus has taken on the work generally carried out by a servant or by a woman of the household. Far from a role marked by prestige or privileged access on the basis of one's attributes of social status (for example, one's class, ethnicity, or gender) or one's formal credentials for leadership (such as ordination), Jesus' role at the supper belongs to those who lack status or who relinquish it in order to serve others.

How long the church actually functioned under such standards for leadership, if it ever did, is not clear. Luke, however, proceeds as if the lesson was, in fact, learned by the church, of which the disciples are here the representatives. The account of their dispute about leadership is followed by a clear statement that they are authorized to carry on the work begun in Jesus (22:28–30). The commission is ironic, for the ensuing narrative makes it clear that these disciples did not manage to stand by Jesus in his times of trial and testing, any more than they appear to have gotten the point about criteria for leadership.

Just as Jesus' earlier vows pointed to the realization of God's reign (22:15–18), so here also it is God's reign once conferred on Jesus that now is handed on to the church so that the long-awaited banquet can finally take place (see the earlier discussion of 14:15). Just as Jesus, especially in his identity as Son of Man, has the role of judge in the final judgment, so that task too—encompassing even the judgment of "the twelve tribes of Israel"—now belongs to the church.

## Peter's Role Foretold (Luke 22:31–34)

22:31 **"Simon, Simon, listen! Satan has demanded to sift all of you like wheat, 32 but I have prayed for you that your own faith may not fail; and you, when once you have turned back, strengthen your brothers." 33 And he said to him, "Lord, I am ready to go with you to prison and to death!"**

[34] Jesus said, "I tell you, Peter, the cock will not crow this day, until you have denied three times that you know me."

The double drama of Jesus' last day and the church's future continues in the words to the one called both Simon and Peter. Like the betrayer whose deed was announced earlier (22:21–23), Peter too has shared in the covenant meal, and is still at table with Jesus when his denials are predicted (unlike in Matthew and Mark, where his denial of Jesus is not mentioned until they have reached the Mount of Olives). Unlike the betrayer's act, however, Peter's denials do not spell the end of his role in the church.

Jesus' words to Peter begin with the assurance of Jesus' sustaining prayer for him (the word "you" in v. 32 is singular) and of Peter's commission to strengthen the others once he himself has "turned back." Following that assurance, Luke makes it clear why it was necessary: Peter's claim of steadfastness notwithstanding, he will fail, and three times he will deny even knowing Jesus. Like the betrayer who shared in the covenant meal, Peter, who will deny Jesus is also clearly an insider. More than simply a member of the community, he is one who will lead the church in the future. Future greatness will not shield him from failing the immediate test, however, nor will that triple failure seal his future.

### Equipment for the Journey (Luke 22:35–38)

22:35 He said to them, "When I sent you out without a purse, bag, or sandals, did you lack anything?" They said, "No, not a thing." [36] He said to them, "But now, the one who has a purse must take it, and likewise a bag. And the one who has no sword must sell his cloak and buy one. [37] For I tell you, this scripture must be fulfilled in me, 'And he was counted among the lawless'; and indeed what is written about me is being fulfilled." [38] They said, "Lord, look, here are two swords." He replied, "It is enough."

Earlier, the twelve (9:1–6) and the seventy (10:1–12) had been sent out without supplies, to rely on the hospitality of those among whom their mission was carried out. Even when hostility would greet them from some people (9:5; 10:3, 10–12), others would welcome and provide for them and would support their ministry (9:4; 10:5–9). Those gentler days have come to an end, however, as the supper draws to a close. Those who accompany Jesus into the Jerusalem night, and who carry on into the life of the church, now must be prepared to provide for themselves and even to protect themselves in the face of hostility.

On the level of the story of Jesus' approaching death, the grounds for the death sentence are established. Their bearing of a sword—even two of them—places Jesus "among the lawless" who disturb the peace and represent a threat to the authorities. On the level of the church, the picture is of a community prepared by Jesus for the struggles that ensued. They are doubly prepared by warnings that their sharing in the covenant meal provides no guarantee against apostasy, strife, or denial, and by the promise that God's saving presence will not desert them. The stage is set for Luke to present Jesus' death as a martyrdom that both reflects the deaths of earlier prophets and provides a model for the disciples when their lives hang in the balance in the years to follow.

## THE MOUNT OF OLIVES
## Luke 22:39–53

### Prayer (Luke 22:39–46)

22:39 **He came out and went, as was his custom, to the Mount of Olives; and the disciples followed him.** 40 **When he reached the place, he said to them, "Pray that you may not come into the time of trial."** 41 **Then he withdrew from them about a stone's throw, knelt down, and prayed,** 42 **"Father, if you are willing, remove this cup from me; yet, not my will but yours be done."** 43 **Then an angel from heaven appeared to him and gave him strength.** 44 **In his anguish he prayed more earnestly, and his sweat became like great drops of blood falling down on the ground.** 45 **When he got up from prayer, he came to the disciples and found them sleeping because of grief,** 46 **and he said to them, "Why are you sleeping? Get up and pray that you may not come into the time of trial."**

The scene on the Mount of Olives includes all the disciples (not just Peter, James, and John, as in Mark and Matthew), who are instructed to pray for themselves (not just to keep watch while Jesus prays). At both the beginning and the end of the scene, he instructs them to pray not to come into the "time of trial" (22:40, 46), which will be so crucial to them and to their future (22:28–30, 31–34). Their falling asleep is attributed to their "grief," making it an understandable human response to the heaviness and foreboding that marked the meal they have just shared with Jesus.

The description of the disciples surrounds the words and actions of Jesus. The resolve expressed in Jesus' vows at the supper continues in Luke's account of the scene on the Mount of Olives. The agitation and struggle that characterize Jesus' words and actions in Matthew 26:36–46 and Mark 14:32–42 are absent from Luke's account. The prayer attributed to Jesus by Luke begins and ends with affirmations of Jesus' commitment to God's will, which surround the plea, "remove this cup from me." The first part of that double affirmation is striking when it is compared to the openings of the prayer in Matthew ("if it is possible") and Mark ("all things are possible"). Both of these introductions suggest a posture of negotiation with God to find another way, or even to change God's own intent in line with Jesus' plea. In Luke, Jesus' focus on God's will never wavers.

Some of the ancient Greek manuscripts of Luke include 22:43–44, while a slightly greater number omit those verses. No parallels are found in Mark or Matthew, however, so if they were not originally in Luke, it is difficult to see where they might have come from. This is particularly true since they could also be read as pointing to Jesus' faltering in his resolve and needing supernatural help to make it through. To draw that conclusion, however, is to misunderstand the imagery of these verses and to overlook the important affirmations about Jesus and about the significance of the unfolding events.

To read 22:44 as suggesting that Jesus' resolve is weakening is to misunderstand both the vocabulary and the imagery involved. The word translated as Jesus' "anguish," like the image of the sweat pouring off his body, comes from the realm of athletics. Both point not to hesitancy or uncertainty, but to the intensely focused energy of an athlete just as a contest is about to begin—for example, of a racer on the blocks, set to run a hundred-meter dash. The prayer finds Jesus focused and ready for the struggle at hand.

Similarly, the angel's ministry (22:43) is not a supernatural prop to diminish the cost to Jesus of the struggle. Instead, the angel reminds Luke's readers that what is at stake here is once again the "trial" or "test" of Jesus by Satan—a struggle for Jesus' very identity and life. Satan's return as an active player in the cast of the unfolding drama (22:3) has already alerted us to the likelihood that this "prosecuting attorney" will resume the work begun early in Jesus' ministry (4:1–13). In his account of that earlier scene, Luke does not mention the presence of any angels serving or "waiting on" Jesus, as do Matthew and Mark (Matt. 4:11; Mark 1:13). Instead, the angel appears in this renewed test, when the legal authorities of Rome and of the temple will be colluding in the trial, and when the stakes are highest of all. Similar to the earlier test in the wilderness, and in contrast to a different garden where Adam failed a test by Satan, Jesus will emerge triumphant once again.

## Arrest (Luke 22:47–53)

22:47 **While he was still speaking, suddenly a crowd came, and the one called Judas, one of the twelve, was leading them. He approached Jesus to kiss him;** [48] **but Jesus said to him, "Judas, is it with a kiss that you are betraying the Son of Man?"** [49] **When those who were around him saw what was coming, they asked, "Lord, should we strike with the sword?"** [50] **Then one of them struck the slave of the high priest and cut off his right ear.** [51] **But Jesus said, "No more of this!" And he touched his ear and healed him.** [52] **Then Jesus said to the chief priests, the officers of the temple police, and the elders who had come for him, "Have you come out with swords and clubs as if I were a bandit?** [53] **When I was with you day after day in the temple, you did not lay hands on me. But this is your hour, and the power of darkness!"**

When they awaken, the disciples who have been sleeping noncombatants find themselves already in the midst of the struggle. A crowd arrives, led by Judas. In Matthew and Mark, Judas announces his plan to betray Jesus with a kiss (Matt. 26:48; Mark 14:44), but in Luke's account Jesus himself identifies the plan to pervert an intimate greeting into the kiss of death. The continued failure of the other disciples to grasp the truth about where life and salvation are lodged is played out in their immediate use of their swords against one of the slaves of the high priest, who have come to carry out the arrest. Jesus cures the injured ear, not as an example of the power of God's reign, but as an embodiment of his own obedience to God's will.

Luke already has explained why Jesus' arrest takes place under cover of night and not when Jesus has been teaching in the temple, on the home turf of the arresting party: The temple officials fear the reaction of the people (22:1–2). Apparently, though, at least some of the people have joined the official delegation, forming a "crowd" whose role throughout the day of arrest, hearings, and execution moves from background to foreground, as the official systems of jurisprudence show themselves not to be equal to their task. Nothing in their administrative guidelines or legal precedents can prepare these forces of order to deal with their "hour, and the power of darkness."

## THE JUDICIAL PROCESS
### Luke 22:54–23:25

### Peter's Denials (Luke 22:54–62)

22:54 **Then they seized him and led him away, bringing him into the high priest's house. But Peter was following at a distance.** [55] **When they had kindled a fire in the middle of the courtyard and sat down together, Peter sat**

among them. [56] Then a servant-girl, seeing him in the firelight, stared at him
and said, "This man also was with him." [57] But he denied it, saying,
"Woman, I do not know him." [58] A little later someone else, on seeing him,
said, "You also are one of them." But Peter said, "Man, I am not!" [59] Then
about an hour later still another kept insisting, "Surely this man also was
with him; for he is a Galilean." [60] But Peter said, "Man, I do not know what
you are talking about!" At that moment, while he was still speaking, the cock
crowed. [61] The Lord turned and looked at Peter. Then Peter remembered the
word of the Lord, how he had said to him, "Before the cock crows today,
you will deny me three times." [62] And he went out and wept bitterly.

Following his arrest, Jesus is kept in custody in the house of the high
priest until morning. In Luke's account, the religious leaders hold no secret meeting to carry out their business under cover of night (as is the case
in Matt. 26:57–68; Mark 14:53–65) but instead, they wait until daybreak.
Two episodes mark the night of Jesus' custody: Peter's denials (22:54–62)
and the mockery of Jesus by the temple police.

In this episode, Peter is called only by that name. He carries out the
deeds predicted for him and that mark him forever in the life of the
church. Peter is with Jesus, yet not with him, when he is arrested. He follows "at a distance" (22:54), but close enough that Jesus can witness his
acts (22:61). The composition of the crowd gathered in the courtyard is
not specified, but it appears to have included some of the arresting party,
perhaps others from the crowd, and people from the high priest's household. A woman and two men identify Peter as one of those who were with
Jesus. The first two times he denies the charge, Peter shows no recognition of how closely he is following the script set for him earlier by Jesus.
When Peter denies the third accusation, and the cock crows, suddenly he
remembers. However, if Jesus' prediction of Peter's denials unfolds exactly as he said, so does Peter's "turning back" (22:32), for "he went out
and wept bitterly." In the very moment of Peter's greatest distance from
Jesus, when Jesus' gaze falls upon him, he is already on the road toward
being able to strengthen the others.

## Mockery by the Guards (Luke 22:63–65)

22:63 Now the men who were holding Jesus began to mock him and beat
him; [64] they also blindfolded him and kept asking him, "Prophesy! Who is it
that struck you?" [65] They kept heaping many other insults on him.

The story of Peter's denials follows closely the script set by Jesus, and
the report of the mockery of Jesus by the guards sounds like a routine case

of physical and verbal abuse of an accused criminal being held in pretrial detention. In this case, however, the abuse reflects the charges that will finally be brought against Jesus by the Jewish authorities meeting in council—charges of being a false prophet or "perverting our nation" (23:2). In contrast to those untrue charges, Luke views Jesus' entire ministry as having borne the hallmark of a true prophet (4:16–30). That role is now being brought to completion in these very experiences of degradation (see 1 Kings 22:24–28; Jer. 28:10–16).

In addition, the challenge to Jesus represented in the charges of false prophecy made in the taunts echoes the first of the tests imposed on Jesus by the devil in the wilderness at the beginning of his ministry (4:1–4): Become the prophet like Moses by turning stones into bread. Just as that test began with the devil's challenge, "If you are the Son of God. . . ," so also the council asks Jesus, "Are you, then, the Son of God?" (22:70). The tests now come not in the barren desert, but in the seats of religious and secular authority, at the hands of those whose "hour"—whether of the day or of the night—belongs to the power of evil (22:53).

## A Hearing before the Council (Luke 22:66–23:1)

22:66 **When day came, the assembly of the elders of the people, both chief priests and scribes, gathered together, and they brought him to their council.** [67] **They said, "If you are the Messiah, tell us." He replied, "If I tell you, you will not believe;** [68] **and if I question you, you will not answer.** [69] **But from now on the Son of Man will be seated at the right hand of the power of God."** [70] **All of them asked, "Are you, then, the Son of God?" He said to them, "You say that I am."** [71] **Then they said, "What further testimony do we need? We have heard it ourselves from his own lips!"**

23:1 **Then the assembly rose as a body and brought Jesus before Pilate.**

Daybreak finds the assembly of the elders, chief priests, and scribes meeting in council. The event is not a formal trial, but rather more like an investigatory hearing. The assembly addresses Jesus twice. The first time they ask if Jesus is the Messiah. His response puts the assembly on notice that it is their faith and testimony that are at issue, and not his. They appear to sit in judgment, but it is really to the Son of Man—by now clearly identified with Jesus himself—that the judgment seat belongs (22:69).

The second time the council addresses Jesus, they ask if he is the Son of God. Although Luke is clear that that is precisely who Jesus is, within the narrative itself a positive answer by Jesus would have made him guilty of blasphemy according to Jewish law. The answer attributed to Jesus is ambiguous. His response could amount to an emphatic "You said it!" or to an equivocal reply such as, "That's what *you* say," or even "*You* said it; I didn't." The reaction of the assembly makes it clear that they understand Jesus' response to the council's question as affirmative.

As serious as his offense would be under Jewish law, however, it would hardly have troubled the Roman authorities. As far as they were concerned, people could make all manner of religious claims as long as public order and the dominant political and economic power of Rome were not jeopardized. Between the investigation by the assembly and the time when they would turn Jesus over to Pilate, there would have to be a repackaging of the charges and a reformulation of the complaint against Jesus.

## A Hearing before Pilate (Luke 23:2–5)

23:2 **They began to accuse him, saying, "We found this man perverting our nation, forbidding us to pay taxes to the emperor, and saying that he himself is the Messiah, a king."** [3] **Then Pilate asked him, "Are you the king of the Jews?" He answered, "You say so."** [4] **Then Pilate said to the chief priests and the crowds, "I find no basis for an accusation against this man."** [5] **But they were insistent and said, "He stirs up the people by teaching throughout all Judea, from Galilee where he began even to this place."**

Pontius Pilate, prefect of Judea, represented Roman authority in Palestine. For the members of the assembly to accuse Jesus before Pilate means that they have concluded that he should be prosecuted for political offenses. According to Luke's narrative, there is no clear break between "Jewish" and "Roman" charges against Jesus. Members of the assembly and the people who surround them not only initiate the charges that Pilate will pursue, but they accompany Jesus through every step of the proceedings that result in the death sentence.

The charges presented to Pilate do not reflect the matters on which the assembly has just examined Jesus, nor do they reflect what Luke has told us about the ministry of Jesus. Luke has been clear from the beginning that Jesus is a true prophet, not a false prophet who leads the people astray. Others have called Jesus "Messiah" and "king" (for example, 9:20; 19:38), but nowhere is Jesus said to make such claims for himself. Jesus' clever reply to an earlier question about paying taxes to Caesar had avoided the trap set by "spies" who intended to turn Jesus over to the authorities, but instead were "amazed by his answer" (20:20–26).

In what is clearly an administrative hearing and not a formal trial, Pilate simply asks Jesus once if he is the king of the Jews. Pilate neither investigates the charges, nor seeks corroborating witnesses, nor (as in Matthew and Mark) presses Jesus concerning his response. Pilate takes Jesus' ambiguous reply, "You say so" (23:3), to be a denial, which, in turn, takes away the basis for their accusation.

This second hearing already establishes the pattern of Luke's assessment of responsibility for Jesus' death. Pilate, the representative of Roman authority, finds no reason to condemn Jesus. The accusations have come from "the assembly of the elders of the people, both chief priests and scribes" (22:66), joined by "the crowds." This same collection of accusers appeals Pilate's ruling with what this time is an accurate charge, stirring up the people with his teaching (23:5)—a charge to which Luke has borne witness many times.

One can sense the bind in which Pilate finds himself in Luke's account. He, the representative of order, has affirmed Jesus' innocence, but Jesus' own religious authorities are clamoring for Pilate to take action against someone they perceive as a threat to order. The loophole they provide him is a jurisdictional technicality: Pilate's authority is based in Jerusalem, whereas Jesus' behavior that they find so offensive had its roots in Galilee.

## A Hearing before Herod (Luke 23:6–12)

23:6 **When Pilate heard this, he asked whether the man was a Galilean. [7] And when he learned that he was under Herod's jurisdiction, he sent him off to Herod, who was himself in Jerusalem at that time. [8] When Herod saw Jesus, he was very glad, for he had been wanting to see him for a long time, because he had heard about him and was hoping to see him perform some sign. [9] He questioned him at some length, but Jesus gave him no answer. [10] The chief priests and the scribes stood by, vehemently accusing him. [11] Even Herod with his soldiers treated him with contempt and mocked him; then he put an elegant robe on him, and sent him back to Pilate. [12] That same day Herod and Pilate became friends with each other; before this they had been enemies.**

Having ascertained that Jesus indeed is a Galilean, Pilate declares the whole case to belong in Herod's jurisdiction, for Herod was Tetrarch in Galilee. Neither Matthew nor Mark records a hearing before Herod, and there is no way to judge the historical accuracy of Luke's account. Clearly, Pilate did have final administrative authority in the matter, as can be seen in his final disposition of the case later in the day (23:13–25). The coincidence of Herod's presence in Jerusalem might be explained by the urgency of the festival crowds, but all in all, Luke's addition to the passion

narrative of the hearing before Herod seems a bit farfetched as a historical report. It does fit Luke's exoneration of Rome in the matter of Jesus'
death, however, because in this episode Herod becomes a second Roman
witness to Jesus' innocence.

Herod has already been mentioned twice in connection with Jesus. He
is mentioned first in 9:7–9, where reports about Jesus' ministry evoke
Herod's puzzlement about Jesus' identity, and again in 13:31, where some
Pharisees tell Jesus that Herod is plotting his death. When Jesus is
brought before Herod, previous hostility at first gives way to curiosity and
to the hope that Jesus might perform some sign (23:8). Herod's extensive
questioning of Jesus, even in the face of Jesus' silence, is in contrast to the
vehement accusations of the chief priests and scribes (23:9–10).

Nothing is said about Herod's conclusions about Jesus on the basis
of his investigation. The mockery of Jesus by Herod and his soldiers—
taunting him and dressing him up like a make-believe king—pokes fun at
the charges apparently forwarded from Pilate that Jesus was calling himself Messiah and king (23:11), without endorsing those charges as true. By
implication, then, Herod joins Pilate as a Roman witness attesting to
Jesus' innocence. Politically, Luke says, dealing with the charges against
Jesus unites the two representatives of civil authority, and friendship re-
places enmity between them: "The rulers take counsel together, against
the LORD and his anointed" (Ps. 2:2).

In the charges and the mockery, however, the second of the devil's earlier temptations is echoed—that Jesus take on the role of king (4:5–8).
Luke is clear that God has conferred "a kingdom" on Jesus, and that Jesus
in turn has the right to confer it on others of his choosing (22:29–30), but
that authority is his on the basis of his faithfulness to God's will, and not
by some collusion with the civil authorities. Once again, Jesus withstands
the test—this time by his eloquent silence.

## A Second Hearing before Pilate:
## The Death Sentence (Luke 23:13–25)

23:13 **Pilate then called together the chief priests, the leaders, and the people, 14 and said to them, "You brought me this man as one who was perverting the people; and here I have examined him in your presence and have
not found this man guilty of any of your charges against him. 15 Neither has
Herod, for he sent him back to us. Indeed, he has done nothing to deserve
death. 16 I will therefore have him flogged and release him."**

**18 Then they all shouted out together, "Away with this fellow! Release
Barabbas for us!" 19 (This was a man who had been put in prison for an in-**

surrection that had taken place in the city, and for murder.) [20] **Pilate, wanting to release Jesus, addressed them again;** [21] **but they kept shouting, "Crucify, crucify him!"** [22] **A third time he said to them, "Why, what evil has he done? I have found in him no ground for the sentence of death; I will therefore have him flogged and then release him."** [23] **But they kept urgently demanding with loud shouts that he should be crucified; and their voices prevailed.** [24] **So Pilate gave his verdict that their demand should be granted.** [25] **He released the man they asked for, the one who had been put in prison for insurrection and murder, and he handed Jesus over as they wished.**

The king in dress-up clothes is taken back to Pilate, who informs "the chief priests, the leaders, and the people" that neither he nor Herod finds Jesus guilty of the charges they have brought against him: "He has done nothing to deserve death" (23:13–15). Pilate, Herod, and the Roman system of administrative justice prove equal to the task of discerning the truth about Jesus. What they lack is the courage to stand up for the truth they have recognized.

Before leaving the stage, Herod has already joined his soldiers in roughing up Jesus before sending him back to Pilate (23:11). Although no taunts or physical harassment of Jesus have yet taken place in Pilate's custody, Pilate's declaration of Jesus' innocence is followed by his decision to subject Jesus to the Roman torture of "flagellation"—a whipping that sometimes even killed the victim—before releasing him (23:16, 22). No explanation is given for such a decision, other than the specter of the audience of Jesus' accusers.

The oldest manuscripts favor omitting 23:17, which echoes Matthew 27:15 and Mark 15:6 in noting the custom of releasing a prisoner during the Passover festival. No corroboration of such a practice is found outside of the Gospels, so Luke may well have chosen not to refer to it here. Without that verse, the drama of Luke's account is further heightened by having even Pilate's order immediately rejected by Jesus' accusers (23:18). Despite their charges that Jesus has been "perverting the people," the accusers plead for the release of another man charged with the same crime because of his participation in an insurrection (23:19). The irony of their request is heightened by the name of the other prisoner, Barabbas. Its form is like that of the name Johnson—literally "son of John"—or Davidson—"son of David." In this case, the name means "son of Abbas." (In fact, some of the oldest Greek manuscripts of Matthew 27:17 identify him as "Jesus Barabbas.") Whether or not Abbas was a real name, it is virtually the same as the Aramaic word Abba, a child's word for "father," which the tradition recognizes as Jesus' characteristic way of referring to God. The name Barabbas thus might mean "Son of the father"—perhaps a terrorist's nickname to preserve anonymity and protect his family—but for Luke it is Jesus who has been repeatedly affirmed as "Son of the Father" or "Son of God." The accusers' shouting for Barabbas underlines their ignorance of Jesus' true identity, as well as their responsibility for his death.

Pilate tries twice more to persuade the accusers to accept Jesus' release, while they cry out for his blood (23:20–23). In the course of the dialogue, Pilate completes the move from a sympathetic to a pathetic figure. He represents the power and authority of Rome. He has the political and legal authority, backed up by the military might of the Roman Empire, but all of that crumbles into the triumph of mob rule (23:24–25). Without ever changing his verdict about Jesus, Pilate decides to grant the accusers' demand. In a cold summary statement, the outcome is pronounced: The man they asked for is released, and Jesus is "handed over."

Matthew, Mark, and Luke agree in using the verb translated as "handed over" to identify Pilate's action. It is the same verb translated as "betray" in relation to Judas. In fact, Jesus is indeed betrayed again. Earlier, the betrayal happened when "one of the twelve"—one of Jesus' own followers—colluded with "the chief priests and officers of the temple police" in his arrest (22:3). This time, Jesus is betrayed when the Roman prefect surrenders to the demands of "the chief priests, the leaders, and the people." Although the religious leaders make the formal accusations (22:67–71; 23:2), the crowd also enters in (23:4–5, 18, 23), and together they finally prevail (23:23). Exactly who would have made up such a crowd is not described. One might imagine that it consisted principally of citizens of Jerusalem who, like the leaders themselves, were drawing a certain benefit from the current arrangement with Rome. Whatever may have been the historical sources of opposition to Jesus among his own people, Luke's verdict is clear: The accusers bent on getting a death sentence against Jesus end by being judged themselves as responsible for his death. In addition, they are judged for preferring the way of insurrection—of Barabbas—to the way of Jesus, a choice Luke knows to be the cause of Jerusalem's downfall less than four decades later, in the disastrous war against Rome that ended in Jerusalem's destruction.

## THE EXECUTION
Luke 23:26–56

### The Walk to the Place
### Called "The Skull" (Luke 23:26–32)

23:26 As they led him away, they seized a man, Simon of Cyrene, who was coming from the country, and they laid the cross on him, and made him carry it behind Jesus. 27 A great number of the people followed him, and among them were women who were beating their breasts and wailing for him. $^{28}$ **But Jesus turned to them and said, "Daughters of Jerusalem, do not weep for me, but weep for yourselves and for your children. $^{29}$ For the days are surely coming when they will say, 'Blessed are the barren, and the wombs that never bore, and the breasts that never nursed.' $^{30}$ Then they will begin to say to the mountains, 'Fall on us'; and to the hills, 'Cover us.' $^{31}$ For if they do this when the wood is green, what will happen when it is dry?"**

$^{32}$ **Two others also, who were criminals, were led away to be put to death with him.**

The grim walk begins toward the place of execution. Crucifixions were common in Jerusalem in Jesus' time. The vertical posts of the crosses were left standing along the principal routes into the city as a constant reminder of their potential use. Condemned criminals would carry to the place of execution the horizontal beam on which they would be fastened with arms outstretched (usually by a combination of ropes and nails). The horizontal beam would then be lifted onto the vertical post, where the body would hang with minimal support until dead. Death would finally be caused by a combination of loss of blood from the flagellation preceding the crucifixion and suffocation from the strain on muscles and diaphragm due to the position of the body on the cross.

The tradition records that, as Jesus made his way to the place of execution, a certain Simon from Cyrene in northern Africa was pressed into service to carry the cross bar (Matt. 27:32; Mark 15:21; Luke 23:26). It was accepted practice for Roman soldiers to require members of their captive populations to carry their packs and other burdens. In this case, Jesus may have been too weak from the torture he had undergone to carry his own cross, so the other man was called to perform the task. This is the only place Simon of Cyrene is mentioned in the Gospels, but the fact that he is mentioned by name (and in Mark as the father of two other named individuals, Alexander and Rufus), suggests that he was important to the memory of the community. He is a disciple who *literally* carries the cross and follows Jesus (14:27); he falls short of being a prototype or model for other disciples, however, on two counts. First, he does not carry the cross of his own will, but only when compelled by the Roman soldiers. Second, we never hear that Simon carries his own "cross" in that long, daily process that for Luke defines true discipleship (9:23; see also 14:26–33).

The description of the journey to Golgotha (23:27–32) is found only in Luke. A crowd of people is again present. Their role is simply to witness what is taking place, and their point of view is left unexplained. Are we to imagine the crowd as including those who had been crying out for Jesus' life? Are any of the disciples who traveled with Jesus in the days of his ministry still with him? At this point, Luke does not say (although later he does describe Jesus' acquaintances as watching from a distance, 23:49). The only members of the crowd specifically identified are the women mourners whose wails lament the impending death. Such women—usually including poor widows who would hope to receive a bit of money for their efforts—had an unofficial but socially recognized role in burial rituals in Jesus' day, where they would accompany the grieving survivors. In the case of political executions where there might not be family members or friends who would dare to exhibit grief at the death for fear of being viewed as guilty too, the "professional" mourners would carry out the ritual grieving on behalf of the family and larger community.

The ritual mourning of the women is turned around, however, when Jesus charges them not to mourn him and his death, but instead, to weep for themselves and their children. The mood has shifted from that in 7:13 and 8:52, where Jesus instructed parents not to weep, even though their beloved children appear to have died. In the earlier stories, the affirmation of life that is the hallmark of Jesus' ministry is the important point. Now, however, the hour of death is approaching, not only for Jesus, but also for the people in general, and weeping is the appropriate response.

In a formal oracle of prophecy that is a tragic reversal of such oracles of promise as Isaiah 40:1–2, 51:16, 62:11–12, and 65:19, these daughters of Jerusalem represent the holy city that Luke recognizes as headed for its own destruction. They also represent the holy people to whom God's promised redemption will come on the other side of harsh judgment. In contrast to the traditional imagery in which women who have been barren are blessed with motherhood, now it will be the barren who are seen as the most greatly blessed for not having borne children to face the awful fate awaiting the city.

In that reversal of the traditional view of barrenness and birth, in the paraphrase of Hosea 10:8 in 23:30, and in the proverb cited in 23:31, Luke's reference to Jerusalem's fall and destruction is clear: The horror they are about to witness in Jesus' death will soon be far surpassed, when the fires consume the city like so much dry kindling. The wailing women are mourning not only Jesus' death, but the fate of Jerusalem as well, and in so doing they speak for Luke.

Despite the presence of "the people" of Jerusalem alongside the religious leaders in the various charges and hearings against Jesus, Luke never gives up hope for the people. Some, at least, will turn from the ways that have ensnared them (23:48; Acts 2:37–42). Beginning with the singing of Zechariah's and Simeon's songs (1:68–79; 2:29–32), Luke has been preparing his audience for this moment of grief, because the salvation that is God's agenda is for all flesh, Jews and Gentiles alike. Luke has not been leading up to a simple passing of the mantle of election from the Jews to the Gentiles. Rather, for Luke, the inability of many in Israel to recognize Jesus, and the horrendous defeat suffered by the Jews in the war with Rome, are tragic events. Jesus' own words on the way to the cross bring the weight of that tragedy home, and in them also is the possibility of its resolution.

The way to the cross ends with the mention of the two "criminals" who are to be executed with Jesus. What was prepared in the citation of Isaiah 53:12 in Luke 22:37 now becomes fact (23:32): He is "counted among the lawless." The charges of the leaders that Jesus was perverting the people are confirmed not in a formal judgment of guilt, but in Pilate's surrender to mob rule. The cry "Crucify, crucify him!" leads not to Jesus' death in splendid isolation, but to his execution in the company of others convicted of crimes against the public order.

## Crucifixion (Luke 23:33–49)

23:33 **When they came to the place that is called The Skull, they crucified Jesus there with the criminals, one on his right and one on his left.** [34] **Then Jesus said, "Father, forgive them; for they do not know what they are doing." And they cast lots to divide his clothing.** [35] **And the people stood by, watching; but the leaders scoffed at him, saying, "He saved others; let him save himself if he is the Messiah of God, his chosen one!"** [36] **The soldiers also mocked him, coming up and offering him sour wine,** [37] **and saying, "If you are the King of the Jews, save yourself!"** [38] **There was also an inscription over him, "This is the King of the Jews."**

[39] **One of the criminals who were hanged there kept deriding him and saying, "Are you not the Messiah? Save yourself and us!"** [40] **But the other rebuked him, saying, "Do you not fear God, since you are under the same sentence of condemnation?** [41] **And we indeed have been condemned justly, for we are getting what we deserve for our deeds, but this man has done nothing wrong."** [42] **Then he said, "Jesus, remember me when you come into your kingdom."** [43] **He replied, "Truly I tell you, today you will be with me in Paradise."**

[44] **It was now about noon, and darkness came over the whole land until three in the afternoon,** [45] **while the sun's light failed; and the curtain of the temple was torn in two.** [46] **Then Jesus, crying with a loud voice, said, "Father, into your hands I commend my spirit." Having said this, he breathed his last.** [47] **When the centurion saw what had taken place, he praised God and said, "Certainly this man was innocent."** [48] **And when all the crowds who had gathered there for this spectacle saw what had taken place, they**

**returned home, beating their breasts. ⁴⁹ But all his acquaintances, including
the women who had followed him from Galilee, stood at a distance, watching these things.**

The matter of the crucifixion itself is handled in a single verse (23:33).
The two criminals occupy the places at Jesus' right and left, places of
honor sought by the disciples (22:24; see Mark 10:37). Now the presence
of the criminals as Jesus' companions in death confirms again that Jesus is
"counted among the lawless."

Jesus' declaration of forgiveness echoes the words later attributed to
Stephen, the first Christian martyr whose story is told in Acts (Acts 7:60).
Manuscript evidence is divided on whether the saying belongs in the account of Jesus' death, suggesting that perhaps it was inserted here on the
assumption that such gracious words attributed to Stephen must have had
their model in Jesus' own words. The saying itself is not typical of Luke's
way of speaking of forgiveness, for usually forgiveness is declared without
condition.

Who are included among those forgiven is not exactly clear. The two
criminals are the most immediate referent for the pronoun "them." If indeed their crime was not ordinary robbery or theft, but rather participating in terrorist raids on others who were profiting from the political and
economic conditions of Roman occupation, the reference to their ignorance would convey Luke's judgment on the futility of terrorism as a political strategy. Tradition, however, has understood Jesus' prayer as encompassing also Jesus' accusers, judges, and executioners. In that case, the
prayer would also convey Luke's judgment on their ignorance of God's
will that is revealed in the triumph of the resurrection. The prayer is also
Luke's affirmation, similar to that of Paul in Romans 8:38–39, that nothing in all creation—not even human efforts to thwart the gospel—can finally prevent the triumph of God's love.

Jesus' prayer is also appropriate to the shift taking place in Luke's narrative from an account of details of traditions surrounding Jesus' death
(such as the casting of lots for his clothing, 23:34b, or the inscription bearing the charge against him, 23:38), to a declaration of God's verdicts on
humankind symbolized in the various perspectives on that death. "The
people," first of all, simply stand by, watching (23:35a). Although earlier
they and the leaders appeared to speak with a single voice demanding
Jesus' crucifixion, now their silent witness distinguishes them from the
leaders' taunts. They stand on a balance-point, no longer where they were,
but not yet at the place where they recognize Jesus as the Christ.

Three others who comment on Jesus' death (leaders, soldiers, and the first of the criminals) do so with mockery, citing charges against him, and daring him to save himself (23:35b, 37, 39). Those taunts echo the third of the temptations by the devil recounted earlier, that Jesus should leap from the pinnacle of the temple, trusting God to save him (4:9–12). Jesus once again refuses to test God, but instead passes his own test. Jesus thus withstands for a second time the test by Satan that, according to Genesis 3, Adam failed. Thus, instead of being expelled from paradise, Jesus has the authority to guard the gates to paradise and the blessing of living there eternally (23:43).

The first of the criminals links this scene with the earlier mockeries of Jesus, but the second criminal adds yet another voice to those of Pilate and Herod (and those of the centurion and—by implication—Joseph of Arimathea, 23:47; 50–53) proclaiming Jesus' innocence. He recognizes the justice of his own punishment, repents, proclaims Jesus' innocence, and recognizes that Jesus' failure to save himself does not contradict the claim that he is the messianic king (seen in his plea that Jesus remember him in his realm). The repentant criminal thus becomes the only person to recognize that rejection and death are for Jesus the way to royal power at the right hand of God. The scene is crucial to Luke, as can be seen not only from its occurrence just before Jesus' death, but also in its continuation of the theme of Jesus' compassion for the outcast (here symbolized in the dying criminal), and by its pointing to the goal of Jesus' way, hidden from almost all human eyes (2:34–35).

Scientists debate the likelihood of astronomic or seismographic events to account for the darkness at noon and for the tearing of the temple curtain exposing the Holy of Holies (23:44–5; Matt. 27:45, 51; Mark 15:33, 38). The point, however, is theological rather than scientific. Not merely the stones (19:40), but the whole cosmos has taken up the cry from the silenced disciples and the dying Jesus. God no longer dwells in the thick darkness of the temple's holiest center, but rather in the darkness that covers the whole earth.

In Luke's account, the moment of death leads not to a cry of Godforsakenness (Matt. 27:46; Mark 15:34), but to an equally strong cry declaring God's presence: "Father, into your hands I commend my spirit" (23:46). With this prayerful quotation of Psalm 31:5, Luke portrays Jesus' faith in God as the God who saves, and having entrusted his spirit or breath (the Greek word means both) to God, Jesus dies.

The centurion grasps the truth of "what had taken place," declaring that Jesus is not simply not guilty of the charges against him (as the word "innocent" in the NRSV might imply). Rather, the Greek word makes the stronger claim tht Jesus is "righteous" (23:47; Isa. 53:11). Jesus is the innocent, righteous victim of the decisions of religious and secular powers, and in his dying he opens the way to life. Jesus the Christ does not save himself, but rather places his own salvation in God's hands. The theme of saving faith is a prominent one in Luke and Acts. That faith encompasses the promises of salvation that God gives and the presence of God in the holy and righteous Christ in whom those promises are secured. The faith that saves is Jesus' own faith, as can be seen from the quotation of Psalm 31:5 attributed to him, and from Luke's reflection on Psalm 16 that is attributed to Jesus in Acts 2 and 13. There it becomes clear that, for Luke, the faith that saves is in particular the faith that God raises the dead. Jesus is the model of that faith, and hence the model for all who follow—a model in faith, as well as in obedience and holiness, of the wholly God-centered life.

Similarly, "what had taken place" pushes the crowd from their pivot-point onto the side of confession (23:48). Their grief marks their turning from the bravado of a lynch mob to readiness to hear Peter's words that will save them (Acts 2). Between this moment and their conversion, however, the heart of Luke's story must be revealed.

The silent witness of Jesus' followers, especially "the women who had followed him from Galilee," is the key to the intervening narrative (23:49). They have witnessed his ministry and his death. Their most important work lies ahead.

## Burial (Luke 23:50–56)

23:50 Now there was a good and righteous man named Joseph, who, though a member of the council, [51] had not agreed to their plan and action. He came from the Jewish town of Arimathea, and he was waiting expectantly for the kingdom of God. [52] This man went to Pilate and asked for the body of Jesus. [53] Then he took it down, wrapped it in a linen cloth, and laid it in a rock-hewn tomb where no one had ever been laid. [54] It was the day of Preparation, and the sabbath was beginning. [55] The women who had come with him from Galilee followed, and they saw the tomb and how his body was laid. [56] Then they returned, and prepared spices and ointments.
On the sabbath they rested according to the commandment.

The principal actor in the next segment of the story is Joseph of Arimathea, recognized in all four Gospels as instrumental in the burial of Jesus' body. He is identified as a member of the Jerusalem council whose charges led to Jesus' death, but as one who was "good and righteous" and "waiting expectantly for the kingdom of God." In other words, as Matthew says explicitly, he was a disciple (Matt. 27:57). His loyalty to Jesus is evident also in his request for the body of the crucified one, for to bury a person was to show honor to that person. To honor a criminal in such an environment would be to expose one's self to suspicion and perhaps to prosecution for similar crimes. The story portrays Joseph as further honoring Jesus by wrapping him in linen and burying him as one would a rich person (Isa. 53:9)—in a new tomb, not one reclaimed after an earlier corpse had fully decayed.

All of this takes place on the day of Preparation, before the beginning of the holy sabbath of the week of Passover. The women—once again identified fully as "the women who had come with him from Galilee"— have duly witnessed the burial and readied the spices and ointments with which to complete the preparation of the body (23:55–56). During Jesus' ministry, sabbath-keeping entailed acting on behalf of life and wholeness. Now that he is dead there is no need to act. Sabbath now is for rest, "according to the commandment."

# 14. "To Make an End Is to Make a Beginning": Stories of Resurrection
*Luke 24:1–53*

Luke presents three stories that point to Jesus' resurrection. Like the other biblical Gospels, Luke does not talk about the event of resurrection itself. (Only the apocryphal Gospel of Peter attempts a description of Jesus' actual rising from the dead, and that account is clearly an imaginative creation.) Instead, Luke tells a story about the finding of the empty tomb (24:1–12) and two stories of appearances of the risen Christ (24:13–35, 36–53).

All of Luke's Easter stories are set in or near Jerusalem, unlike John's, which take place both in Jerusalem and in Galilee, and Matthew's, which are set in Galilee. The oldest manuscripts of Mark—those least likely to have been influenced by the resurrection accounts in Matthew and Luke—contain no appearance stories at all, though some medieval manuscripts have added to Mark a digest of appearance stories from all three other Gospels. Mark's version of the empty tomb story (Mark 16:7) joins Matthew's witness that Galilee is the place where the risen one will be found. The Jerusalem location is significant for Luke, because it is in Jerusalem that the Holy Spirit will come upon the church (24:49; Acts 1:4; 2:1–13), and it is from Jerusalem that the church's witness will go out "to the ends of the earth" (Acts 1:8).

In Luke, all of the appearance stories are indeed Easter stories, since all are set on the very same day. This is true even of the story of Jesus' ascension (24:50–53), which Acts 1:3–11 describes as taking place forty days later. Also according to Acts, the intervening days are marked by additional appearances of the risen Christ (Acts 1:3). Since both Luke and Acts come from the same author, the discrepancy is puzzling. Attempts to rationalize it end up sounding apologetic. Luke's point, however, is to testify to experience rather than to report facts. For that reason, the differences in detail between the accounts are of less importance than the implications they hold in common for the witness and self-understanding of the church. Less surprising is the fact that John's appearance stories (and, by implication, Matthew's, since the journey to Galilee would take some time) are spread out over some time, and are not confined to Easter itself (Matthew 28; John 20—21).

The long Easter day of Luke's Gospel begins in confusion and wonder, and by day's end has taken on liturgical rhythms and shape, as memory forms a bridge from the present back to the past and forward into the future.

## THE EMPTY TOMB
## Luke 24:1–12

24:1 But on the first day of the week, at early dawn, they came to the tomb, taking the spices that they had prepared. [2] They found the stone rolled away from the tomb, [3] but when they went in, they did not find the body. [4] While they were perplexed about this, suddenly two men in dazzling clothes stood beside them. [5] The women were terrified and bowed their faces to the ground, but the men said to them, "Why do you look for the living among the dead? He is not here, but has risen. [6] Remember how he told you, while he was still in Galilee, [7] that the Son of Man must be handed over to sinners, and be crucified, and on the third day rise again." [8] Then they remembered his words, [9] and returning from the tomb, they told all this to the eleven and to all the rest. [10] Now it was Mary Magdalene, Joanna, Mary the mother of James, and the other women with them who told this to the apostles. [11] But these words seemed to them an idle tale, and they did not believe them. [12] But Peter got up and ran to the tomb; stooping and looking in, he saw the linen cloths by themselves; then he went home, amazed at what had happened.

An economy of words shows the passage of time following the burial of Jesus. The women who followed Jesus from Galilee provide the thread of continuity from crucifixion (23:49), to burial, preparation of spices, and sabbath rest (23:55–56), and finally to the visit to the tomb at dawn on the day following the sabbath (24:1). Their continuous presence, not only through these events, but through Jesus' earlier ministry as well (8:1–3), makes them thoroughly qualified and reliable witnesses of what follows, even though their testimony is said to be dismissed by the apostles as an "idle tale" (24:11).

The reference to the women at the beginning of the story (24:1) and the list of some of their names at the end (24:10) frames the account. Of those named (in addition to others who were also there), Mary Magdalene and Joanna were also named on the list in 8:1–3, whereas Mary the mother of James is new to the story. The report of Peter's visit to the tomb (24:12) is sometimes omitted from Luke, both because it is not found in some of the oldest Greek manuscripts of the Gospel and because it seems to echo Peter's role in John 20:3–10, whereas otherwise Peter has no role in Luke's story of the empty tomb. (Even the later reference to an appearance to him mentions not Peter, but Simon, 24:34.) The evidence in favor of omitting the verse, however, is not very strong, and it should probably be considered as part of Luke's account.

The story begins simply, with none of Matthew's drama of an earthquake opening the tomb (Matt. 28:2–4), or Mark's report of the women's conversation about how they will manage the stone (Mark 16:3–4). In Luke's version, the women have come to prepare the body. The story takes them quickly toward that purpose—they arrive, find the stone rolled back, and enter the tomb. Suddenly the story hits a "speed bump" in the road, for they do not find the body (24:1–3). Having thus been brought with them to a sudden stop, we join them in looking around.

The sight—or, more appropriately, the vision—takes us into a realm of awe and wonder, for suddenly two men appear (24:4). They bring to mind the sudden appearance of Moses and Elijah in the Transfiguration story (9:30), though this time it is the men's clothing that is dazzling, whereas in the Transfiguration story it was Jesus who acquired the heavenly glow. This time also, the witnesses are not the three principal disciples (Peter, James, and John) who have been selected to accompany Jesus at prayer, but a gathering of women engaged in their traditional task of caring for the body of a loved one—a member of their new family—who has died. Cleopas and his companion will later identify the two men as "angels" (24:23), but in the story of the empty tomb they are not given that label. In fact, they do not even get an angel's task, which is to provide new information to their human audience (see 1:11–20, 26–38; 2:8–14). The role of these two is to ask a question, and to remind the women of what Jesus has already told them (24:5–7), which is a role followed also by the two men in white robes who serve as interpreters of Jesus' ascension in Acts 1:10–11.

The place of memory is crucial to Luke's interpretation of the resurrection of Jesus. In the first place, since the women indeed "remember" (24:8), Luke obviously intends to present them as part of the inner circle of disciples with whom such information was shared (see 9:18–22; 18: 31–34, which suggest a limited audience of Jesus' teachings). The memory, however, has apparently not been available to the women to help them understand the events they have witnessed in the preceding days, for no mention of such predictions is ever made in the course of or aftermath to the story of Jesus' arrest, hearings, and execution (Luke 22 and 23). The chaos and horror of the actual events have blotted out the memory. Only later, as they prepare to engage in one of the rituals of mourning, are they able to remember what they know.

Furthermore, once that memory is recovered, it impels them forward to tell "all this to the eleven and to all the rest" (24:9). "All this" clearly includes what is remembered as well as what is witnessed at the tomb. "All the rest" reminds Luke's audience that those who receive and, in turn, must testify to the news of the resurrection form an inclusive, not a restricted group (see also 24:33; Acts 1:12–15). In fact, in an interesting twist, the apostles—despite their special commission and preparation for their task of bearing witness to Jesus and his mission—are apparently not able to "remember." When they are said to dismiss the women's words as "an idle tale" (24:11), they reveal that they are not yet able to cross the bridge of memory that can take them from their days with Jesus, through the events of the passion, into the future of the church's mission. That task requires more workers than just the twelve (now reduced to eleven) or even the seventy.

With the role of memory, however, the additional witnesses come into place. In fact, all who hear or read Luke's Gospel join their ranks, for we also remember the words that give meaning and shape to the events to which we are to bear witness. We, the readers, become participants in the final chapter of Luke's Gospel as part of "all the rest" who can be helped to remember. Where the memories of our hearts fail us, and, like the apostles, we dismiss all this as a fantastic or "idle" tale, the liturgical memory of the church perhaps can lead us over that bridge into God's tomorrow.

## THE JOURNEY TO EMMAUS
## Luke 24:13–35

24:13 Now on that same day two of them were going to a village called Emmaus, about seven miles from Jerusalem, ¹⁴ and talking with each other about all these things that had happened. ¹⁵ While they were talking and discussing, Jesus himself came near and went with them, ¹⁶ but their eyes were kept from recognizing him. [17] And he said to them, "What are you discussing with each other while you walk along?" They stood still, looking sad. [18] Then one of them, whose name was Cleopas, answered him, "Are you the only stranger in Jerusalem who does not know the things that have taken place there in these days?" [19] He asked them, "What things?" They replied, "The things about Jesus of Nazareth, who was a prophet mighty in deed and word before God and all the people, [20] and how our chief priests and leaders handed him over to be condemned to death and crucified him. [21] But we had hoped that he was the one to redeem Israel. Yes, and besides all this, it is now the third day since these things took place. [22] Moreover, some women of our group astounded us. They were at the tomb early this morning, [23] and when they did not find his body there, they came back and told us that they had indeed seen a vision of angels who said that he was alive. [24] Some of those who were with us went to the tomb and found it just as the women had said; but they did not see him." [25] Then he said to them, "Oh, how foolish you are, and how slow of heart to believe all that the prophets have declared! [26] Was it not necessary that the Messiah should suffer these things and then enter into his glory?" [27] Then beginning with Moses and all the prophets, he interpreted to them the things about himself in all the scriptures.

[28] As they came near the village to which they were going, he walked ahead as if he were going on. [29] But they urged him strongly, saying, "Stay with us, because it is almost evening and the day is now nearly over." So he went in to stay with them. [30] When he was at the table with them, he took bread, blessed and broke it, and gave it to them. [31] Then their eyes were opened, and they recognized him; and he vanished from their sight. [32] They said to each other, "Were not our hearts burning within us while he was talking to us on the road, while he was opening the scriptures to us?" [33] That same hour they got up and returned to Jerusalem; and they found the eleven and their companions gathered together. [34] They were saying, "The Lord has risen indeed, and he has appeared to Simon!" [35] Then they told what had happened on the road, and how he had been made known to them in the breaking of the bread.

The scene shifts to later on the same day, on the road to Emmaus. The characters are first identified simply as "two of them," and it is not immediately clear to whom the pronoun refers. The apostles are the group most recently named, but the name "Cleopas" (24:18) is not found on any of the lists of the twelve. Since that group appears to remain fixed in number and composition (see Acts 1:13; 15–26), the pronoun probably refers to "the eleven and all the rest" (24:9). Cleopas figures nowhere else in the Gospels. John 19:25 lists "Mary the wife of Clopas" among the witnesses to the crucifixion, but most commentators conclude that the two are not the same, because Cleopas is Greek in form, whereas Clopas looks like an adaptation of a Semitic name. In fact, however, the experience of immigrants in any age points to just such variation in names when people move from one language context to another, and it is not impossible that both Gospels refer to the same early Christian witness. The companion of Cleopas in Luke's story is unnamed, which is a fate suffered particularly by many women throughout history. Given that fact, the travelers may indeed represent another missionary couple in the early church (like Prisca or Priscilla and Aquila, for example [see Acts 18:2, 18, 26; Rom. 16:3; 1 Cor. 16:19; 2 Tim. 4:19])—Cleopas and "Mrs. Cleopas," the woman John knows as another Mary.

As they walk along on their journey, the two discuss the events that have taken place. Not idle reminiscences, these memories themselves make Jesus present again with them (24:13–15). The memories and stories themselves are not enough to make them recognize Jesus; as Luke noted earlier, some things require revelation (10:22). That revelation does not come with bolts of lightning or heavenly voices, but in three simple human acts. First, the two travelers retell the gospel story of Jesus' crucifixion and resurrection (24:19–24). Second, that story is interpreted in the context of scripture—of Moses and the prophets (24:25–27; see 16:31; 24:44–47). Finally, the bread is broken (24:28–31a).

The meal starts as a simple supper, the sharing of hospitality at the end of the day's journey. At the meal, the travelers' still unrecognized companion "took bread, blessed and broke it, and gave it to them." The words have a familiar cadence. They take us back to the last supper Jesus shared with the disciples (22:19), and even further back to the time (perhaps even the many times) when the hungry crowd was fed (9:10–17). Suddenly it all comes together: "Their eyes were opened, and they recognized him" (24:31a); in other words, they remember (24:8). That sudden recognition then works backwards, revealing the memory that has been hovering just below the surface all along, in the words of scripture as well as in the breaking of the bread (24:32).

The events of the story follow the pattern of what we know about early Christian worship, as well as continuing liturgical practice: Two or more are gathered together, telling the stories that recall Jesus' presence, reflecting on scripture, and breaking bread together. These activities give birth to the memory that reveals the truth embodied in the events. Although the moment of revelation itself is fleeting (24:31b), it continues to fuel the memory (24:32) and to empower the weary travelers to carry on their journey.

In this case, their journey takes them back to where other disciples ("the eleven and their companions") are gathered. There they discover that their experience has been echoed, and each bears witness to the others of what has happened to them (24:33–35). In this time, before the coming of the Holy Spirit on the community (Acts 2), they still bear witness only within the community of believers. They tell the stories from one believer to another, and they share the awakening memories of one who has been with them from the beginning. Peter is even called by his old name "Simon" (see 4:38–39; 5:3–10; 6:14; 22:31) during this period of transition or rite of passage, when followers of Jesus were becoming witnesses to the Risen One.

## THE APPEARANCE IN JERUSALEM
## Luke 24:36–53

### Revelation and Commission (Luke 24:36–49)

24:36 **While they were talking about this, Jesus himself stood among them and said to them, "Peace be with you."** [37] **They were startled and terrified, and thought that they were seeing a ghost.** [38] **He said to them, "Why are you frightened, and why do doubts arise in your hearts?** [39] **Look at my hands and my feet; see that it is I myself. Touch me and see; for a ghost does not have flesh and bones as you see that I have."** [40] **And when he had said this, he showed them his hands and his feet.** [41] **While in their joy they were disbelieving and still wondering, he said to them, "Have you anything here to eat?"** [42] **They gave him a piece of broiled fish,** [43] **and he took it and ate in their presence.**

[44] **Then he said to them, "These are my words that I spoke to you while I was still with you—that everything written about me in the law of Moses, the prophets, and the psalms must be fulfilled."** [45] **Then he opened their minds to understand the scriptures,** [46] **and he said to them, "Thus it is written, that the Messiah is to suffer and to rise from the dead on the third day,** [47] **and that repentance and forgiveness of sins is to be proclaimed in his name to all nations, beginning from Jerusalem.** [48] **You are witnesses of these things.** [49] **And see, I am sending upon you what my Father promised; so stay here in the city until you have been clothed with power from on high."**

While they are in the midst of sharing their stories, it happens again: Suddenly Jesus is in their midst. Despite the greeting, "Peace be with you," the disciples' recently stirred memories and understandings are gone, replaced by terror, fear, and doubt (24:36–37). Ghosts or hallucinations are explanations more readily accepted than resurrection. The evidence of the scars from the torture that preceded the crucifixion is Luke's testimony that this is no ghost story and no case of mistaken identity, nor is it proof of the immortality of the soul (24:39–40; see also the story of "doubting Thomas" in John 20:24–29). The one who is alive in their midst is the same Jesus whose execution they witnessed, and resurrection is always resurrection of the body—transformed, but still a body.

Their response moves over into joy, but joy still tinged with disbelief and amazement (24:41). Once again, memory is solidified with food (24:42). The broiled fish echoes the story of the feeding of the crowd in 9:10–17 and also recalls John's story of when the risen Jesus shares breakfast on the beach with the disciples (John 21:1–14). More important, however, the fact that *Jesus* is said to eat the fish draws Luke's readers back to the last supper, to Jesus' vows not to eat the Passover meal or drink the wine until God's reign comes (22:15–18). Although this is not a formal Passover meal, it still falls in Passover week and the setting—with the disciples in Jerusalem—is the same: Perhaps that means God's reign has dawned.

As was the case in the previous story, both Jesus' own words and the interpretation of scripture join the symbolic meal to give liturgical shape to the event. The verb tenses—"These *are* my words that I *spoke*"—establish continuity between what Jesus said and what the risen Christ says (24:44a, emphasis added). The reference to the law of Moses, the prophets, the psalms, and Jesus' words about his own fate and about the church's mission (24:44b–47) establish the continuity of God's saving purpose that encompasses both Israel and the Gentiles. That continuity is to be the subject of their witness (21:12–15), for which they will be empowered just as Jesus was empowered for his own ministry (4:14), by the Holy Spirit (24:48–49).

With that commission, the liturgy of the community draws toward its close. Only the final blessing remains unspoken.

## Blessing and Departure (Luke 24:50–53)

24:50 **Then he led them out as far as Bethany, and, lifting up his hands, he blessed them.** 51 **While he was blessing them, he withdrew from them and was carried up into heaven.** 52 **And they worshiped him, and returned to Jerusalem with great joy;** 53 **and they were continually in the temple blessing God.**

For the final blessing, the community goes out to the place that has provided nightly refuge from the threats and the crowds that have surrounded them during Jesus' ministry in Jerusalem (19:47–48; 20:19, 26; 21:37–38). The blessing signals Jesus' departure from them into heaven (see 22:69). In the Gospel of Luke, the blessing and Jesus' departure bring closure to Easter day, whereas in Acts these events come some forty days later (Acts 1:2–3, 9–11). In both cases, the emphasis is not on the time frame, but on the risen Jesus' departure from them (see also 24:31). That departure is not a punishment, but the crucial step between the story of Jesus and the story of the church. It comes when Jesus' work on earth is finished—when the life-giving memory has been awakened, and the liturgical rhythms are in place to keep that memory alive in the community.

This time, the disciples' joy is untempered (see 24:41). They "worship" Jesus, and that worship leads them back to the temple, where they are "continually" (literally, "through everything") blessing God. Luke's Gospel ends where it began with Zechariah, Simeon, and Anna—in the temple in Jerusalem, the house of prayer where God is properly worshiped (19:46).

However, as Luke and his audience know, the temple is gone, and so is Jerusalem itself. Thus, although Luke's Gospel ends there, the gospel has barely gotten started on its journey (24:46–49; Acts 1:8). In the syntax of God, "To make an end is to make a beginning."

# For Further Reading

Craddock, Fred B. *Luke. Interpretation.* Louisville, Ky.: Westminster/ John Knox Press, 1990.

Crossan, John Dominic. *The Historical Jesus: The Life of a Mediterranean Jewish Peasant.* San Francisco: Harper Collins, 1991.

Danker, Frederick W. *Jesus and the New Age: A Commentary on St. Luke's Gospel.* Philadelphia: Fortress Press, 1987.

Fitzmyer, Joseph A., S.J. *The Gospel According to Luke.* 2 vols. Garden City, N.Y.: Doubleday & Company, Inc. (Anchor Bible 28, 28A), 1981 and 1985.

Horsley, Richard A. *Jesus and the Spiral of Violence: Popular Jewish Resistance in Roman Palestine.* San Francisco: Harper & Row, 1987.

Malina, Bruce J., and Richard L. Rohrbaugh. *Social-Science Commentary on the Synoptic Gospels.* Minneapolis: Fortress Press, 1992.

Neyrey, Jerome H., ed. *The Social World of Luke–Acts: Models for Interpretation.* Peabody, Mass.: Hendrickson Publishers, 1991.

Powell, Mark Allan. *What Are They Saying about Luke?* New York: Paulist Press, 1989.

Talbert, Charles H. *Reading Luke: A Literary and Theological Commentary on the Third Gospel.* New York: Crossroad Publishing Co., 1986.

Tannehill, Robert C. *The Narrative Unity of Luke–Acts: A Literary Interpretation.* 2 vols. Philadelphia and Minneapolis: Fortress Press (Foundations and Facets), 1986 and 1990.

Tiede, David L. *Luke.* Minneapolis: Augsburg Publishing House (Augsburg Commentary on the New Testament), 1988.